STAR WARS®
KNIGHT ERRANT

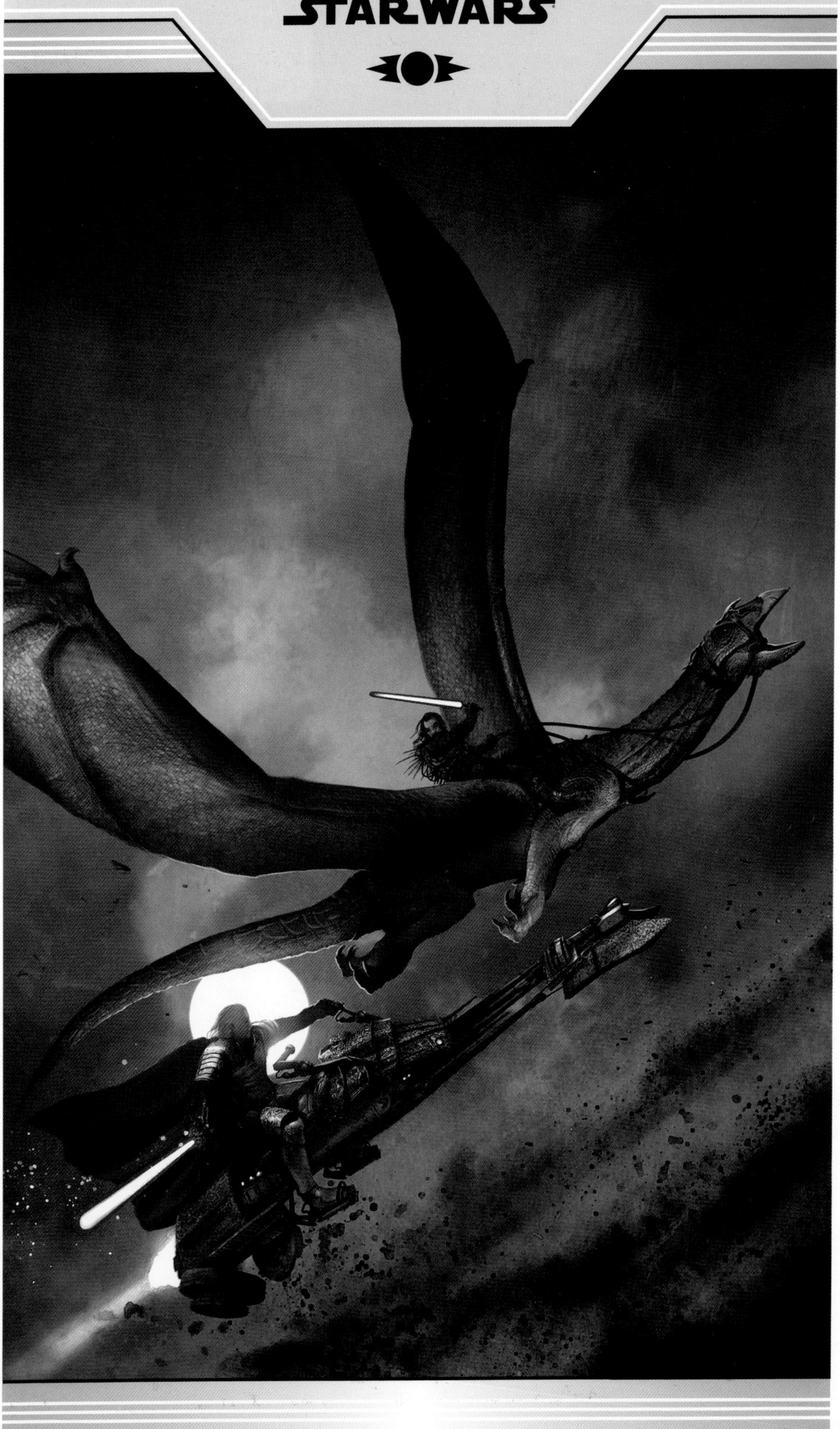
STAR WARS

ILLUSTRATION BY BENJAMIN CARRÉ

STAR WARS
KNIGHT ERRANT

VOLUME THREE
ESCAPE

Script
JOHN JACKSON MILLER

Pencils
MARCO CASTIELLO

Pencil Assists
ANDREA CHELLA

Inks
VINCENZO ACUNZO

Colors
MICHAEL ATIYEH

Letters
MICHAEL HEISLER

Cover Art
BENJAMIN CARRÉ

DARK HORSE BOOKS

THE OLD REPUBLIC
(25,000–1,000 years before the Battle of Yavin)

The Old Republic was the legendary government that united a galaxy under the rule of the Senate. In this era, the Jedi are numerous, and serve as guardians of peace and justice. The *Tales of the Jedi* comics series takes place in this era, chronicling the immense wars fought by the Jedi of old, and the ancient Sith.

This story takes place approximately 1,032 years before *Star Wars:* Episode IV—*A New Hope.*

President and Publisher
MIKE RICHARDSON

Collection Designer
KAT LARSON

Editor
DAVE MARSHALL

Assistant Editor
FREDDYE LINS

NEIL HANKERSON Executive Vice President TOM WEDDLE Chief Financial Officer RANDY STRADLEY Vice President of Publishing MICHAEL MARTENS Vice President of Book Trade Sales ANITA NELSON Vice President of Business Affairs SCOTT ALLIE Editor in Chief MATT PARKINSON Vice President of Marketing DAVID SCROGGY Vice President of Product Development DALE LAFOUNTAIN Vice President of Information Technology DARLENE VOGEL Senior Director of Print, Design, and Production KEN LIZZI General Counsel DAVEY ESTRADA Editorial Director CHRIS WARNER Senior Books Editor DIANA SCHUTZ Executive Editor CARY GRAZZINI Director of Print and Development LIA RIBACCHI Art Director CARA NIECE Director of Scheduling TIM WIESCH Director of International Licensing MARK BERNARDI Director of Digital Publishing

Special thanks to Jennifer Heddle, Leland Chee, Troy Alders, Carol Roeder, Jann Moorhead, and David Anderman at Lucas Licensing.

STAR WARS: KNIGHT ERRANT—ESCAPE

This volume collects issues #1–#5 of the Dark Horse comic-book series *Star Wars: Knight Errant—Escape.*

Published by
Dark Horse Books
A division of Dark Horse Comics, Inc.
10956 SE Main Street
Milwaukie, OR 97222

DarkHorse.com
StarWars.com

To find a comics shop in your area, call the Comic Shop Locator Service toll-free at 1-888-266-4226

Library of Congress Cataloging-in-Publication Data

Miller, John Jackson.
Star wars, knight errant. volume 3, Escape / script, John Jackson Miller ; pencils, Marco Castiello ; pencil assists, Andrea Chella ; inks, Vincenzo Acunzo ; colors, Michael Atiyeh ; letters, Michael Heisler ; cover art, Benjamin Carré.
   p. cm.
Summary: Jedi Knight Kerra Holt is deep in Sith territory, hoping to find the truth about her missing parents, and prevent a dangerous relic from falling into the wrong hands.
ISBN 978-1-61655-076-9
1. Star Wars fiction. 2. Extraterrestrial beings--Comic books, strips, etc. 3. Extraterrestrial beings--Juvenile fiction. 4. Space warfare--Comic books, strips, etc. 5. Space warfare--Juvenile fiction. 6. Graphic novels. [1. Graphic novels. 2. Extraterrestrial beings--Fiction. 3. Space warfare--Fiction.] I. Carré, Benjamin (Benjamin C.), ill. II. Title. III. Title: Knight errant. IV. Title: Escape.
PZ7.7.M535Stk 2013
741.5'973--dc23
                2012040398

First edition: April 2013
ISBN 978-1-61655-076-9

1 3 5 7 9 10 8 6 4 2
Printed in China

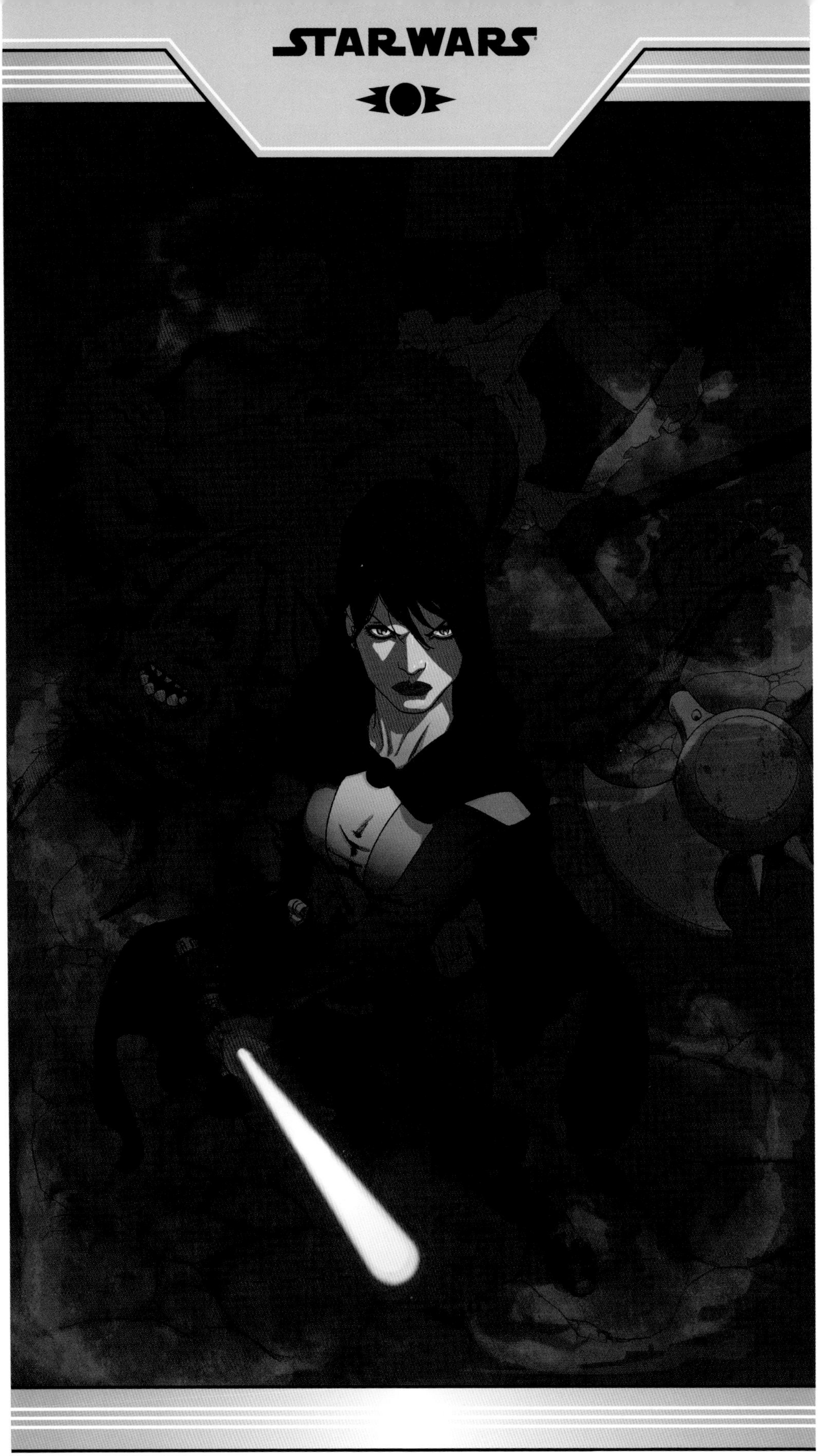
STAR WARS

ILLUSTRATION BY MIKE HAWTHORNE

ESCAPE

There is no peace for the people of the sectors under Sith rule—but there is hope. Hope in the form of Kerra Holt, a young Jedi orphaned years earlier, who has now ventured into the regions abandoned by the Republic to protect—and rescue—as many innocents as possible.

But while Kerra has no living family, it is sibling rivalry that presents the most danger to the people of the Grumani Sector. Lord Daiman, who imagines himself the universe's creator, wars with his elder brother, Lord Odion, who sees himself as its destroyer.

Kerra has wreaked havoc on Daiman's regime. But Odion's is, in many ways, the more diabolical—a suicide cult centering on the mentally damaged Sith Lord, who finds the existence of other living beings painful because of his connection to the Force. It is only a matter of time before Odion acts to blot out the light, once and for all . . .

This story takes place approximately 1,032 years before *Star Wars:* Episode IV— *A New Hope*.

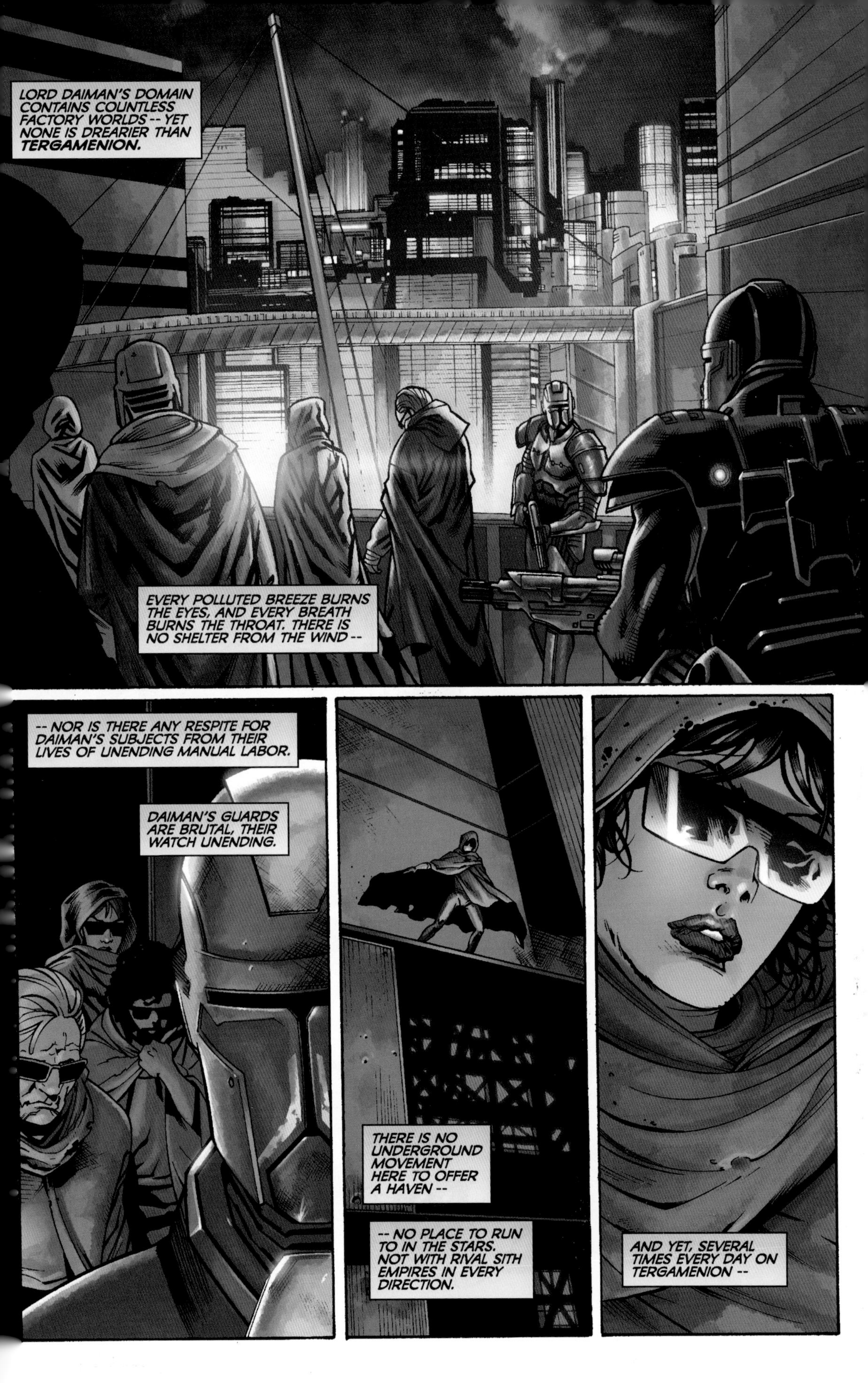
LORD DAIMAN'S DOMAIN CONTAINS COUNTLESS FACTORY WORLDS -- YET NONE IS DREARIER THAN TERGAMENION.
EVERY POLLUTED BREEZE BURNS THE EYES, AND EVERY BREATH BURNS THE THROAT. THERE IS NO SHELTER FROM THE WIND --
-- NOR IS THERE ANY RESPITE FOR DAIMAN'S SUBJECTS FROM THEIR LIVES OF UNENDING MANUAL LABOR.
DAIMAN'S GUARDS ARE BRUTAL, THEIR WATCH UNENDING.
THERE IS NO UNDERGROUND MOVEMENT HERE TO OFFER A HAVEN --
-- NO PLACE TO RUN TO IN THE STARS. NOT WITH RIVAL SITH EMPIRES IN EVERY DIRECTION.
AND YET, SEVERAL TIMES EVERY DAY ON TERGAMENION --

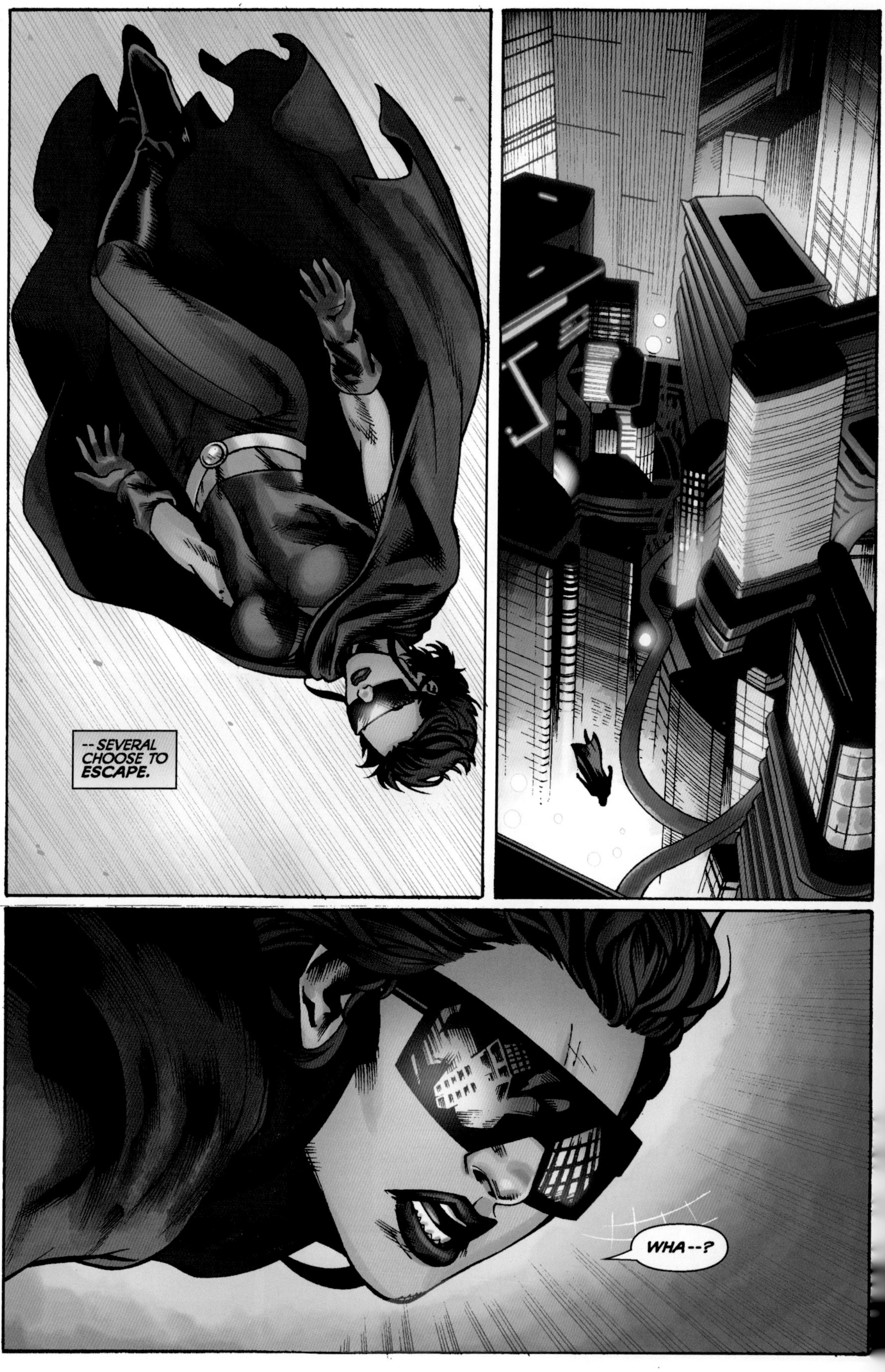
--SEVERAL CHOOSE TO ESCAPE.
WHA--?

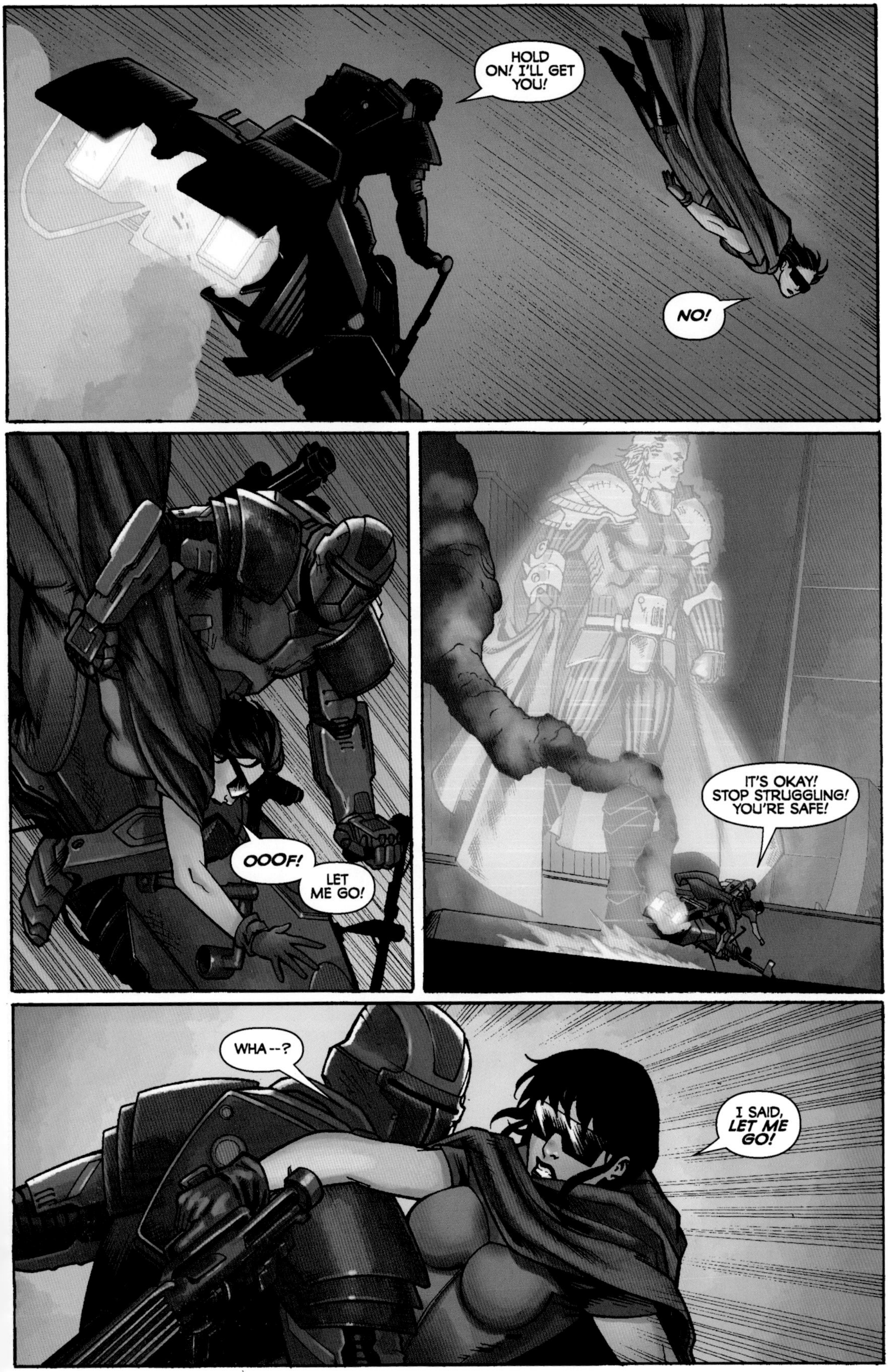
HOLD ON! I'LL GET YOU!
NO!
OOOF!
LET ME GO!
IT'S OKAY! STOP STRUGGLING! YOU'RE SAFE!
WHA--?
I SAID, *LET ME GO!*

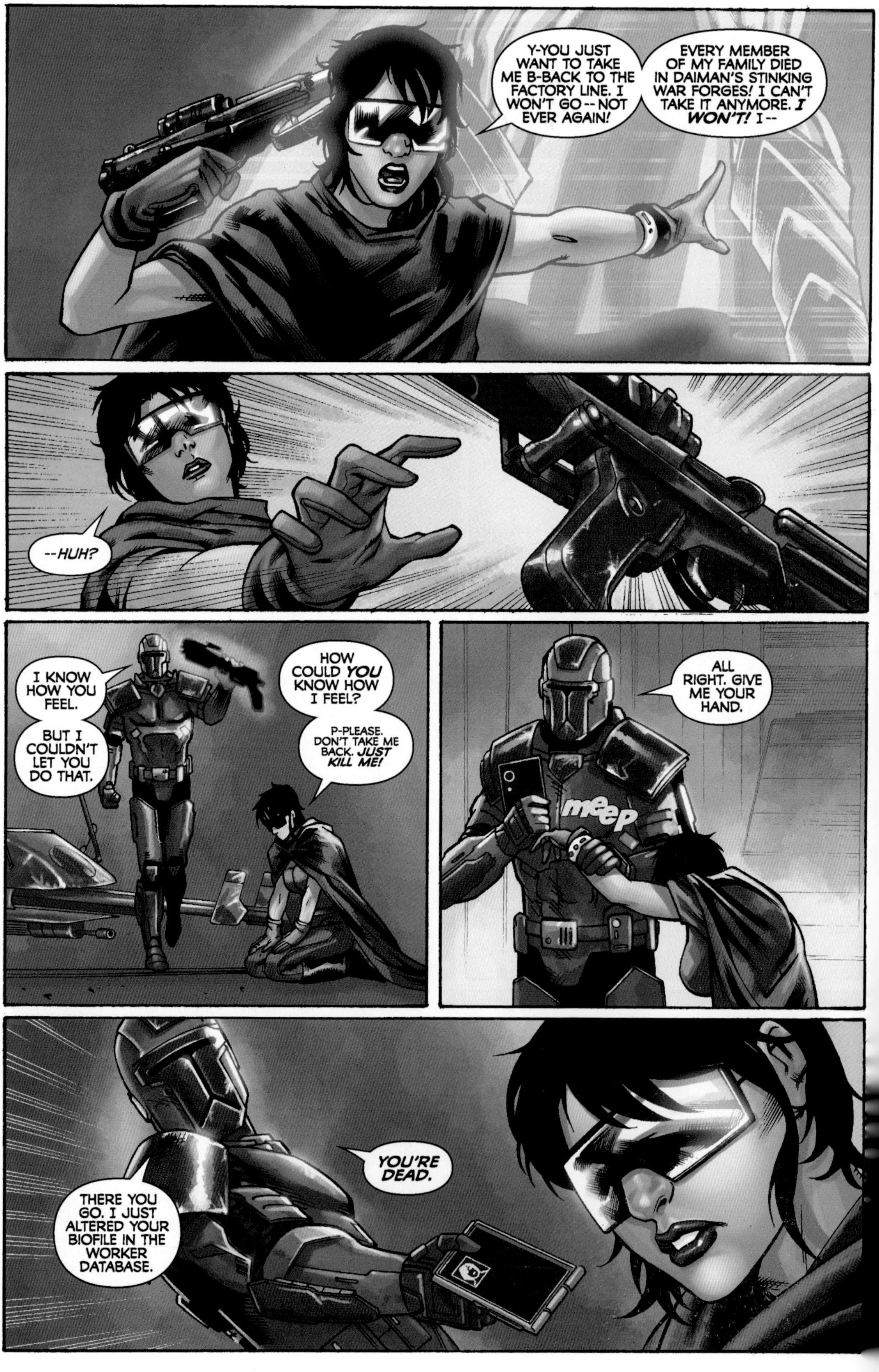
Y-YOU JUST WANT TO TAKE ME B-BACK TO THE FACTORY LINE. I WON'T GO--NOT EVER AGAIN!
EVERY MEMBER OF MY FAMILY DIED IN DAIMAN'S STINKING WAR FORGES! I CAN'T TAKE IT ANYMORE. I WON'T! I--
--HUH?
I KNOW HOW YOU FEEL.
BUT I COULDN'T LET YOU DO THAT.
HOW COULD YOU KNOW HOW I FEEL?
P-PLEASE. DON'T TAKE ME BACK. JUST KILL ME!
ALL RIGHT. GIVE ME YOUR HAND.
meep
THERE YOU GO. I JUST ALTERED YOUR BIOFILE IN THE WORKER DATABASE.
YOU'RE DEAD.

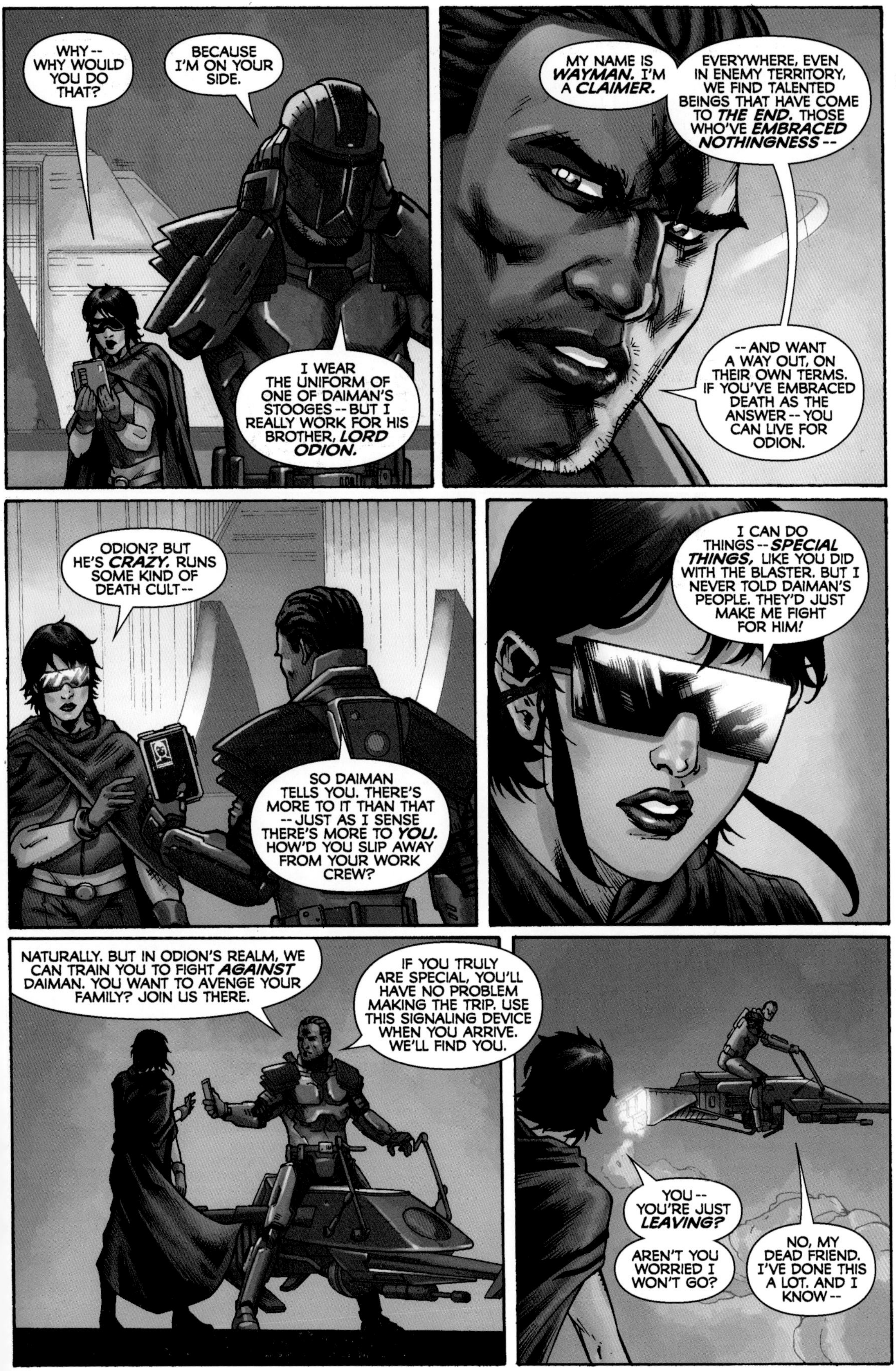
WHY -- WHY WOULD YOU DO THAT?
BECAUSE I'M ON YOUR SIDE.
I WEAR THE UNIFORM OF ONE OF DAIMAN'S STOOGES -- BUT I REALLY WORK FOR HIS BROTHER, LORD ODION.
MY NAME IS WAYMAN. I'M A CLAIMER.
EVERYWHERE, EVEN IN ENEMY TERRITORY, WE FIND TALENTED BEINGS THAT HAVE COME TO THE END. THOSE WHO'VE EMBRACED NOTHINGNESS --
-- AND WANT A WAY OUT, ON THEIR OWN TERMS. IF YOU'VE EMBRACED DEATH AS THE ANSWER -- YOU CAN LIVE FOR ODION.
ODION? BUT HE'S CRAZY. RUNS SOME KIND OF DEATH CULT--
SO DAIMAN TELLS YOU. THERE'S MORE TO IT THAN THAT -- JUST AS I SENSE THERE'S MORE TO YOU. HOW'D YOU SLIP AWAY FROM YOUR WORK CREW?
I CAN DO THINGS -- SPECIAL THINGS, LIKE YOU DID WITH THE BLASTER. BUT I NEVER TOLD DAIMAN'S PEOPLE. THEY'D JUST MAKE ME FIGHT FOR HIM!
NATURALLY. BUT IN ODION'S REALM, WE CAN TRAIN YOU TO FIGHT AGAINST DAIMAN. YOU WANT TO AVENGE YOUR FAMILY? JOIN US THERE.
IF YOU TRULY ARE SPECIAL, YOU'LL HAVE NO PROBLEM MAKING THE TRIP. USE THIS SIGNALING DEVICE WHEN YOU ARRIVE. WE'LL FIND YOU.
YOU -- YOU'RE JUST LEAVING?
AREN'T YOU WORRIED I WON'T GO?
NO, MY DEAD FRIEND. I'VE DONE THIS A LOT. AND I KNOW --

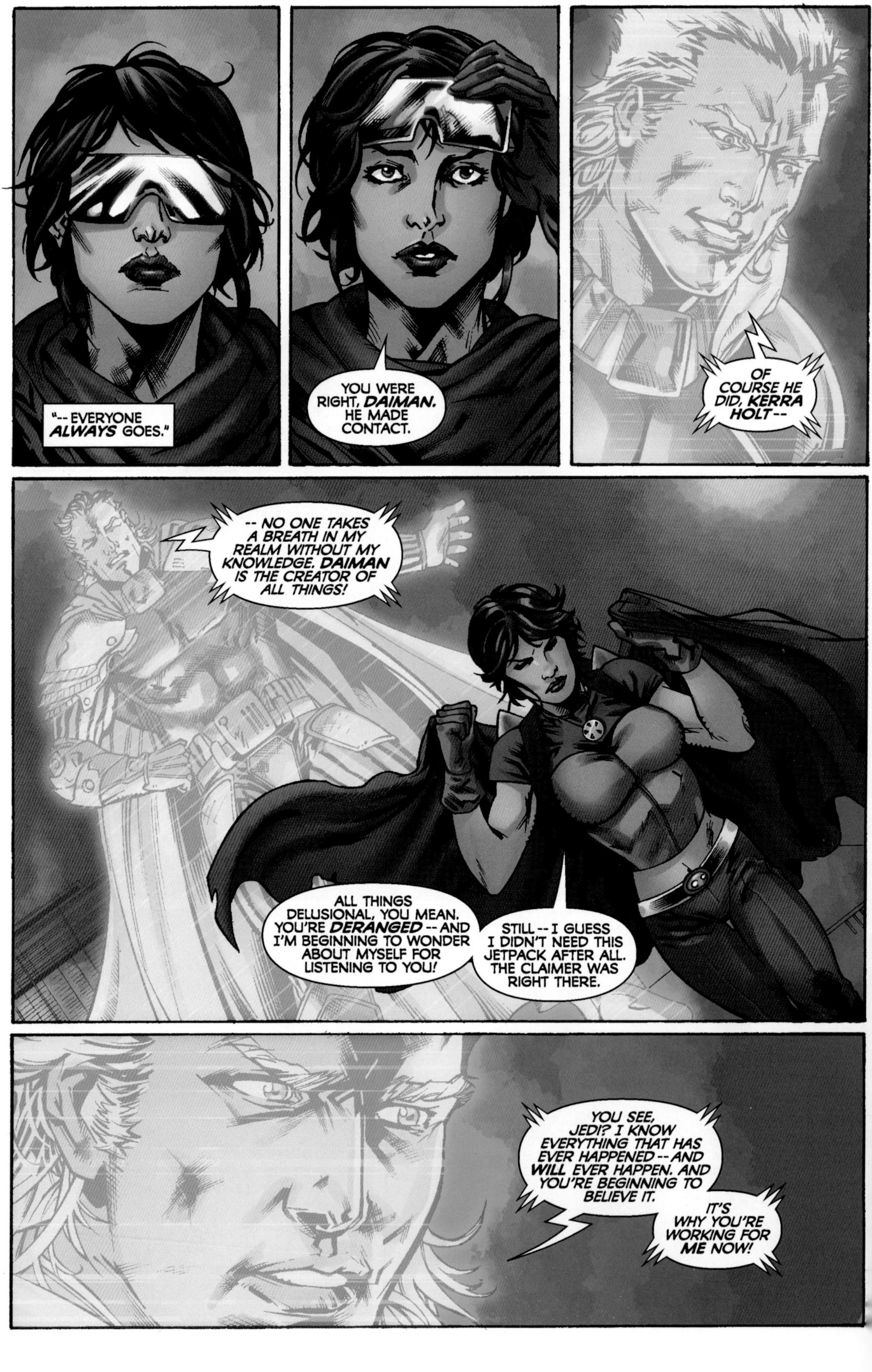
"-- EVERYONE ALWAYS GOES."
YOU WERE RIGHT, DAIMAN. HE MADE CONTACT.
OF COURSE HE DID, KERRA HOLT--
-- NO ONE TAKES A BREATH IN MY REALM WITHOUT MY KNOWLEDGE. DAIMAN IS THE CREATOR OF ALL THINGS!
ALL THINGS DELUSIONAL, YOU MEAN. YOU'RE DERANGED -- AND I'M BEGINNING TO WONDER ABOUT MYSELF FOR LISTENING TO YOU!
STILL -- I GUESS I DIDN'T NEED THIS JETPACK AFTER ALL. THE CLAIMER WAS RIGHT THERE.
YOU SEE, JEDI? I KNOW EVERYTHING THAT HAS EVER HAPPENED -- AND WILL EVER HAPPEN. AND YOU'RE BEGINNING TO BELIEVE IT.
IT'S WHY YOU'RE WORKING FOR ME NOW!

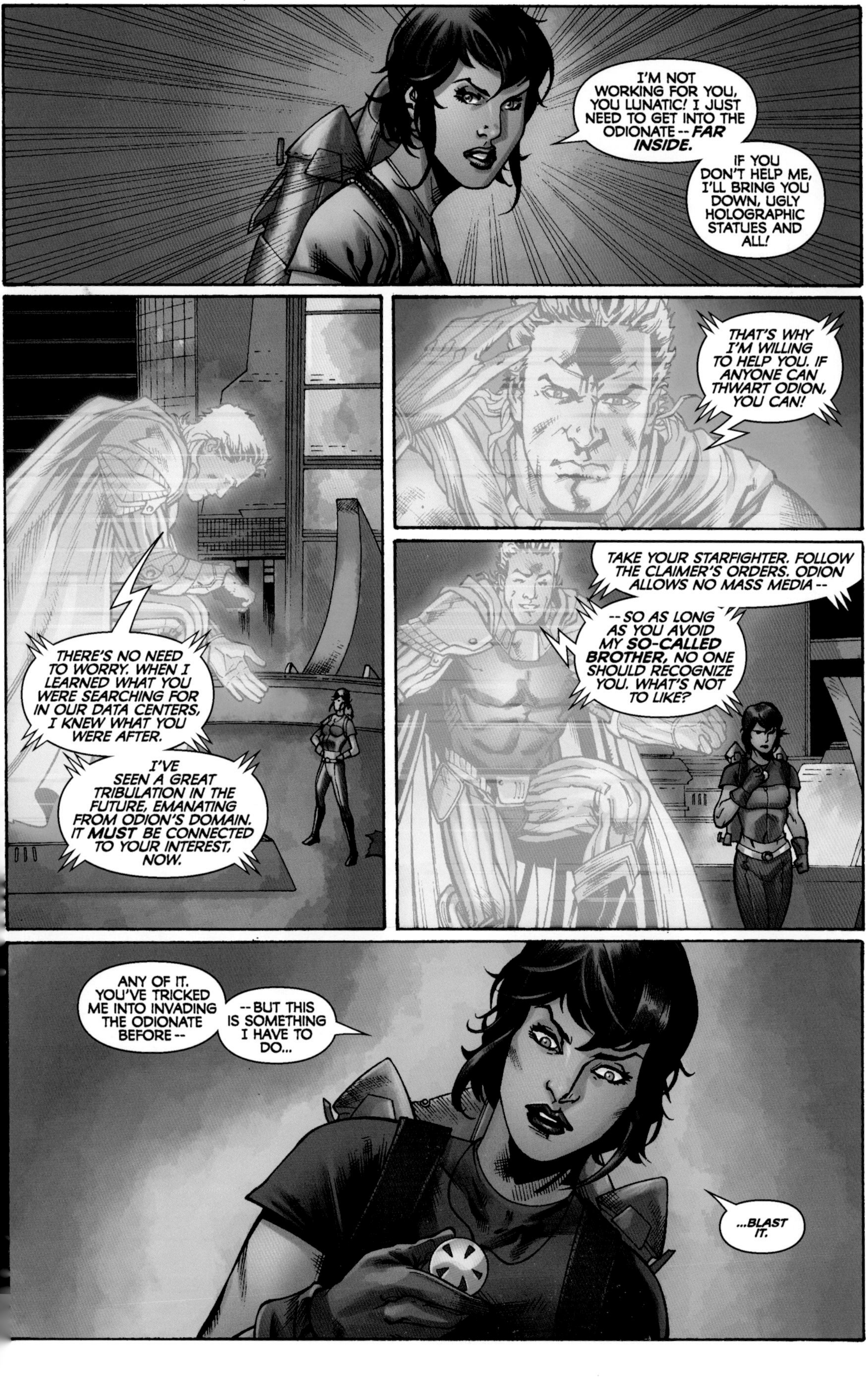

I'M NOT WORKING FOR YOU, YOU LUNATIC! I JUST NEED TO GET INTO THE ODIONATE -- FAR INSIDE.
IF YOU DON'T HELP ME, I'LL BRING YOU DOWN, UGLY HOLOGRAPHIC STATUES AND ALL!
THERE'S NO NEED TO WORRY. WHEN I LEARNED WHAT YOU WERE SEARCHING FOR IN OUR DATA CENTERS, I KNEW WHAT YOU WERE AFTER.
I'VE SEEN A GREAT TRIBULATION IN THE FUTURE, EMANATING FROM ODION'S DOMAIN. IT MUST BE CONNECTED TO YOUR INTEREST, NOW.
THAT'S WHY I'M WILLING TO HELP YOU. IF ANYONE CAN THWART ODION, YOU CAN!
TAKE YOUR STARFIGHTER. FOLLOW THE CLAIMER'S ORDERS. ODION ALLOWS NO MASS MEDIA --
-- SO AS LONG AS YOU AVOID MY SO-CALLED BROTHER, NO ONE SHOULD RECOGNIZE YOU. WHAT'S NOT TO LIKE?
ANY OF IT. YOU'VE TRICKED ME INTO INVADING THE ODIONATE BEFORE --
-- BUT THIS IS SOMETHING I HAVE TO DO...
...BLAST IT.

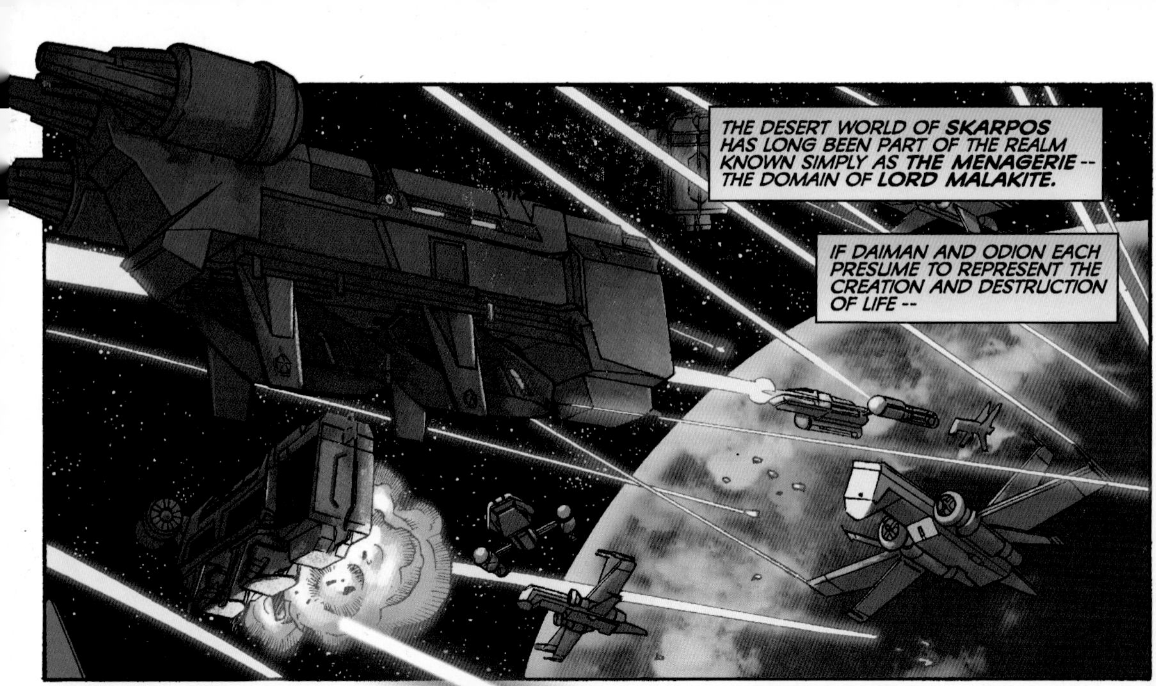
THE DESERT WORLD OF SKARPOS HAS LONG BEEN PART OF THE REALM KNOWN SIMPLY AS THE MENAGERIE -- THE DOMAIN OF LORD MALAKITE.
IF DAIMAN AND ODION EACH PRESUME TO REPRESENT THE CREATION AND DESTRUCTION OF LIFE --

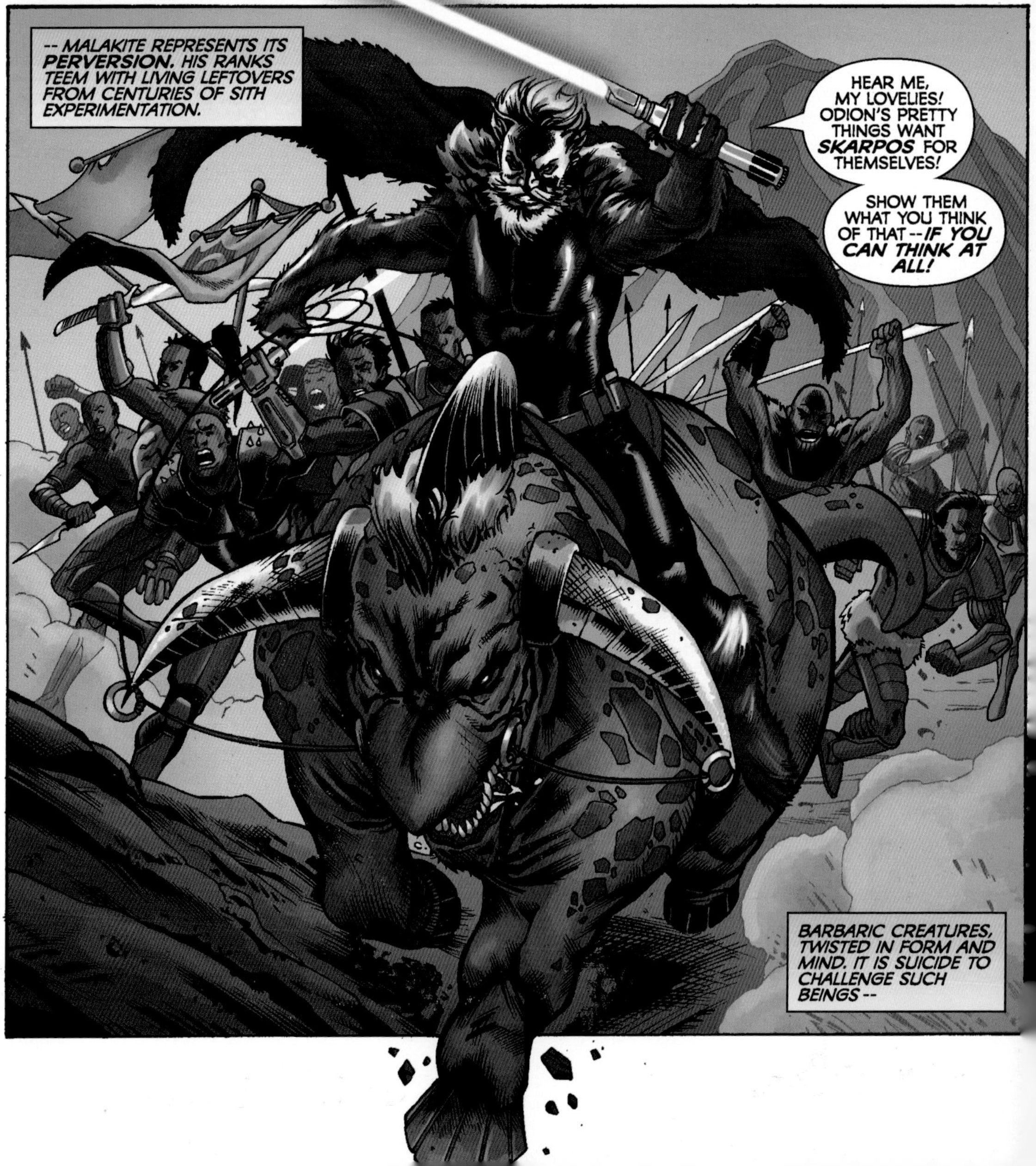
-- MALAKITE REPRESENTS ITS PERVERSION. HIS RANKS TEEM WITH LIVING LEFTOVERS FROM CENTURIES OF SITH EXPERIMENTATION.
HEAR ME, MY LOVELIES! ODION'S PRETTY THINGS WANT SKARPOS FOR THEMSELVES!
SHOW THEM WHAT YOU THINK OF THAT -- IF YOU CAN THINK AT ALL!
BARBARIC CREATURES, TWISTED IN FORM AND MIND. IT IS SUICIDE TO CHALLENGE SUCH BEINGS --

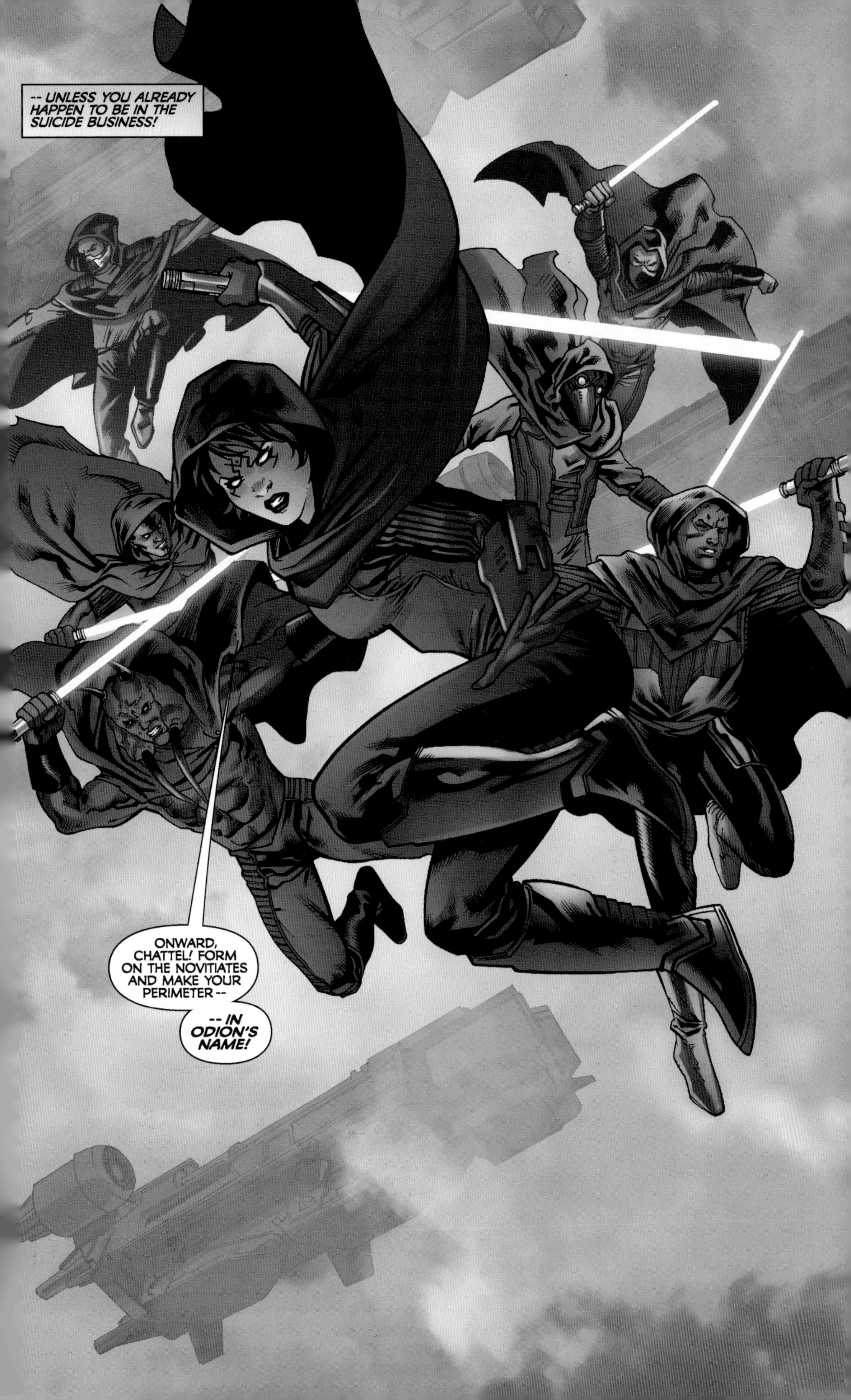
-- UNLESS YOU ALREADY HAPPEN TO BE IN THE SUICIDE BUSINESS!
ONWARD, CHATTEL! FORM ON THE NOVITIATES AND MAKE YOUR PERIMETER --
-- IN ODION'S NAME!

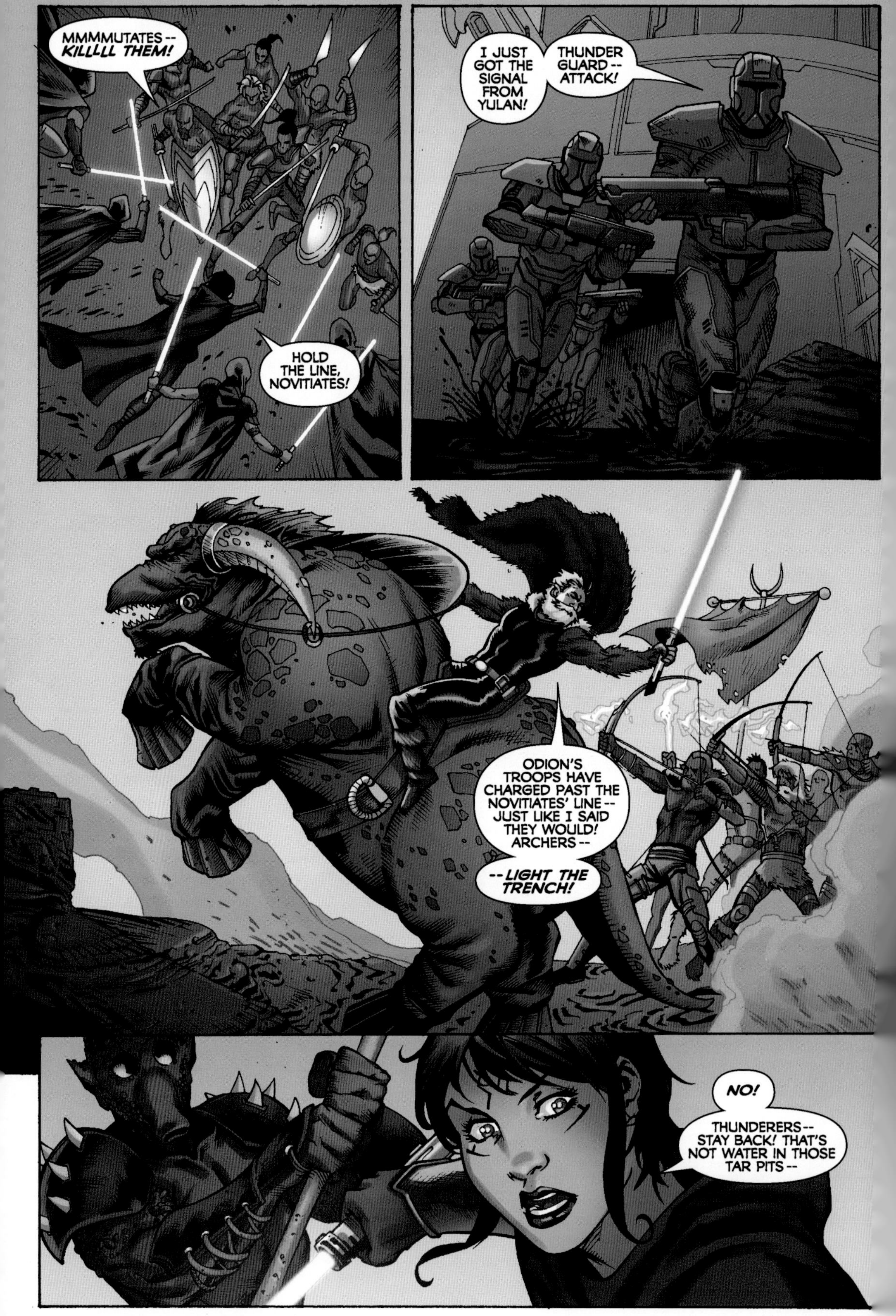
MMMMUTATES -- KILLLLL THEM!
HOLD THE LINE, NOVITIATES!
I JUST GOT THE SIGNAL FROM YULAN!
THUNDER GUARD -- ATTACK!
ODION'S TROOPS HAVE CHARGED PAST THE NOVITIATES' LINE -- JUST LIKE I SAID THEY WOULD! ARCHERS --
-- LIGHT THE TRENCH!
NO!
THUNDERERS -- STAY BACK! THAT'S NOT WATER IN THOSE TAR PITS --

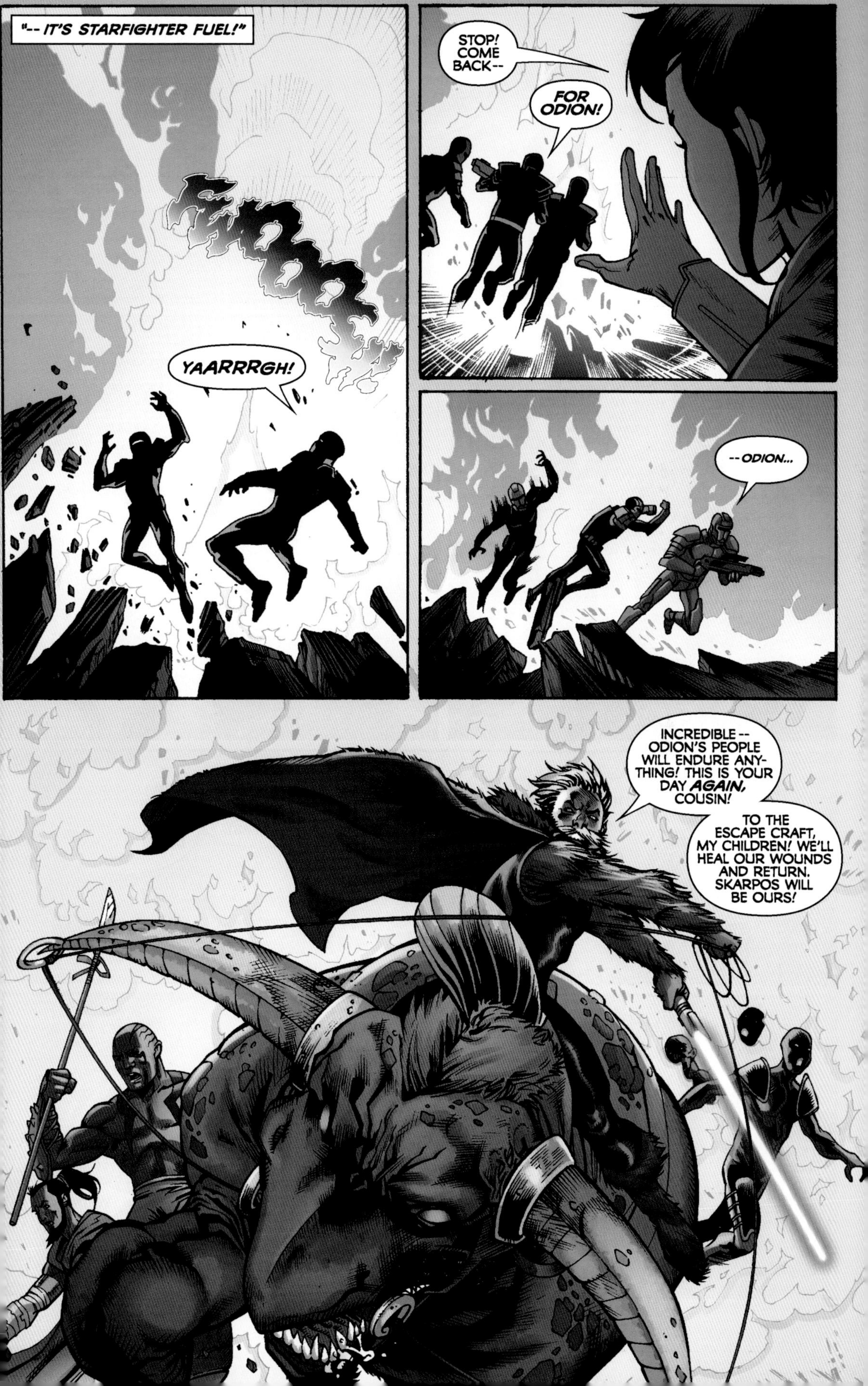
"-- IT'S STARFIGHTER FUEL!"
YAARRRGH!
STOP! COME BACK--
FOR ODION!
--ODION...
INCREDIBLE -- ODION'S PEOPLE WILL ENDURE ANYTHING! THIS IS YOUR DAY AGAIN, COUSIN!
TO THE ESCAPE CRAFT, MY CHILDREN! WE'LL HEAL OUR WOUNDS AND RETURN. SKARPOS WILL BE OURS!

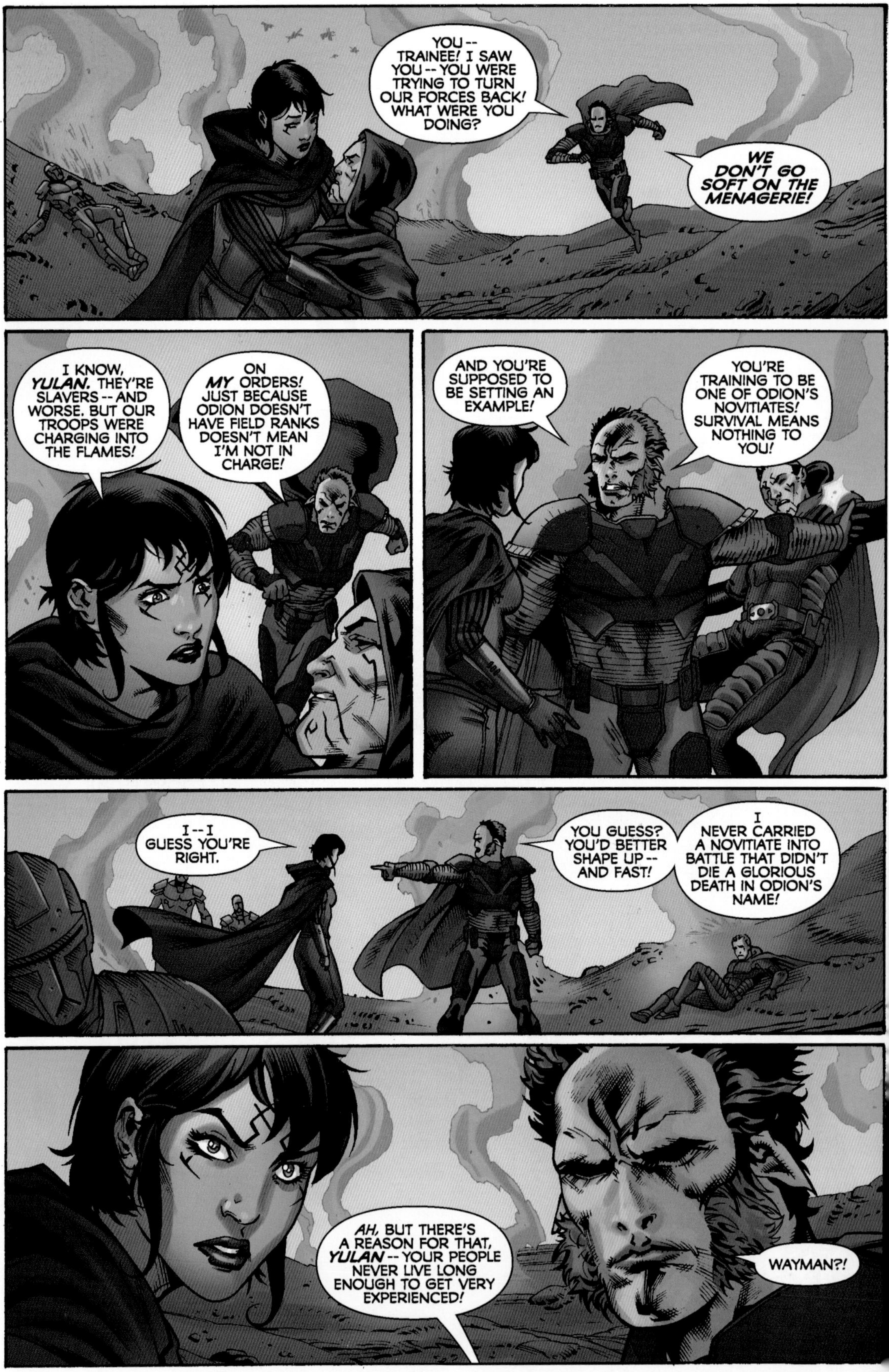
YOU -- TRAINEE! I SAW YOU -- YOU WERE TRYING TO TURN OUR FORCES BACK! WHAT WERE YOU DOING?
WE DON'T GO SOFT ON THE MENAGERIE!
I KNOW, YULAN. THEY'RE SLAVERS -- AND WORSE. BUT OUR TROOPS WERE CHARGING INTO THE FLAMES!
ON MY ORDERS! JUST BECAUSE ODION DOESN'T HAVE FIELD RANKS DOESN'T MEAN I'M NOT IN CHARGE!
AND YOU'RE SUPPOSED TO BE SETTING AN EXAMPLE!
YOU'RE TRAINING TO BE ONE OF ODION'S NOVITIATES! SURVIVAL MEANS NOTHING TO YOU!
I -- I GUESS YOU'RE RIGHT.
YOU GUESS? YOU'D BETTER SHAPE UP -- AND FAST!
I NEVER CARRIED A NOVITIATE INTO BATTLE THAT DIDN'T DIE A GLORIOUS DEATH IN ODION'S NAME!
AH, BUT THERE'S A REASON FOR THAT, YULAN -- YOUR PEOPLE NEVER LIVE LONG ENOUGH TO GET VERY EXPERIENCED!
WAYMAN?!

I'M NOT COMPLAINING -- YOU KEEP ME AND THE OTHER CLAIMERS PRETTY BUSY LOOKING FOR REPLACEMENTS.

BUT I HAVE HIGH HOPES FOR THIS ONE.

DON'T KNOW WHY. CALLS HERSELF *MERCY* -- AND I THINK IT'S GONE TO HER HEAD.

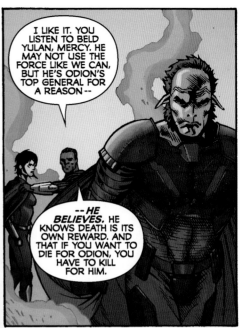

I LIKE IT. YOU LISTEN TO BELD YULAN, MERCY. HE MAY NOT USE THE FORCE LIKE WE CAN, BUT HE'S ODION'S TOP GENERAL FOR A REASON --

-- *HE BELIEVES*. HE KNOWS DEATH IS ITS OWN REWARD. AND THAT IF YOU WANT TO DIE FOR ODION, YOU HAVE TO KILL FOR HIM.

AND YOU'RE ABOUT TO GET THE CHANCE. I'VE JUST COME FROM *JUBALENE*. LORD ODION WANTS A SQUAD OF NOVITIATES FOR A BIG ASSIGNMENT.

JUBALENE? *ODION'S CAPITAL?*

HIS CAPITAL IS WHEREVER *HE* IS -- BUT YES. I'VE VOLUNTEERED THIS TEAM FOR THE MISSION. YULAN'S FLEET IS TO MEET US THERE.

YOU HEAR THAT, YULAN?

HMMM?

OH. YES -- WE'LL BE THERE. I JUST... NEED A QUICK STOP ON *VANAHAME* TO REARM.

WAYMAN -- DOES JUBALENE HAVE DATA CENTERS? THEY PUT US IN THE FIELD SO FAST -- I'D LIKE TO LEARN MORE ABOUT ODION'S TEACHINGS.

THAT'S THE SPIRIT. YES, THERE'S A LOT TO SEE --

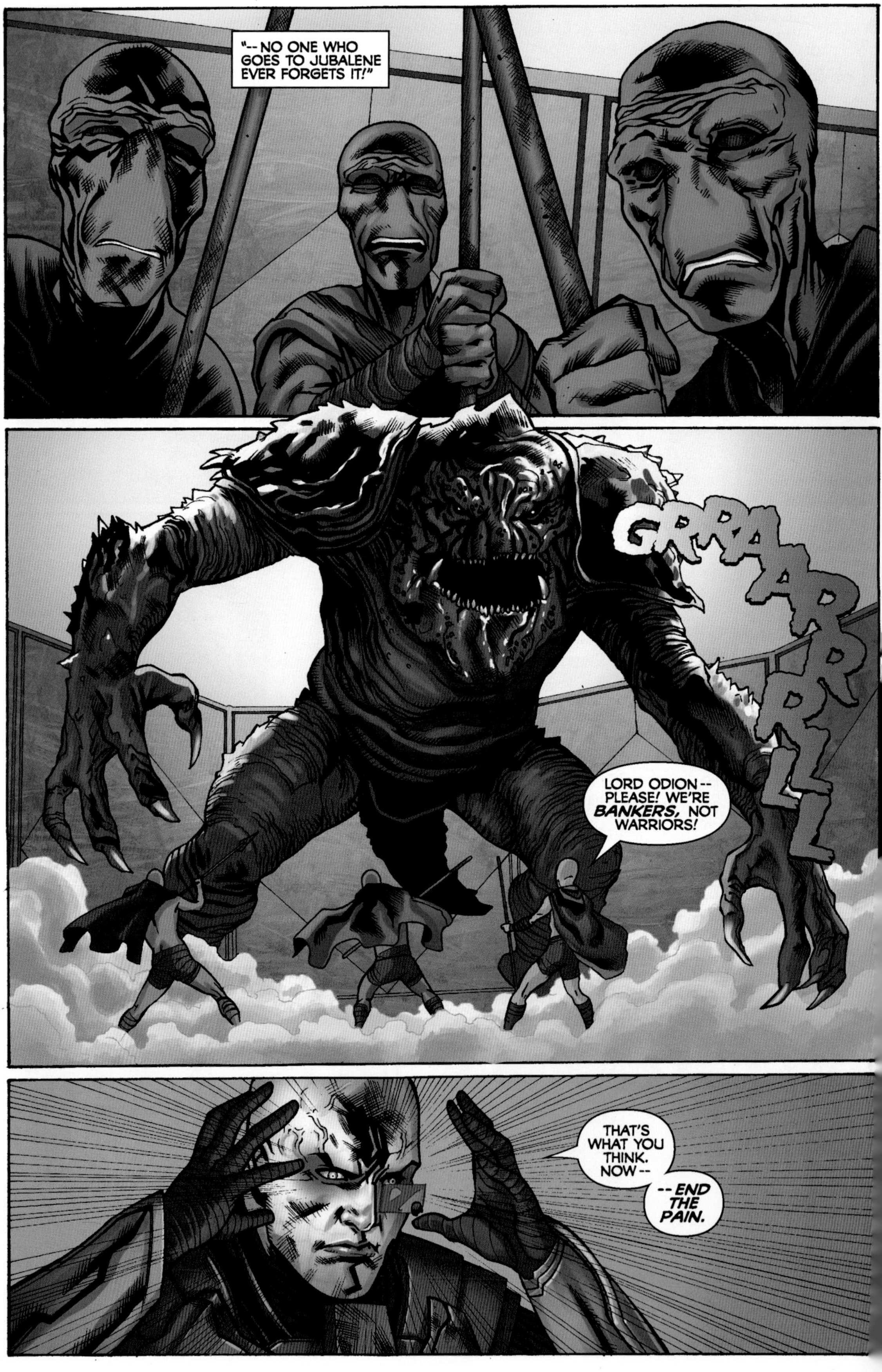
"-- NO ONE WHO GOES TO JUBALENE EVER FORGETS IT!"
GRRAARRRLL
LORD ODION -- PLEASE! WE'RE *BANKERS,* NOT WARRIORS!
THAT'S WHAT YOU THINK. NOW --
-- *END THE PAIN.*

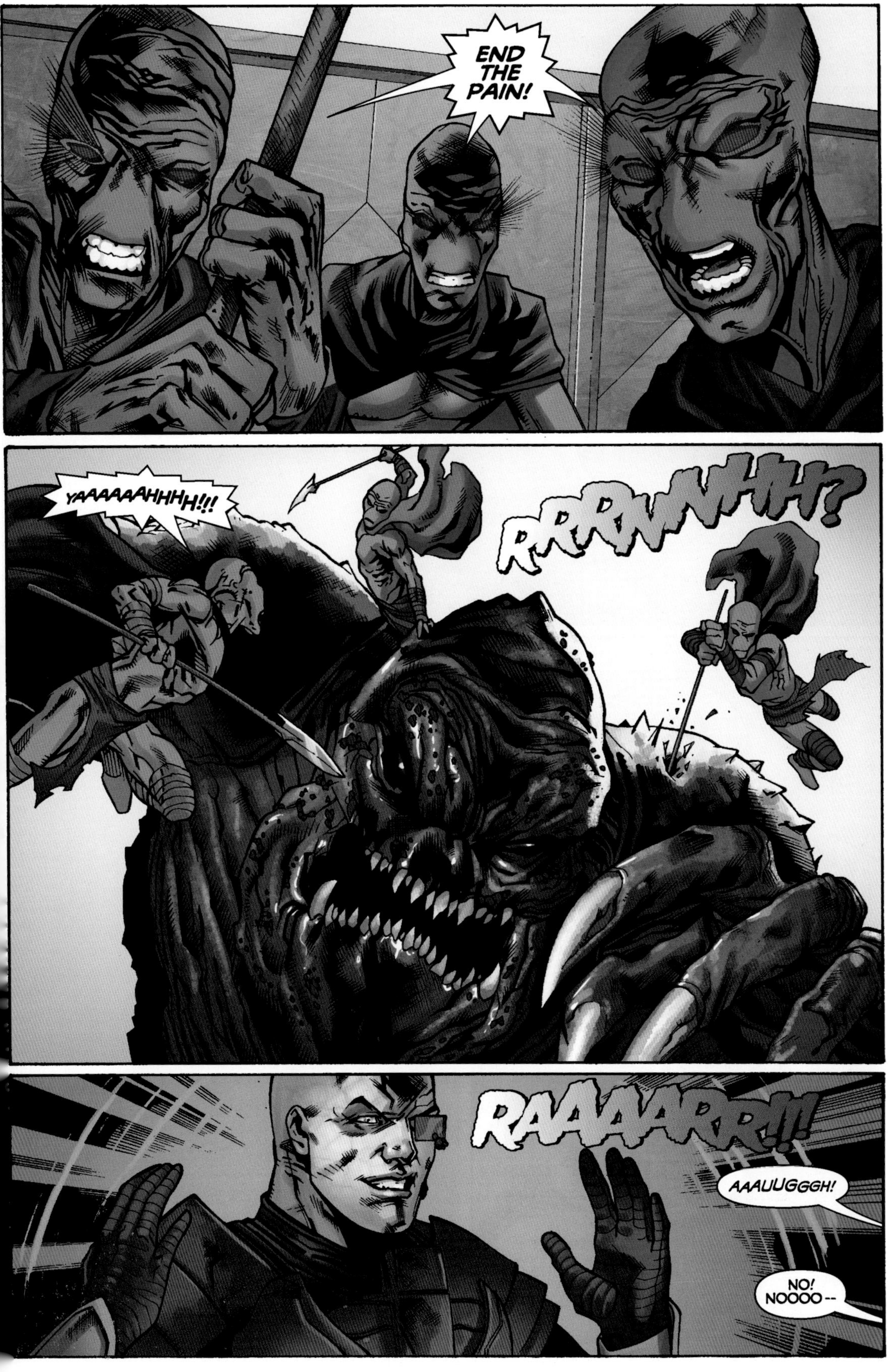
END THE PAIN!
YAAAAAAHHHH!!!
RRRRWWHHH?
RAAAAARRR!!!
AAAUUGGGH!
NO! NOOOO--

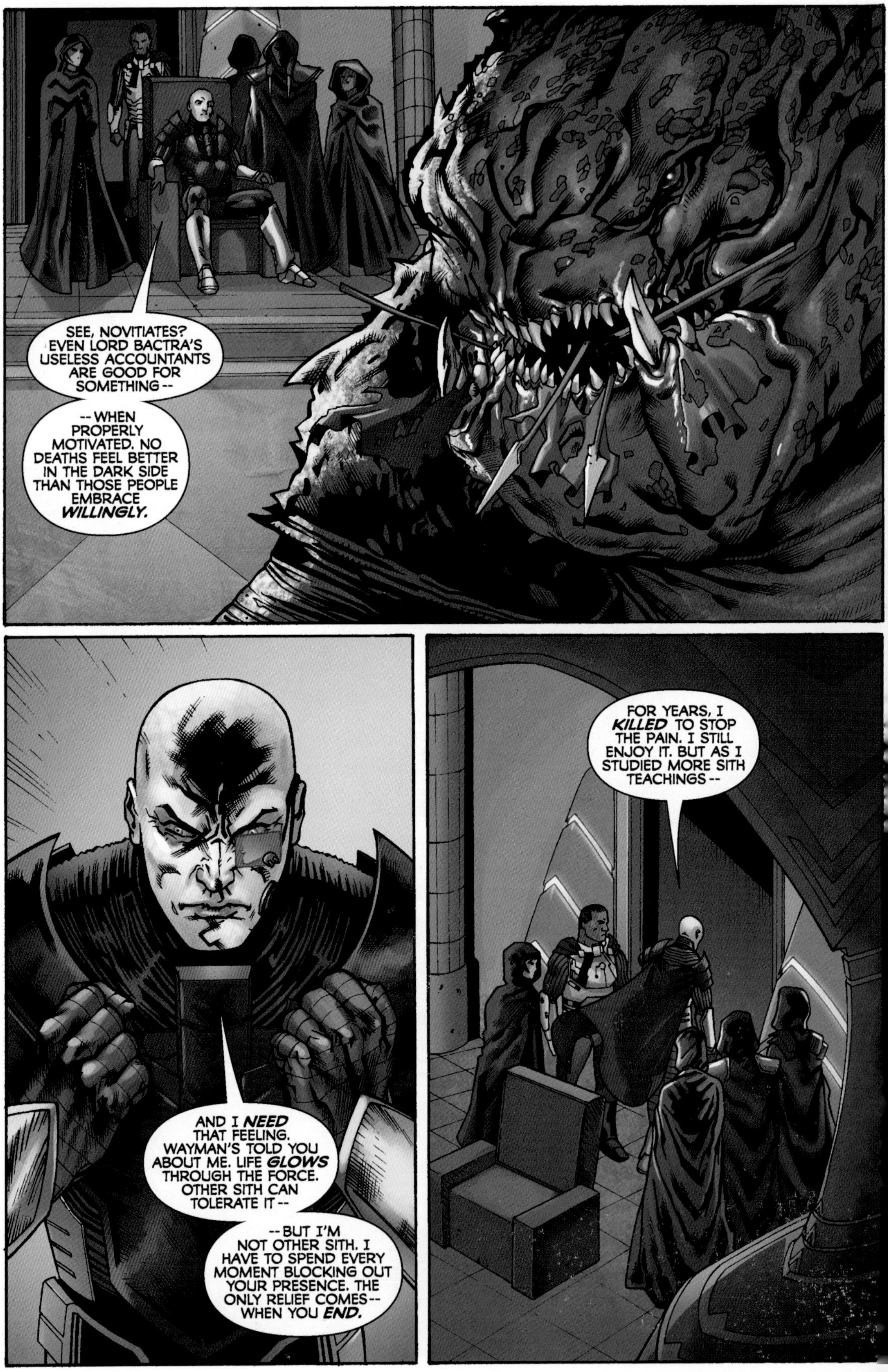

SEE, NOVITIATES? EVEN LORD BACTRA'S USELESS ACCOUNTANTS ARE GOOD FOR SOMETHING --
-- WHEN PROPERLY MOTIVATED. NO DEATHS FEEL BETTER IN THE DARK SIDE THAN THOSE PEOPLE EMBRACE WILLINGLY.
AND I NEED THAT FEELING. WAYMAN'S TOLD YOU ABOUT ME. LIFE GLOWS THROUGH THE FORCE. OTHER SITH CAN TOLERATE IT --
-- BUT I'M NOT OTHER SITH. I HAVE TO SPEND EVERY MOMENT BLOCKING OUT YOUR PRESENCE. THE ONLY RELIEF COMES -- WHEN YOU END.
FOR YEARS, I KILLED TO STOP THE PAIN. I STILL ENJOY IT. BUT AS I STUDIED MORE SITH TEACHINGS --

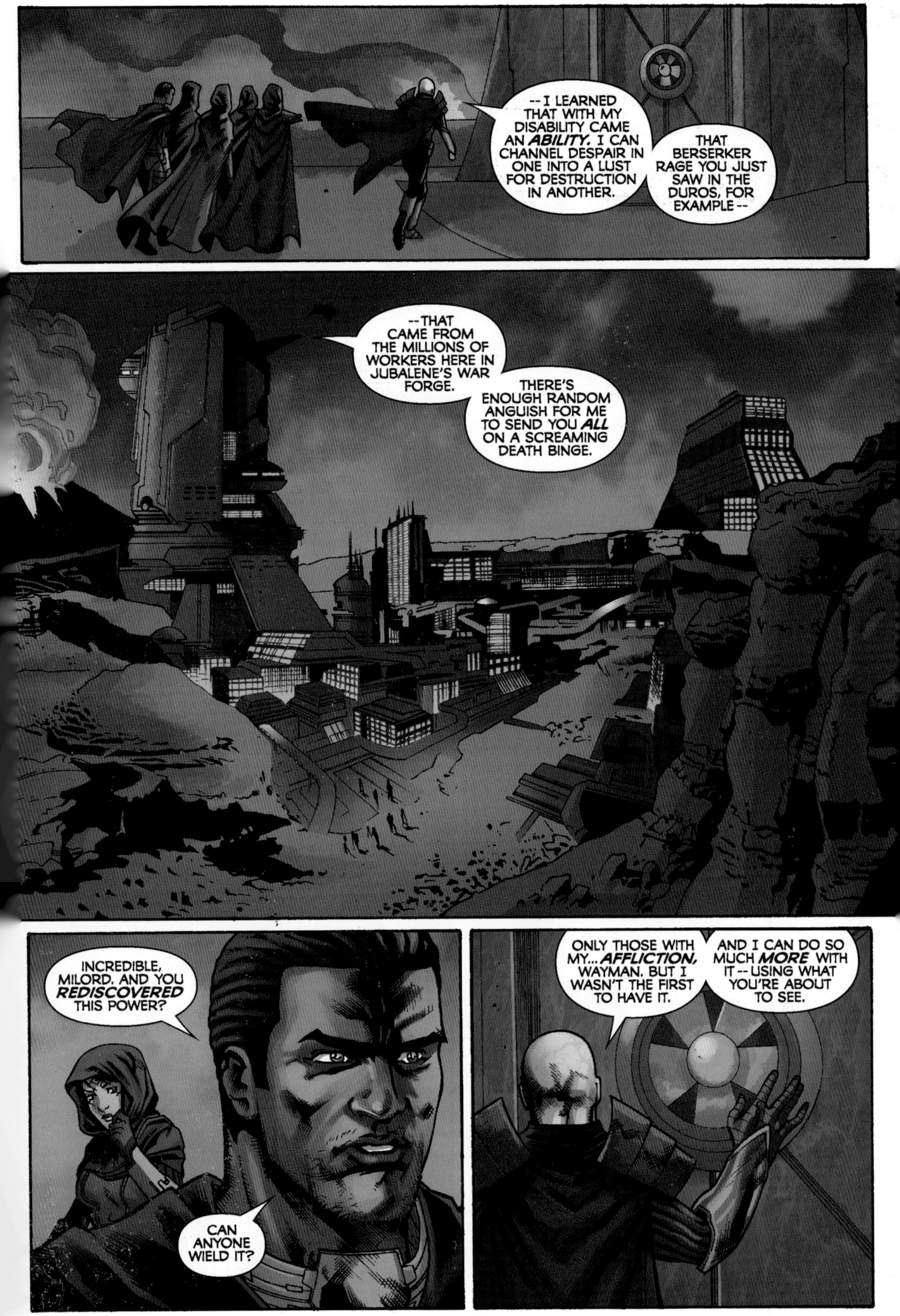
--I LEARNED THAT WITH MY DISABILITY CAME AN ABILITY. I CAN CHANNEL DESPAIR IN ONE INTO A LUST FOR DESTRUCTION IN ANOTHER.
THAT BERSERKER RAGE YOU JUST SAW IN THE DUROS, FOR EXAMPLE--
--THAT CAME FROM THE MILLIONS OF WORKERS HERE IN JUBALENE'S WAR FORGE.
THERE'S ENOUGH RANDOM ANGUISH FOR ME TO SEND YOU ALL ON A SCREAMING DEATH BINGE.
INCREDIBLE, MILORD. AND YOU REDISCOVERED THIS POWER?
CAN ANYONE WIELD IT?
ONLY THOSE WITH MY...AFFLICTION, WAYMAN. BUT I WASN'T THE FIRST TO HAVE IT.
AND I CAN DO SO MUCH MORE WITH IT--USING WHAT YOU'RE ABOUT TO SEE.

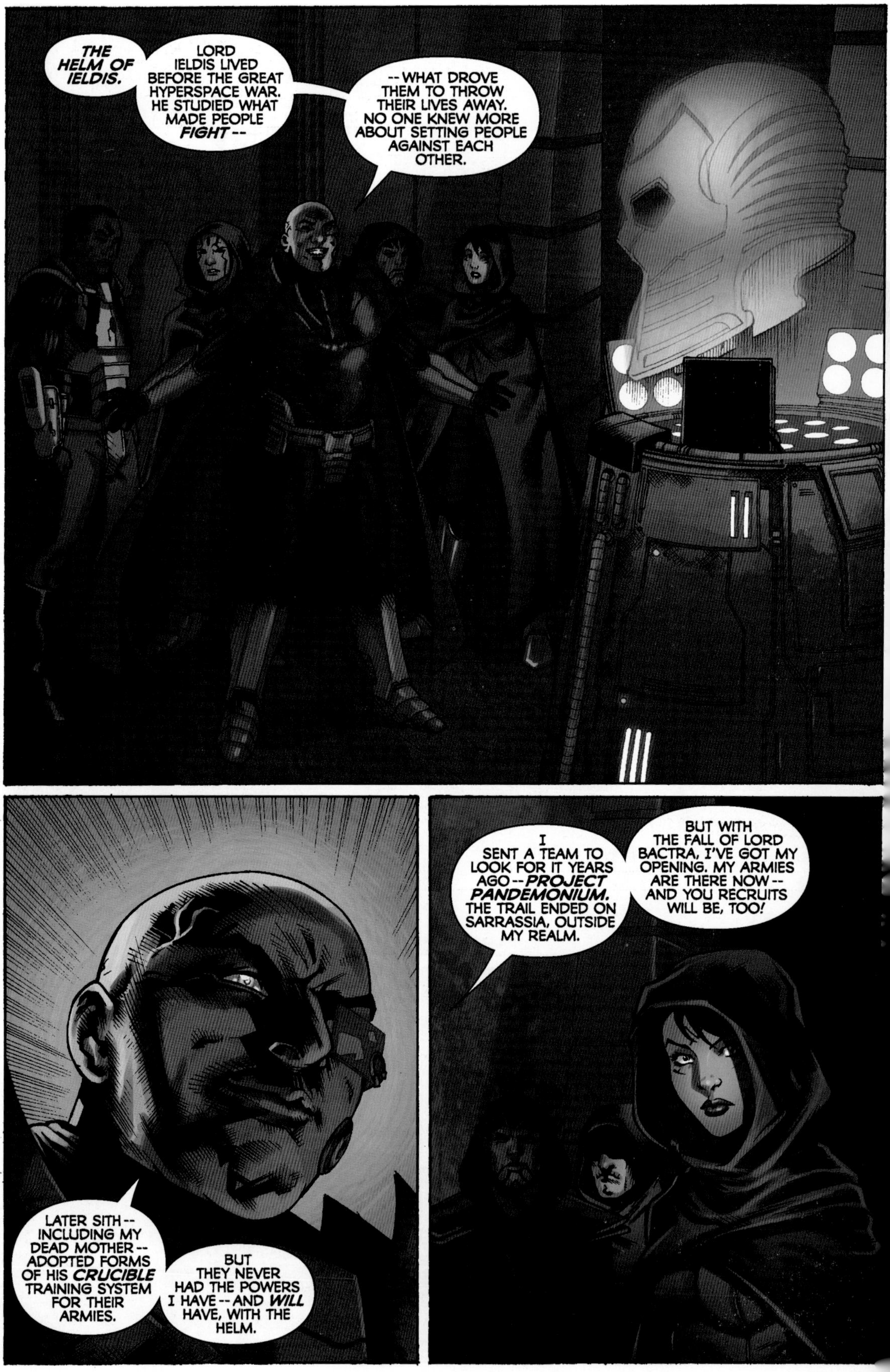
THE HELM OF IELDIS.
LORD IELDIS LIVED BEFORE THE GREAT HYPERSPACE WAR. HE STUDIED WHAT MADE PEOPLE FIGHT--
--WHAT DROVE THEM TO THROW THEIR LIVES AWAY. NO ONE KNEW MORE ABOUT SETTING PEOPLE AGAINST EACH OTHER.
LATER SITH--INCLUDING MY DEAD MOTHER--ADOPTED FORMS OF HIS CRUCIBLE TRAINING SYSTEM FOR THEIR ARMIES.
BUT THEY NEVER HAD THE POWERS I HAVE--AND WILL HAVE, WITH THE HELM.
I SENT A TEAM TO LOOK FOR IT YEARS AGO--PROJECT PANDEMONIUM. THE TRAIL ENDED ON SARRASSIA, OUTSIDE MY REALM.
BUT WITH THE FALL OF LORD BACTRA, I'VE GOT MY OPENING. MY ARMIES ARE THERE NOW--AND YOU RECRUITS WILL BE, TOO!

WE'RE HONORED, MILORD. BUT I'M SURPRISED YOU'RE NOT GOING THERE YOURSELF --

I DON'T DIG AROUND IN GRAVES, WAYMAN -- I *FILL* THEM. BETWEEN DAIMAN AND MY IDIOT COUSINS, I'VE GOT MY HANDS FULL.

BUT YOUR TEAM WILL TAKE UP THE RESEARCH, BEGINNING WITH THE MATERIAL IN THIS ROOM. THEN I CAN CLAIM THE HELM, ONCE AND FOR --

-- *WAIT.* SOMEONE'S HERE --

-- SOMEONE I *KNOW.*

THE HEADACHES HAVE BEEN GETTING WORSE LATELY -- EVERYTHING'S A BLUR.

BUT THERE'S SOMEONE I COULD NEVER FORGET --

-- *YULAN!* HOW WAS VANAHAME, WIDOWMAKER?

WE'RE REARMED AND READY, MY LORD. MY FLEET AWAITS YOUR TEAM. THOSE SARRASSIANS WON'T KNOW WHAT HIT THEM!

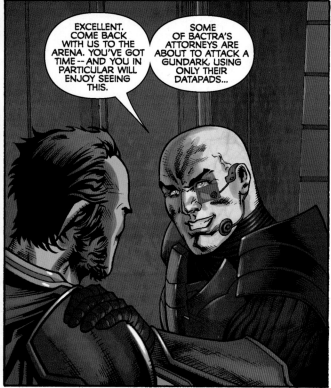

EXCELLENT. COME BACK WITH US TO THE ARENA. YOU'VE GOT TIME -- AND YOU IN PARTICULAR WILL ENJOY SEEING THIS.

SOME OF BACTRA'S ATTORNEYS ARE ABOUT TO ATTACK A GUNDARK, USING ONLY THEIR DATAPADS...

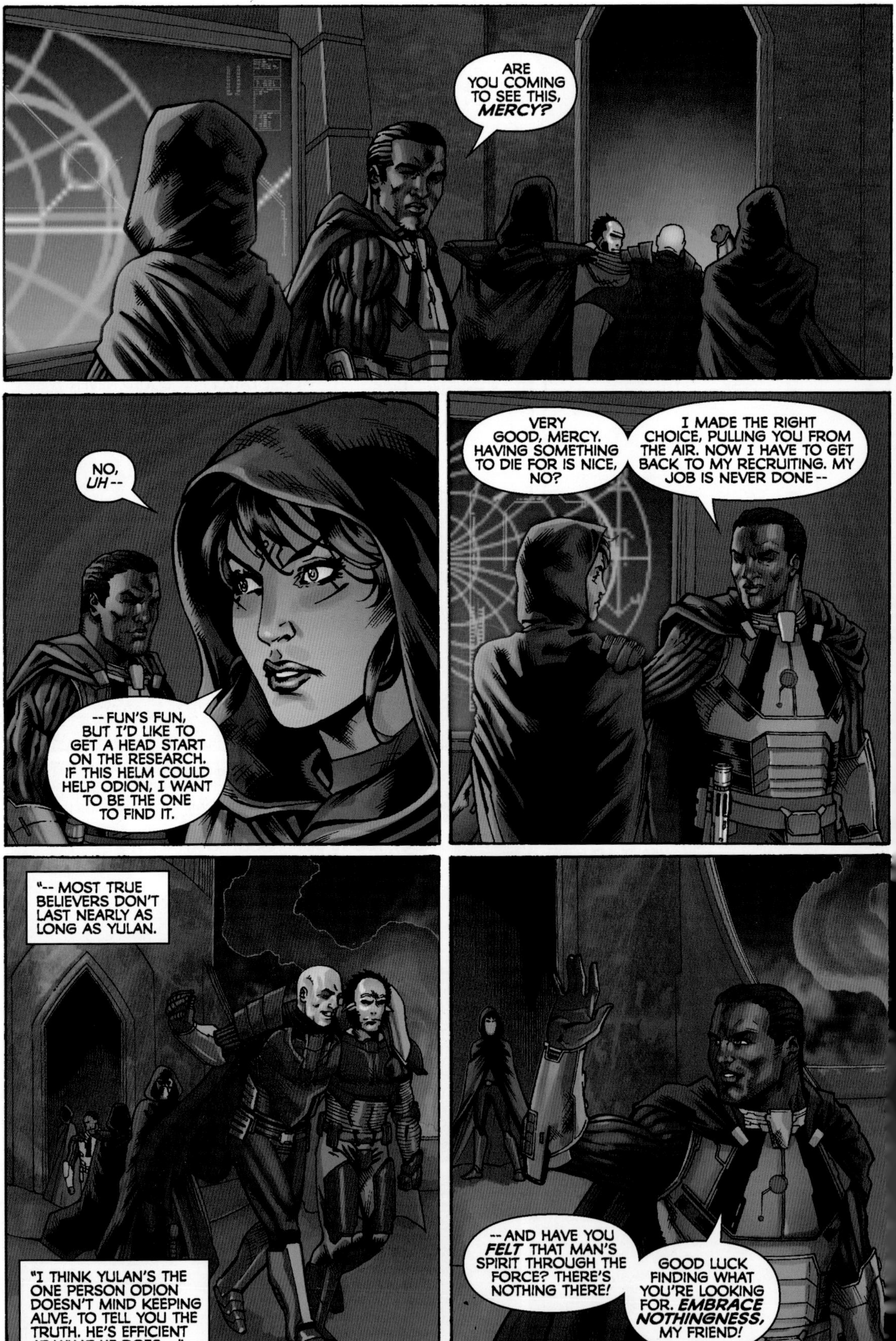
ARE YOU COMING TO SEE THIS, *MERCY?*
NO, *UH*--
--FUN'S FUN, BUT I'D LIKE TO GET A HEAD START ON THE RESEARCH. IF THIS HELM COULD HELP ODION, I WANT TO BE THE ONE TO FIND IT.
VERY GOOD, MERCY. HAVING SOMETHING TO DIE FOR IS NICE, NO?
I MADE THE RIGHT CHOICE, PULLING YOU FROM THE AIR. NOW I HAVE TO GET BACK TO MY RECRUITING. MY JOB IS NEVER DONE--
"-- MOST TRUE BELIEVERS DON'T LAST NEARLY AS LONG AS YULAN.
"I THINK YULAN'S THE ONE PERSON ODION DOESN'T MIND KEEPING ALIVE, TO TELL YOU THE TRUTH. HE'S EFFICIENT AT WHAT HE DOES --"
--AND HAVE YOU *FELT* THAT MAN'S SPIRIT THROUGH THE FORCE? THERE'S NOTHING THERE!
GOOD LUCK FINDING WHAT YOU'RE LOOKING FOR. *EMBRACE NOTHINGNESS,* MY FRIEND!

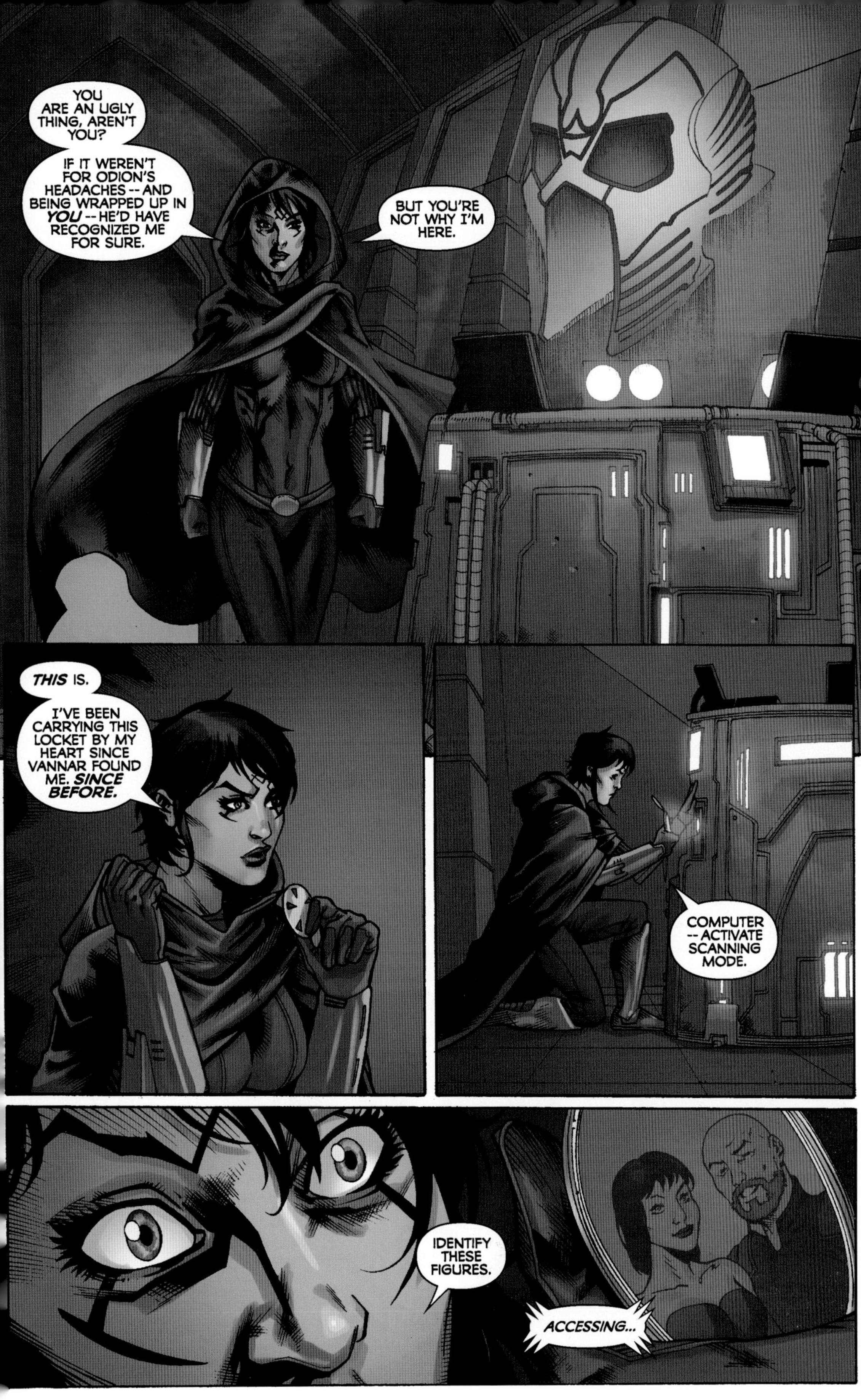
YOU ARE AN UGLY THING, AREN'T YOU?
IF IT WEREN'T FOR ODION'S HEADACHES -- AND BEING WRAPPED UP IN *YOU* -- HE'D HAVE RECOGNIZED ME FOR SURE.
BUT YOU'RE NOT WHY I'M HERE.
THIS IS.
I'VE BEEN CARRYING THIS LOCKET BY MY HEART SINCE VANNAR FOUND ME. *SINCE BEFORE.*
COMPUTER -- ACTIVATE SCANNING MODE.
IDENTIFY THESE FIGURES.
ACCESSING...

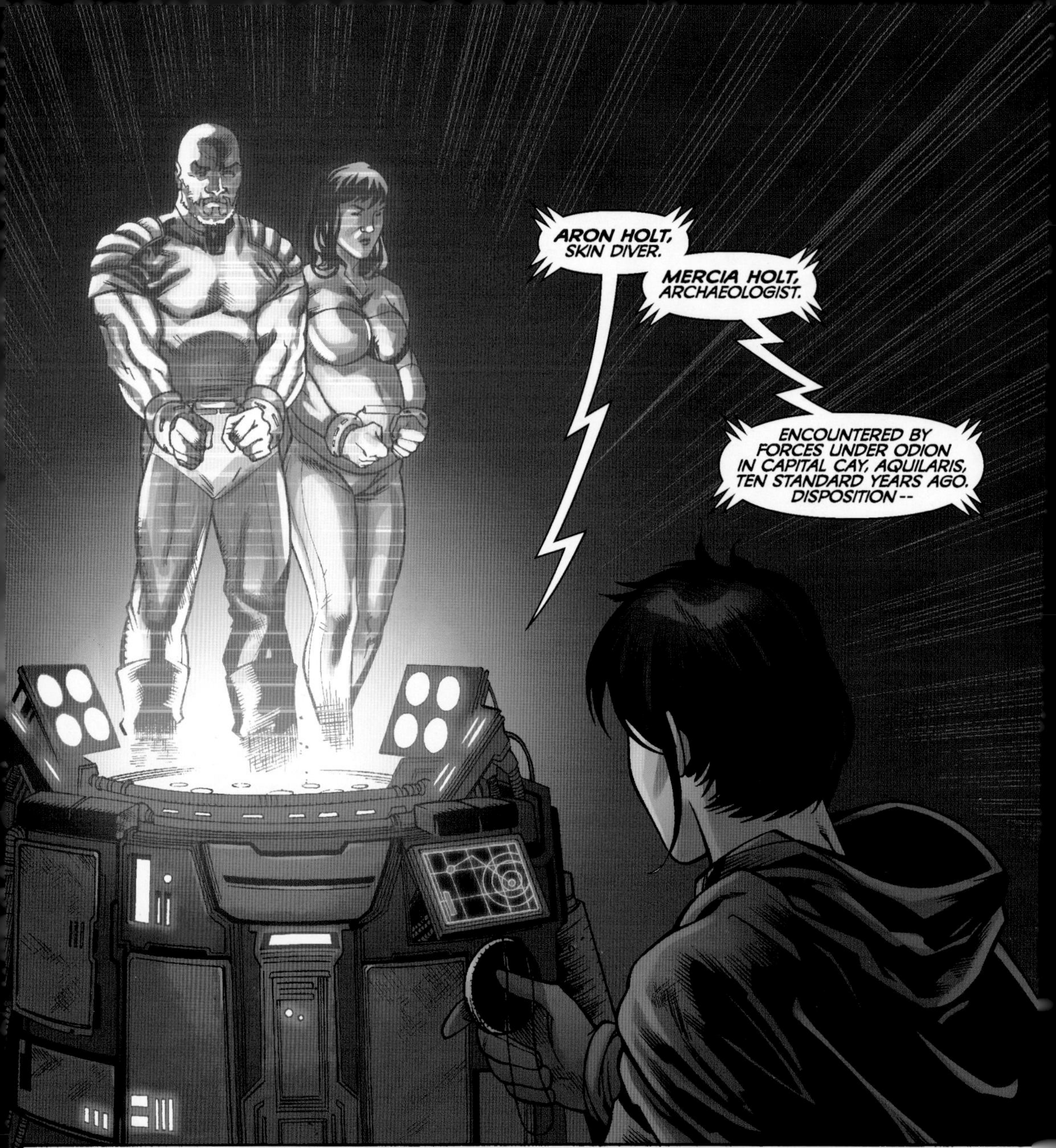
ARON HOLT, SKIN DIVER.
MERCIA HOLT, ARCHAEOLOGIST.
ENCOUNTERED BY FORCES UNDER ODION IN CAPITAL CAY, AQUILARIS, TEN STANDARD YEARS AGO. DISPOSITION --

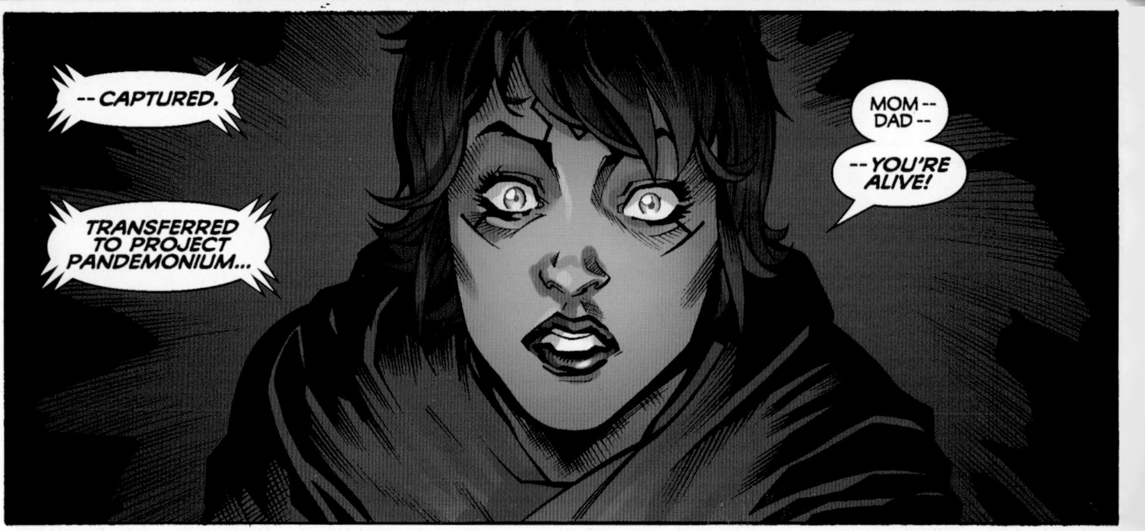
-- CAPTURED.
TRANSFERRED TO PROJECT PANDEMONIUM...
MOM -- DAD --
-- YOU'RE ALIVE!

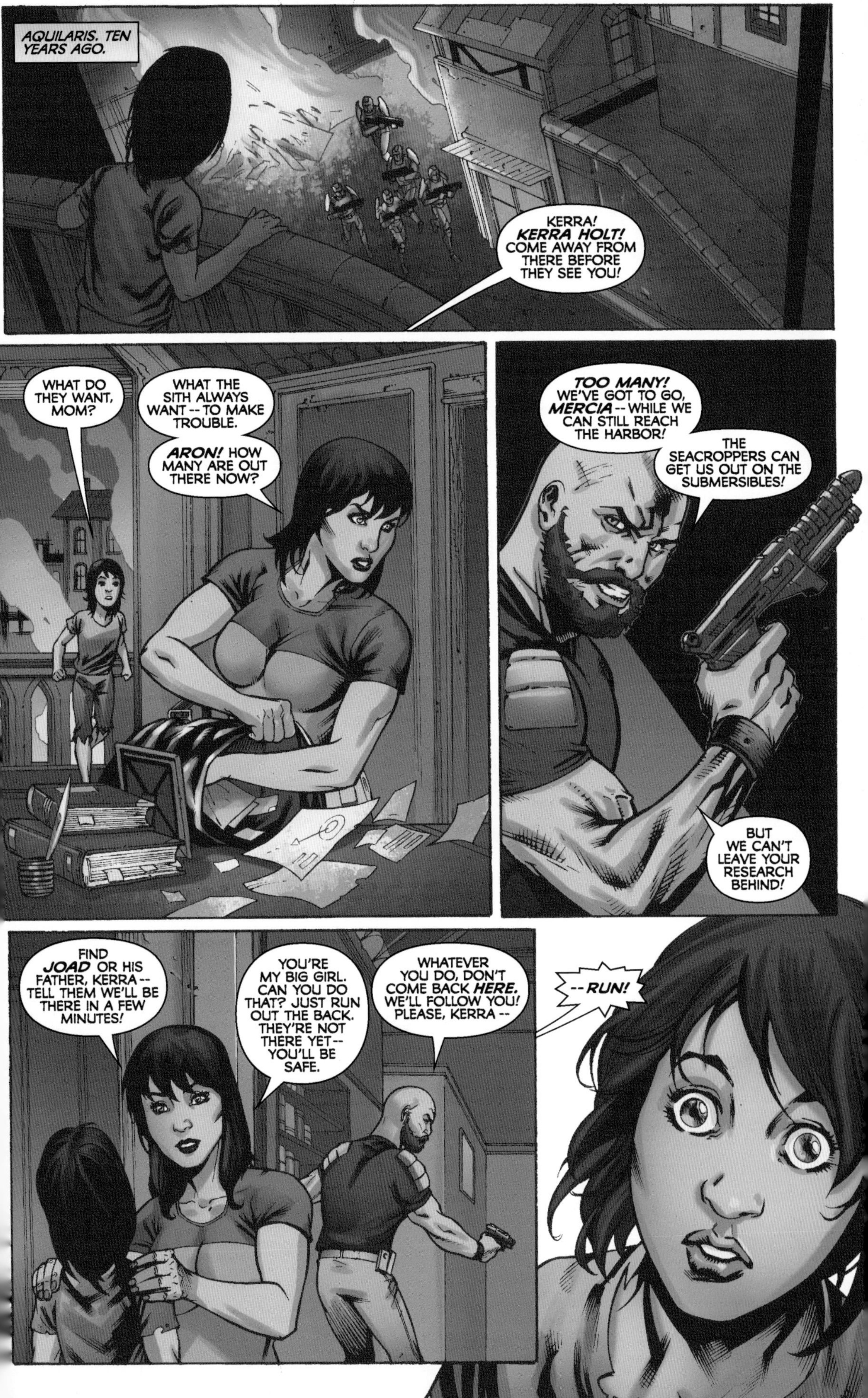
AQUILARIS. TEN YEARS AGO.
KERRA! KERRA HOLT! COME AWAY FROM THERE BEFORE THEY SEE YOU!
WHAT DO THEY WANT, MOM?
WHAT THE SITH ALWAYS WANT -- TO MAKE TROUBLE.
ARON! HOW MANY ARE OUT THERE NOW?
TOO MANY! WE'VE GOT TO GO, MERCIA -- WHILE WE CAN STILL REACH THE HARBOR!
THE SEACROPPERS CAN GET US OUT ON THE SUBMERSIBLES!
BUT WE CAN'T LEAVE YOUR RESEARCH BEHIND!
FIND JOAD OR HIS FATHER, KERRA -- TELL THEM WE'LL BE THERE IN A FEW MINUTES!
YOU'RE MY BIG GIRL. CAN YOU DO THAT? JUST RUN OUT THE BACK. THEY'RE NOT THERE YET -- YOU'LL BE SAFE.
WHATEVER YOU DO, DON'T COME BACK HERE. WE'LL FOLLOW YOU! PLEASE, KERRA --
-- RUN!

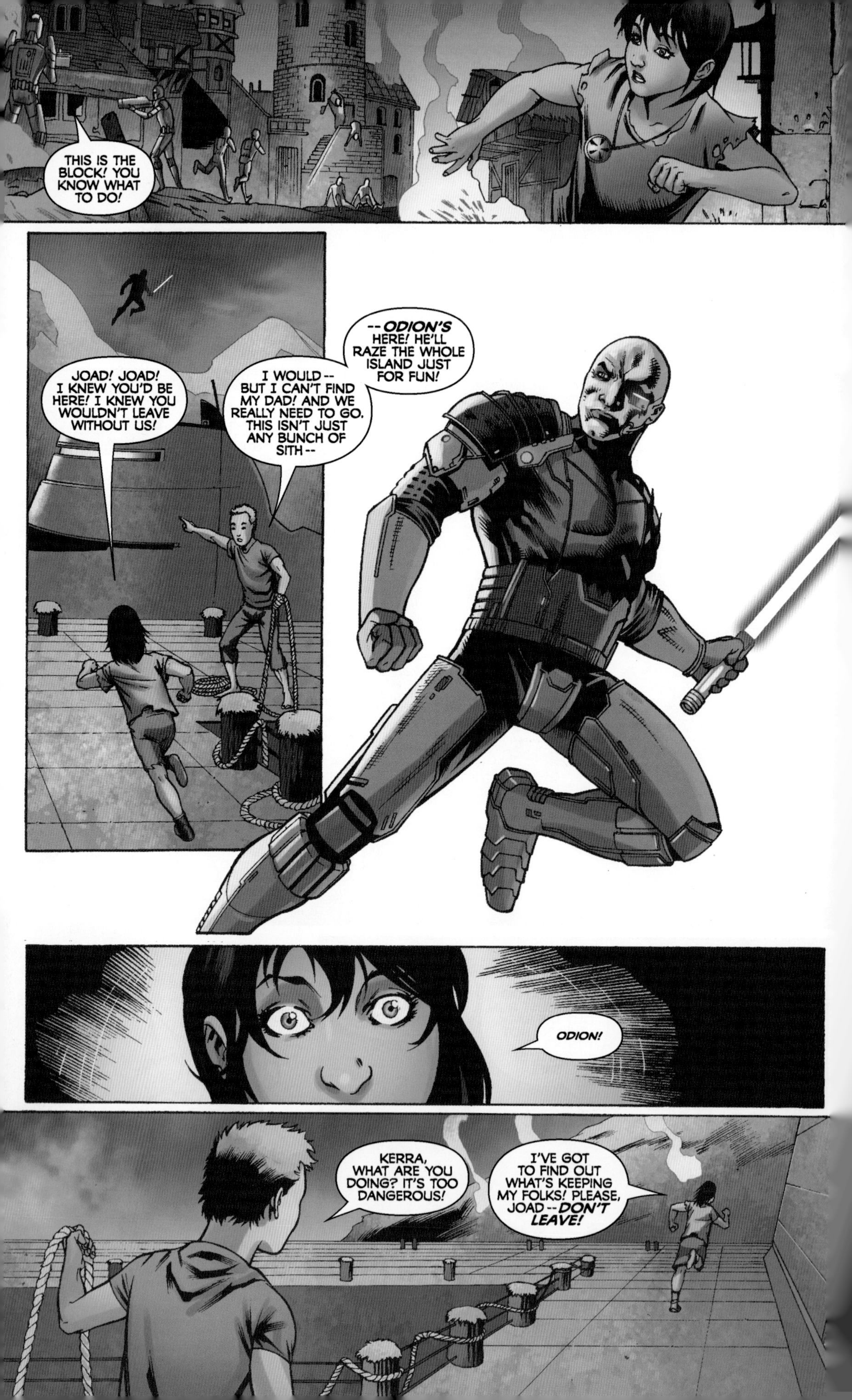
THIS IS THE BLOCK! YOU KNOW WHAT TO DO!
JOAD! JOAD! I KNEW YOU'D BE HERE! I KNEW YOU WOULDN'T LEAVE WITHOUT US!
I WOULD -- BUT I CAN'T FIND MY DAD! AND WE REALLY NEED TO GO. THIS ISN'T JUST ANY BUNCH OF SITH --
-- ODION'S HERE! HE'LL RAZE THE WHOLE ISLAND JUST FOR FUN!
ODION!
KERRA, WHAT ARE YOU DOING? IT'S TOO DANGEROUS!
I'VE GOT TO FIND OUT WHAT'S KEEPING MY FOLKS! PLEASE, JOAD -- DON'T LEAVE!

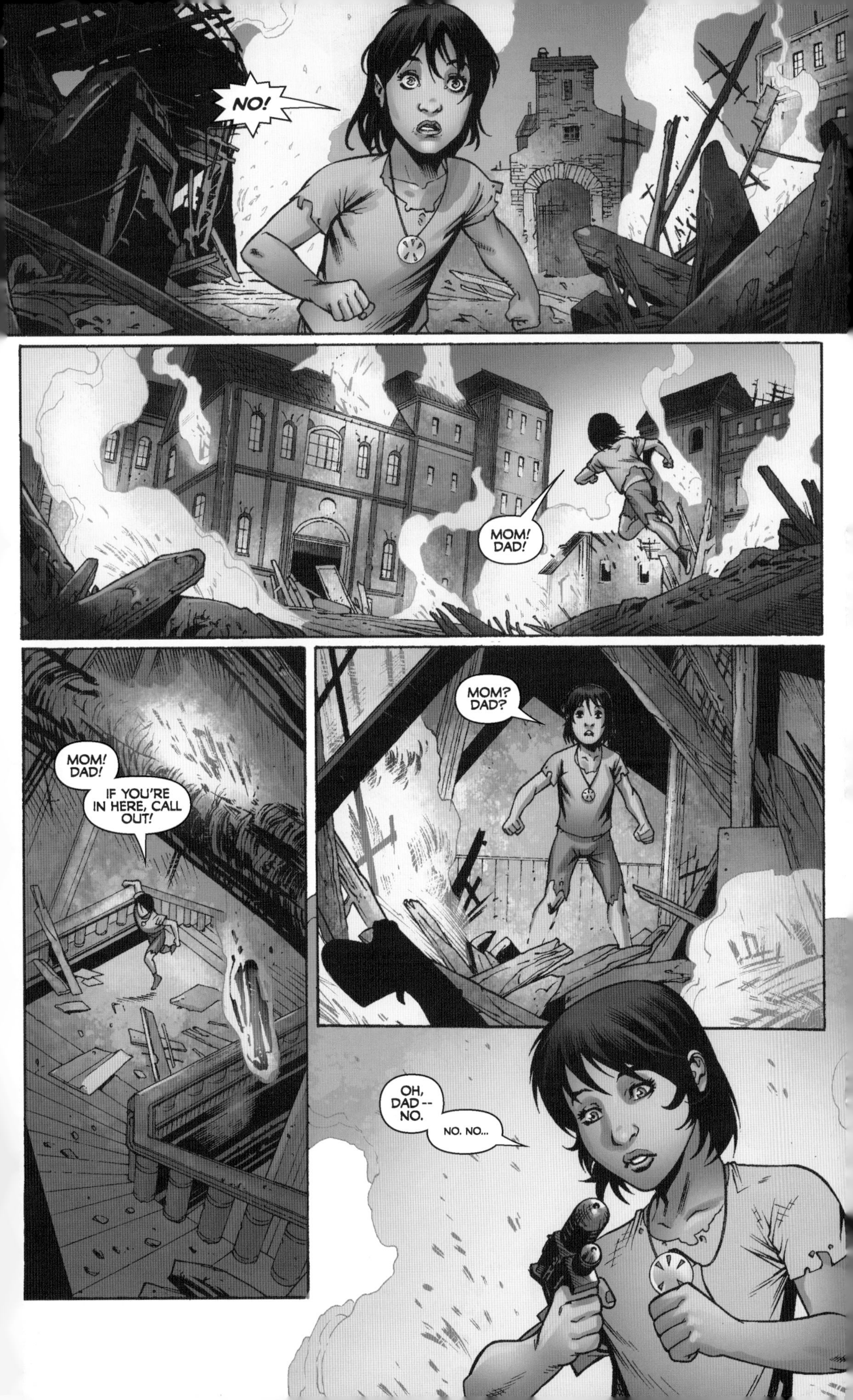
NO!
MOM! DAD!
MOM! DAD!
IF YOU'RE IN HERE, CALL OUT!
MOM? DAD?
OH, DAD -- NO.
NO. NO...

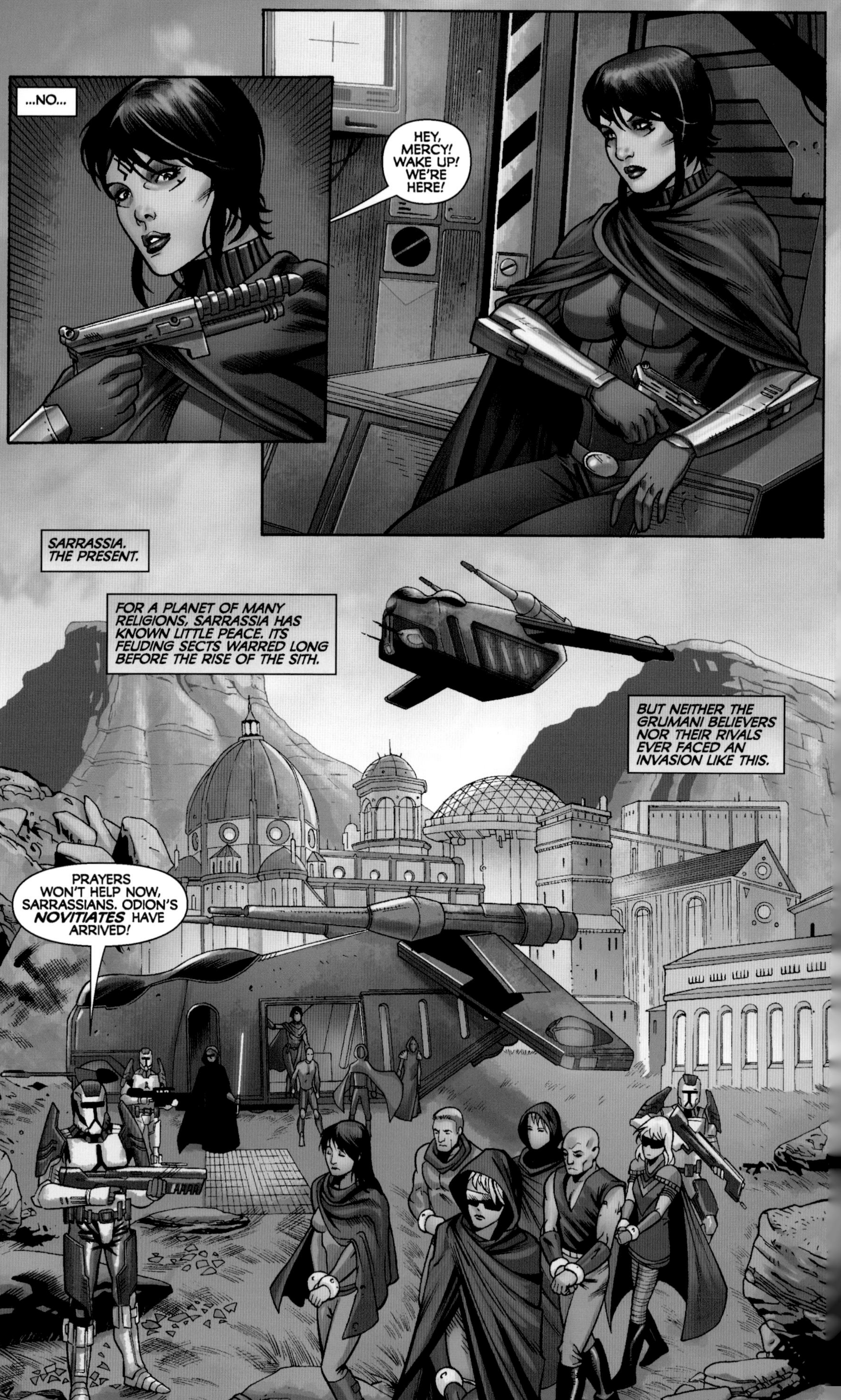
...NO...
HEY, MERCY! WAKE UP! WE'RE HERE!
SARRASSIA. THE PRESENT.
FOR A PLANET OF MANY RELIGIONS, SARRASSIA HAS KNOWN LITTLE PEACE. ITS FEUDING SECTS WARRED LONG BEFORE THE RISE OF THE SITH.
BUT NEITHER THE GRUMANI BELIEVERS NOR THEIR RIVALS EVER FACED AN INVASION LIKE THIS.
PRAYERS WON'T HELP NOW, SARRASSIANS. ODION'S NOVITIATES HAVE ARRIVED!

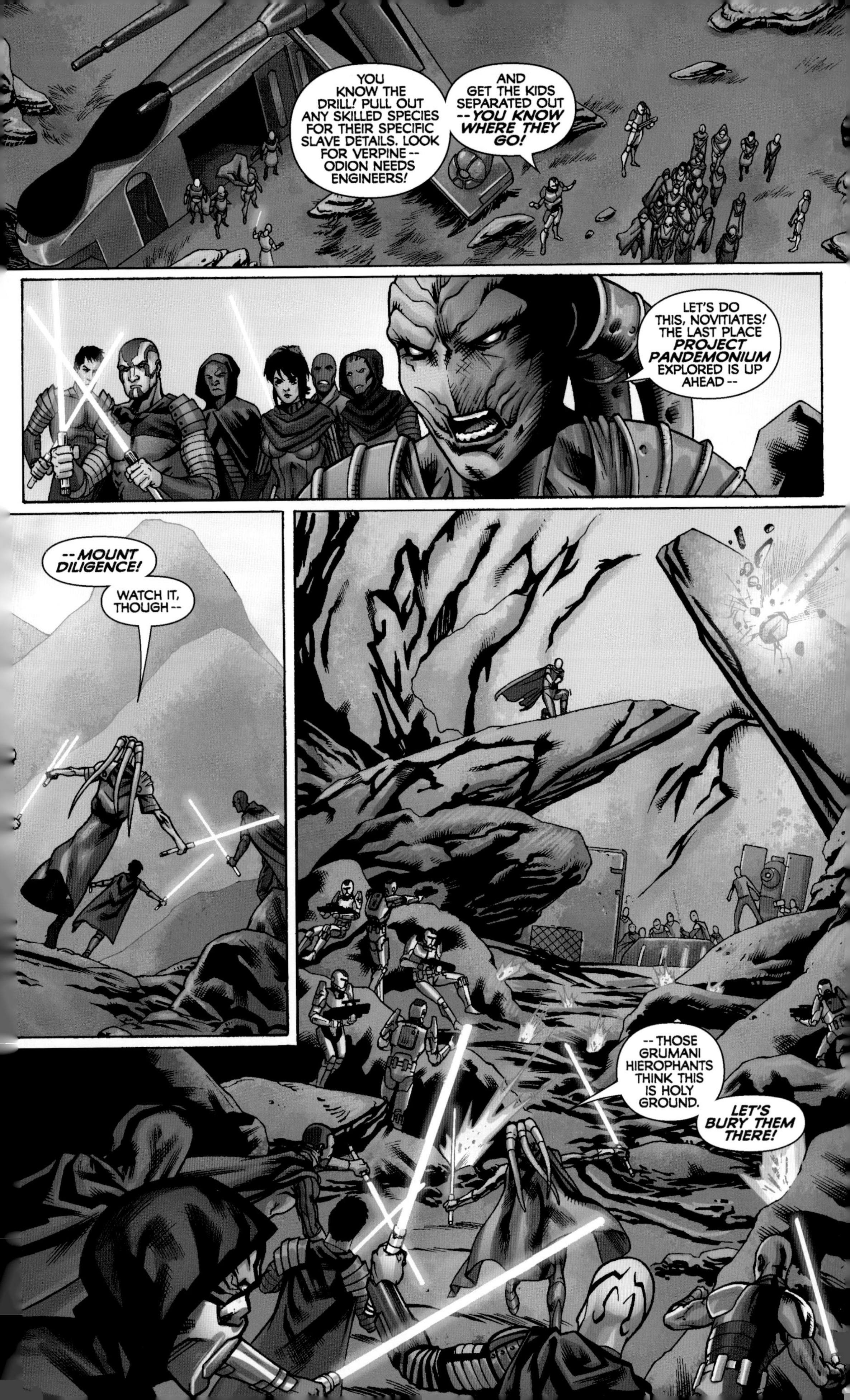
YOU KNOW THE DRILL! PULL OUT ANY SKILLED SPECIES FOR THEIR SPECIFIC SLAVE DETAILS. LOOK FOR VERPINE -- ODION NEEDS ENGINEERS!
AND GET THE KIDS SEPARATED OUT -- YOU KNOW WHERE THEY GO!
LET'S DO THIS, NOVITIATES! THE LAST PLACE PROJECT PANDEMONIUM EXPLORED IS UP AHEAD --
-- MOUNT DILIGENCE!
WATCH IT, THOUGH --
-- THOSE GRUMANI HIEROPHANTS THINK THIS IS HOLY GROUND.
LET'S BURY THEM THERE!

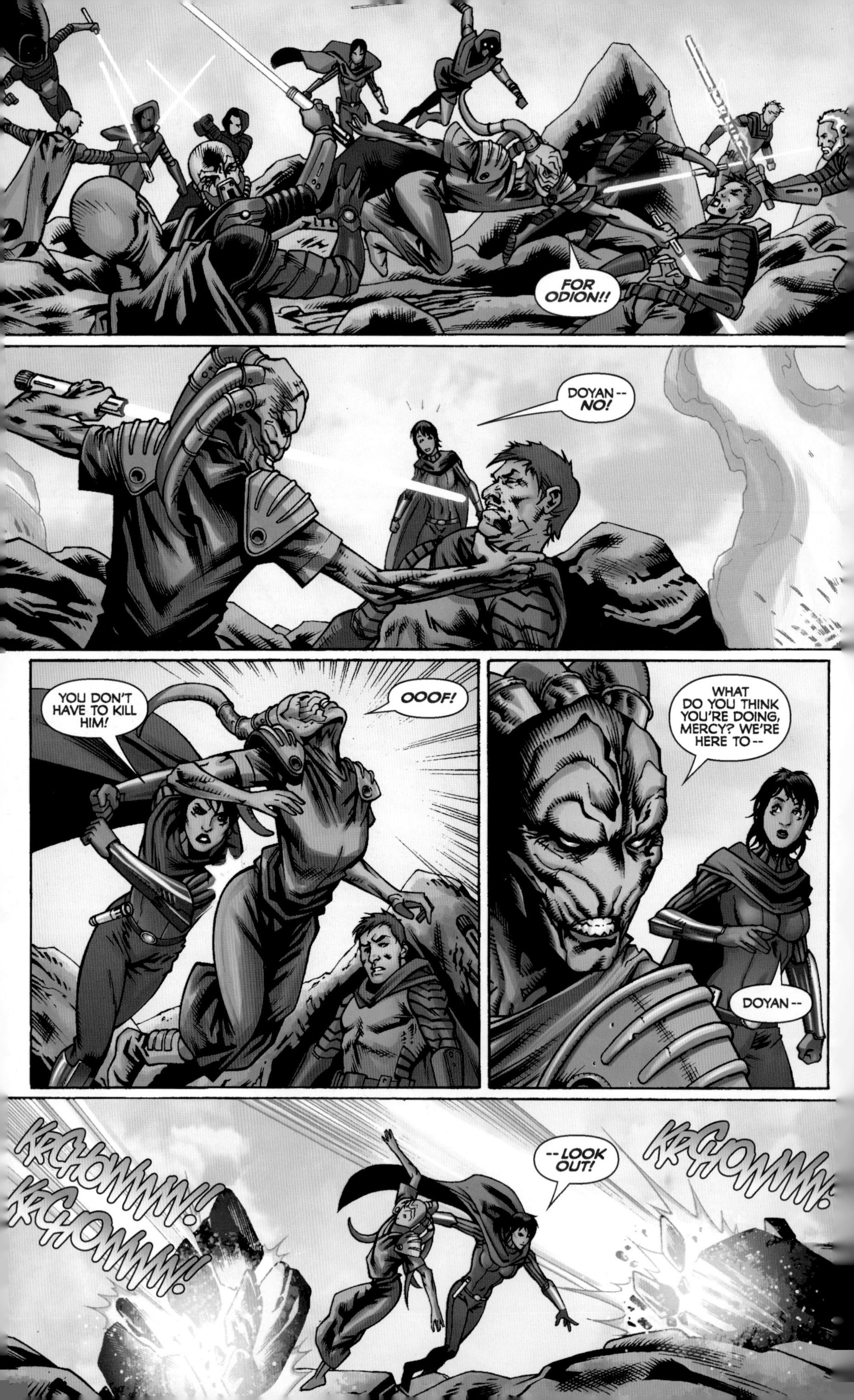
FOR ODION!!
DOYAN -- NO!
YOU DON'T HAVE TO KILL HIM!
OOOF!
WHAT DO YOU THINK YOU'RE DOING, MERCY? WE'RE HERE TO --
DOYAN --
KRCHOWWW!
KRCHOWWW!
--LOOK OUT!
KRCHOWWW!

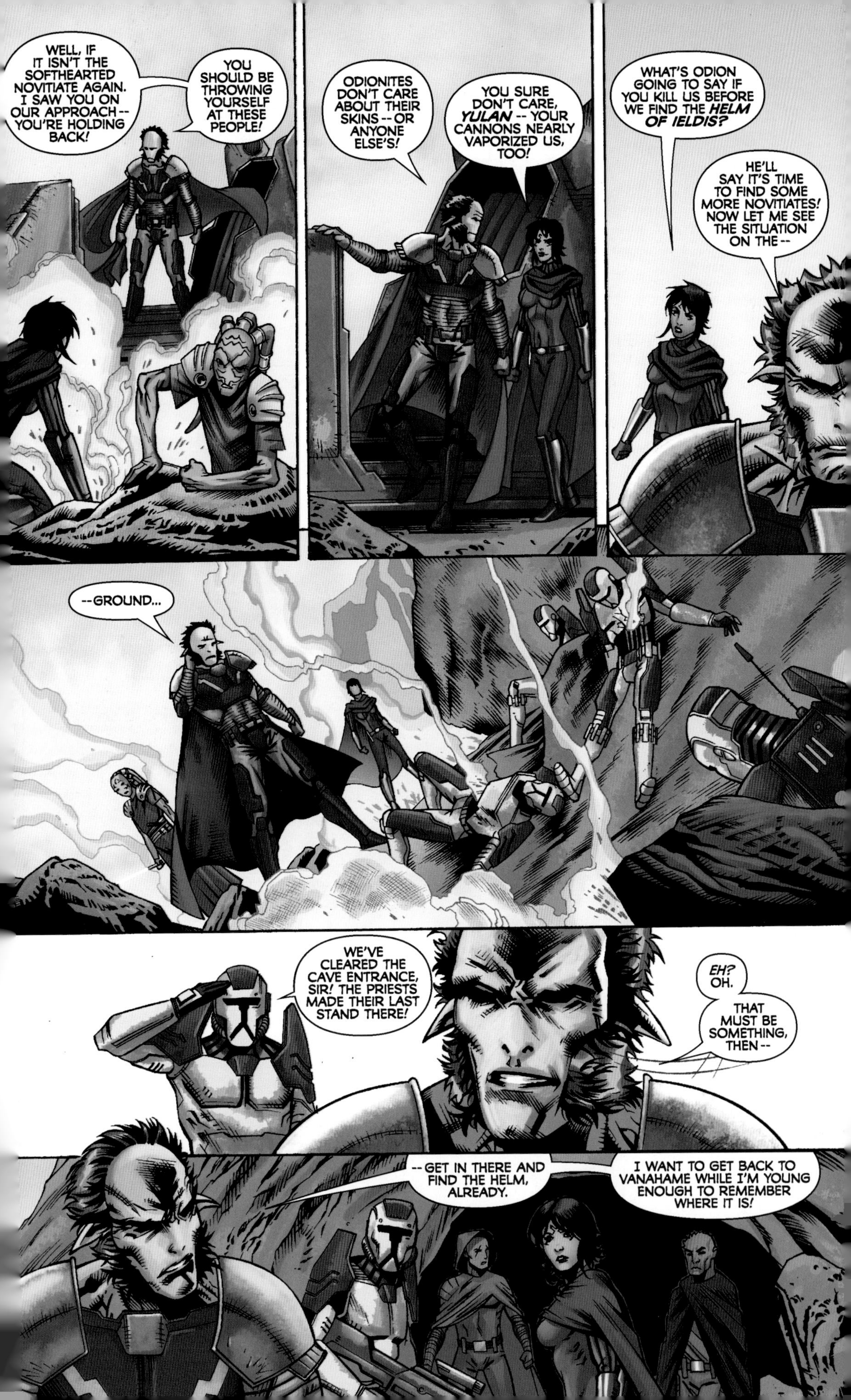
WELL, IF IT ISN'T THE SOFTHEARTED NOVITIATE AGAIN. I SAW YOU ON OUR APPROACH -- YOU'RE HOLDING BACK!
YOU SHOULD BE THROWING YOURSELF AT THESE PEOPLE!
ODIONITES DON'T CARE ABOUT THEIR SKINS -- OR ANYONE ELSE'S!
YOU SURE DON'T CARE, YULAN -- YOUR CANNONS NEARLY VAPORIZED US, TOO!
WHAT'S ODION GOING TO SAY IF YOU KILL US BEFORE WE FIND THE HELM OF IELDIS?
HE'LL SAY IT'S TIME TO FIND SOME MORE NOVITIATES! NOW LET ME SEE THE SITUATION ON THE --
--GROUND...
WE'VE CLEARED THE CAVE ENTRANCE, SIR! THE PRIESTS MADE THEIR LAST STAND THERE!
EH? OH.
THAT MUST BE SOMETHING, THEN --
-- GET IN THERE AND FIND THE HELM, ALREADY.
I WANT TO GET BACK TO VANAHAME WHILE I'M YOUNG ENOUGH TO REMEMBER WHERE IT IS!

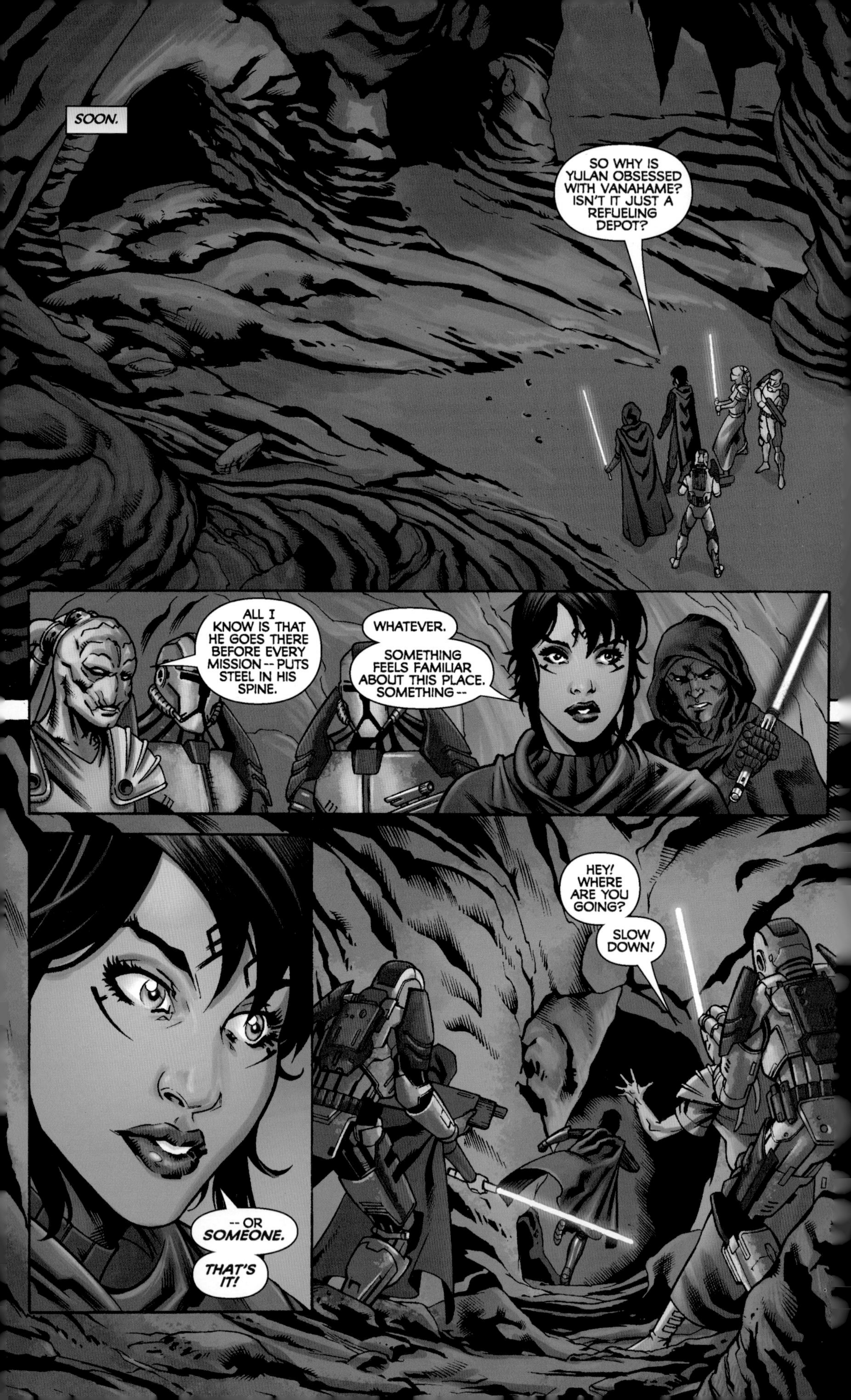
SOON.
SO WHY IS YULAN OBSESSED WITH VANAHAME? ISN'T IT JUST A REFUELING DEPOT?
ALL I KNOW IS THAT HE GOES THERE BEFORE EVERY MISSION -- PUTS STEEL IN HIS SPINE.
WHATEVER.
SOMETHING FEELS FAMILIAR ABOUT THIS PLACE. SOMETHING --
-- OR SOMEONE.
THAT'S IT!
HEY! WHERE ARE YOU GOING?
SLOW DOWN!

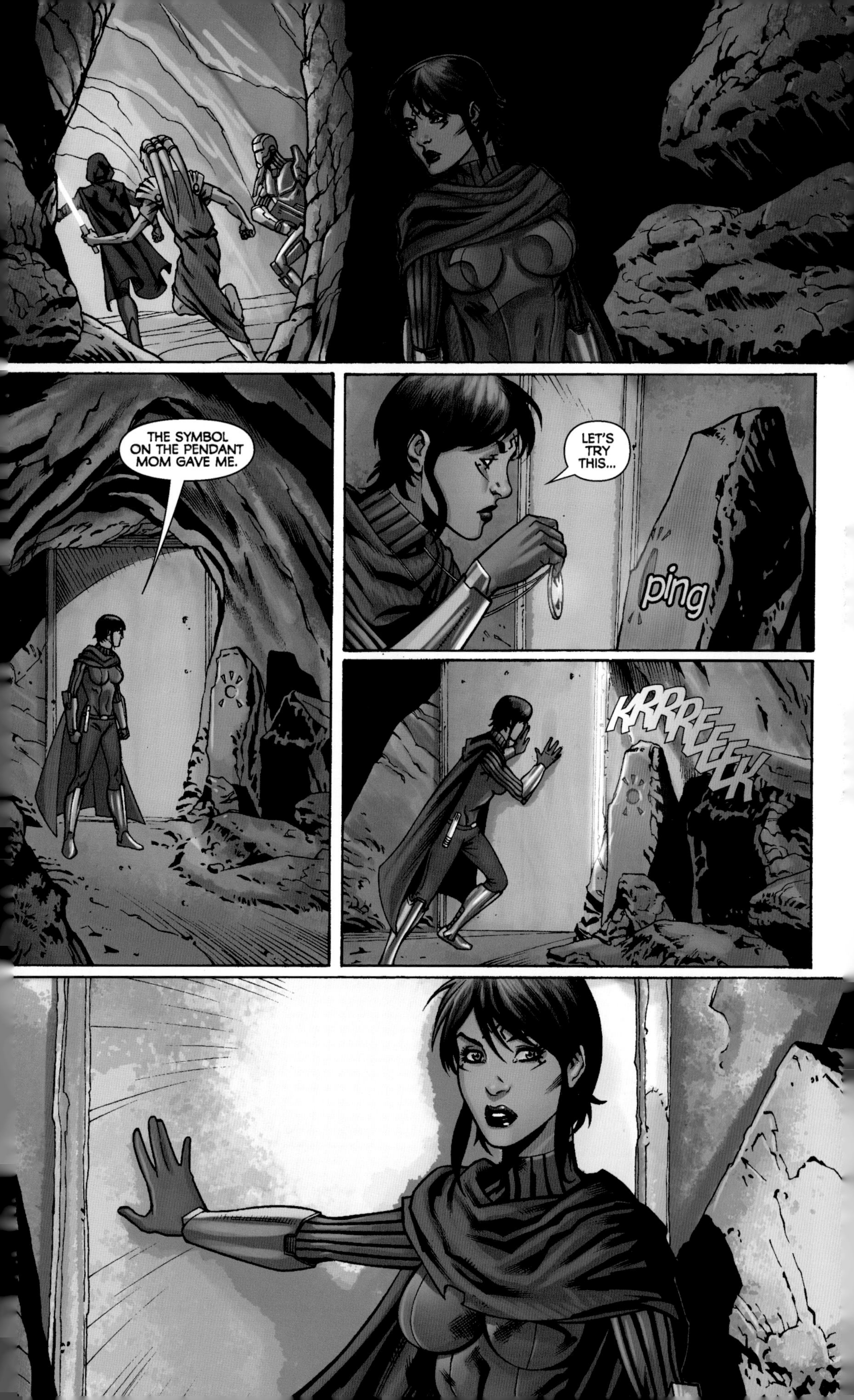
THE SYMBOL ON THE PENDANT MOM GAVE ME.
LET'S TRY THIS...
ping
KRRREEEEK

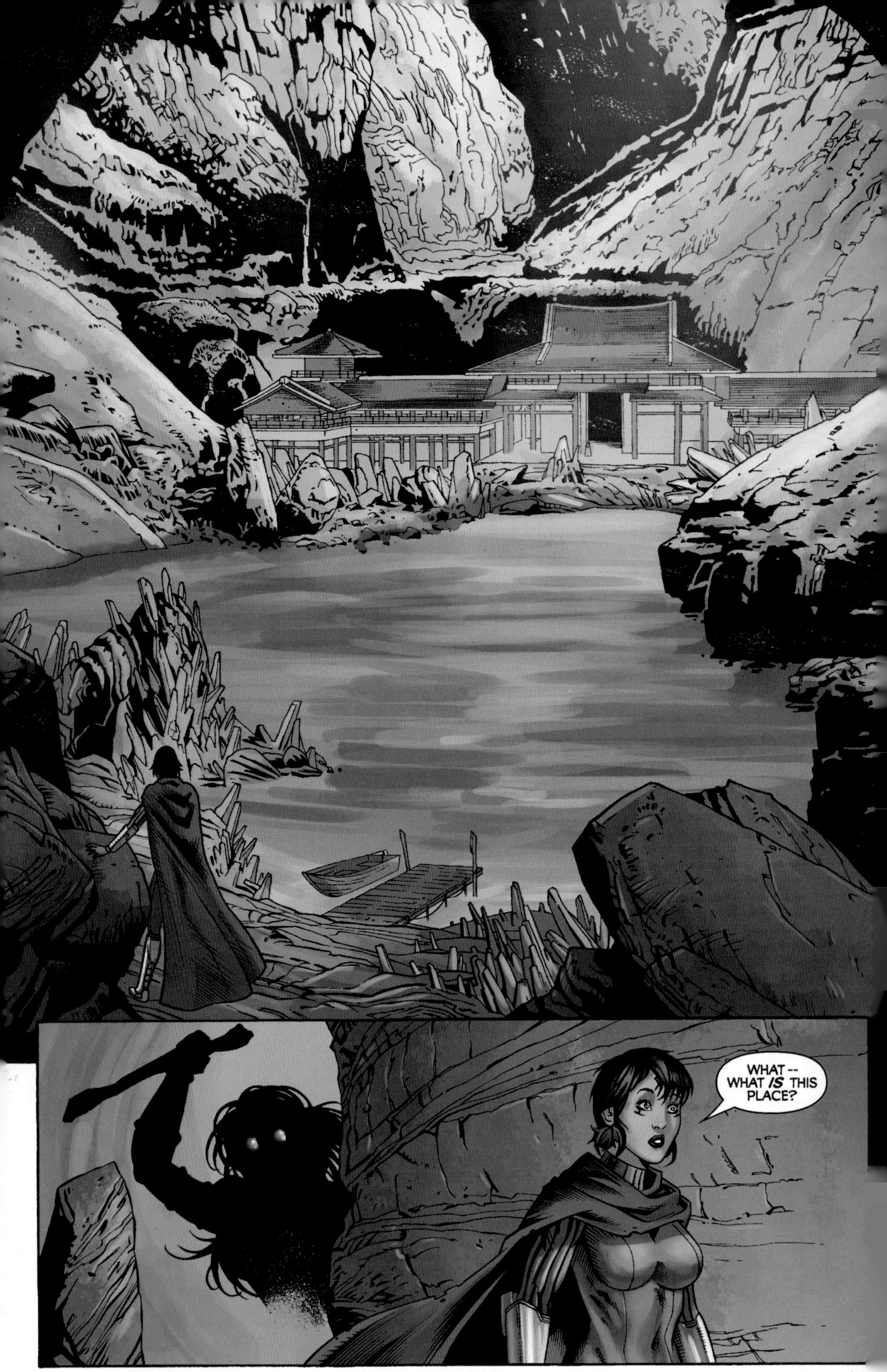
WHAT -- WHAT *IS* THIS PLACE?

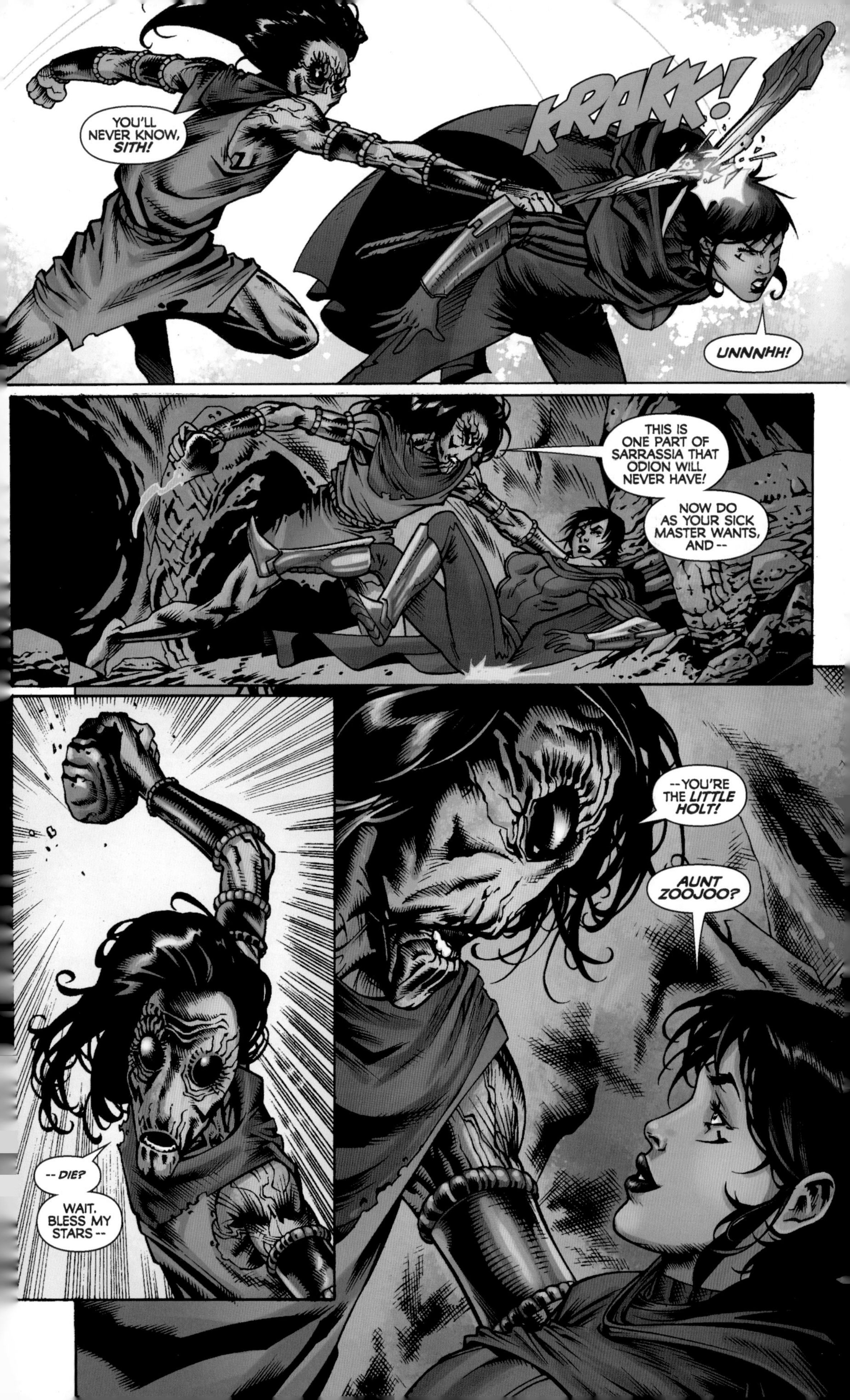

YOU'LL NEVER KNOW, SITH!
KRAKK!
UNNNHH!
THIS IS ONE PART OF SARRASSIA THAT ODION WILL NEVER HAVE!
NOW DO AS YOUR SICK MASTER WANTS, AND --
-- DIE?
WAIT. BLESS MY STARS --
-- YOU'RE THE LITTLE HOLT!
AUNT ZOOJOO?

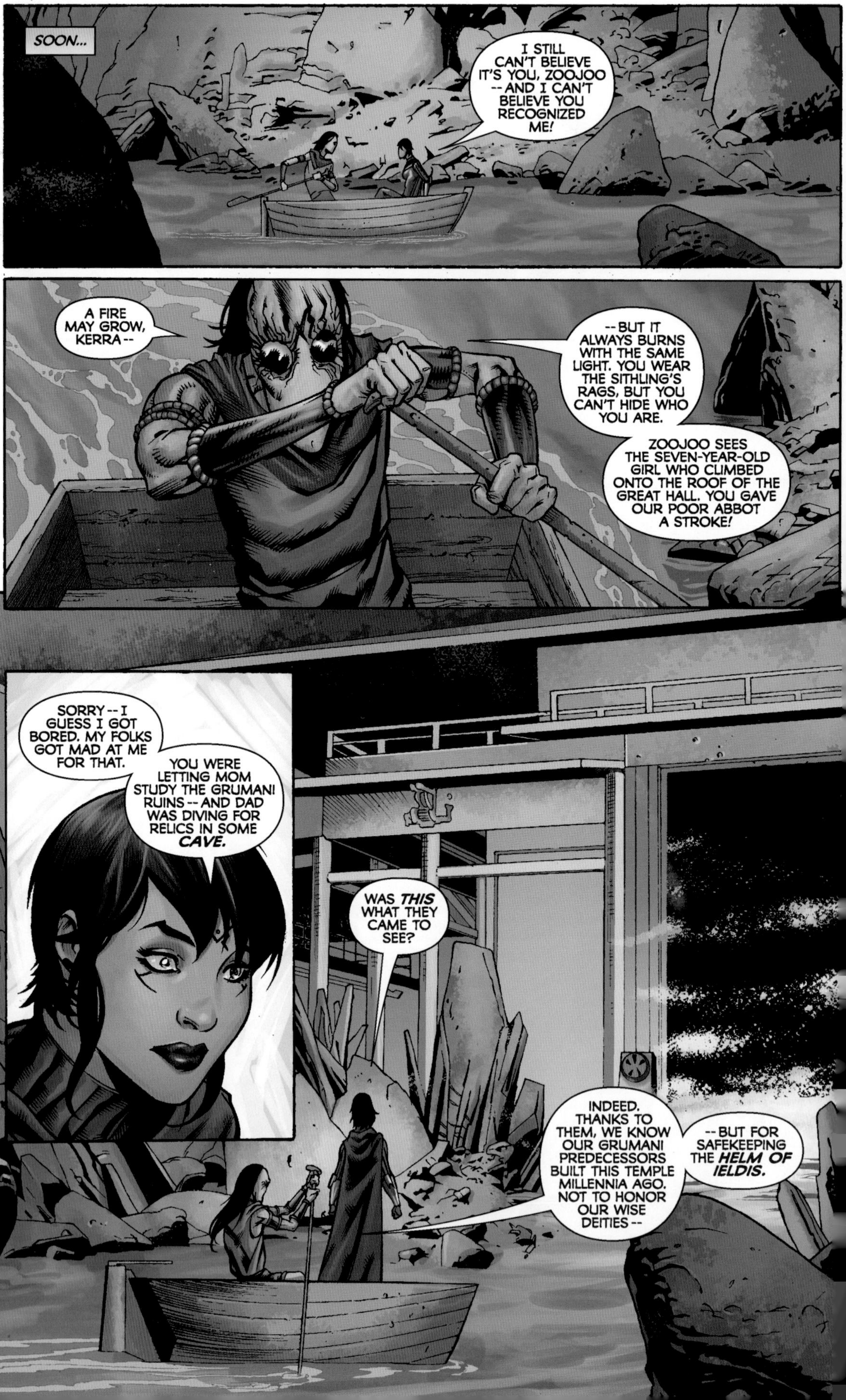
SOON...
I STILL CAN'T BELIEVE IT'S YOU, ZOOJOO --AND I CAN'T BELIEVE YOU RECOGNIZED ME!
A FIRE MAY GROW, KERRA--
--BUT IT ALWAYS BURNS WITH THE SAME LIGHT. YOU WEAR THE SITHLING'S RAGS, BUT YOU CAN'T HIDE WHO YOU ARE.
ZOOJOO SEES THE SEVEN-YEAR-OLD GIRL WHO CLIMBED ONTO THE ROOF OF THE GREAT HALL. YOU GAVE OUR POOR ABBOT A STROKE!
SORRY--I GUESS I GOT BORED. MY FOLKS GOT MAD AT ME FOR THAT.
YOU WERE LETTING MOM STUDY THE GRUMANI RUINS--AND DAD WAS DIVING FOR RELICS IN SOME CAVE.
WAS THIS WHAT THEY CAME TO SEE?
INDEED. THANKS TO THEM, WE KNOW OUR GRUMANI PREDECESSORS BUILT THIS TEMPLE MILLENNIA AGO. NOT TO HONOR OUR WISE DEITIES--
--BUT FOR SAFEKEEPING THE HELM OF IELDIS.

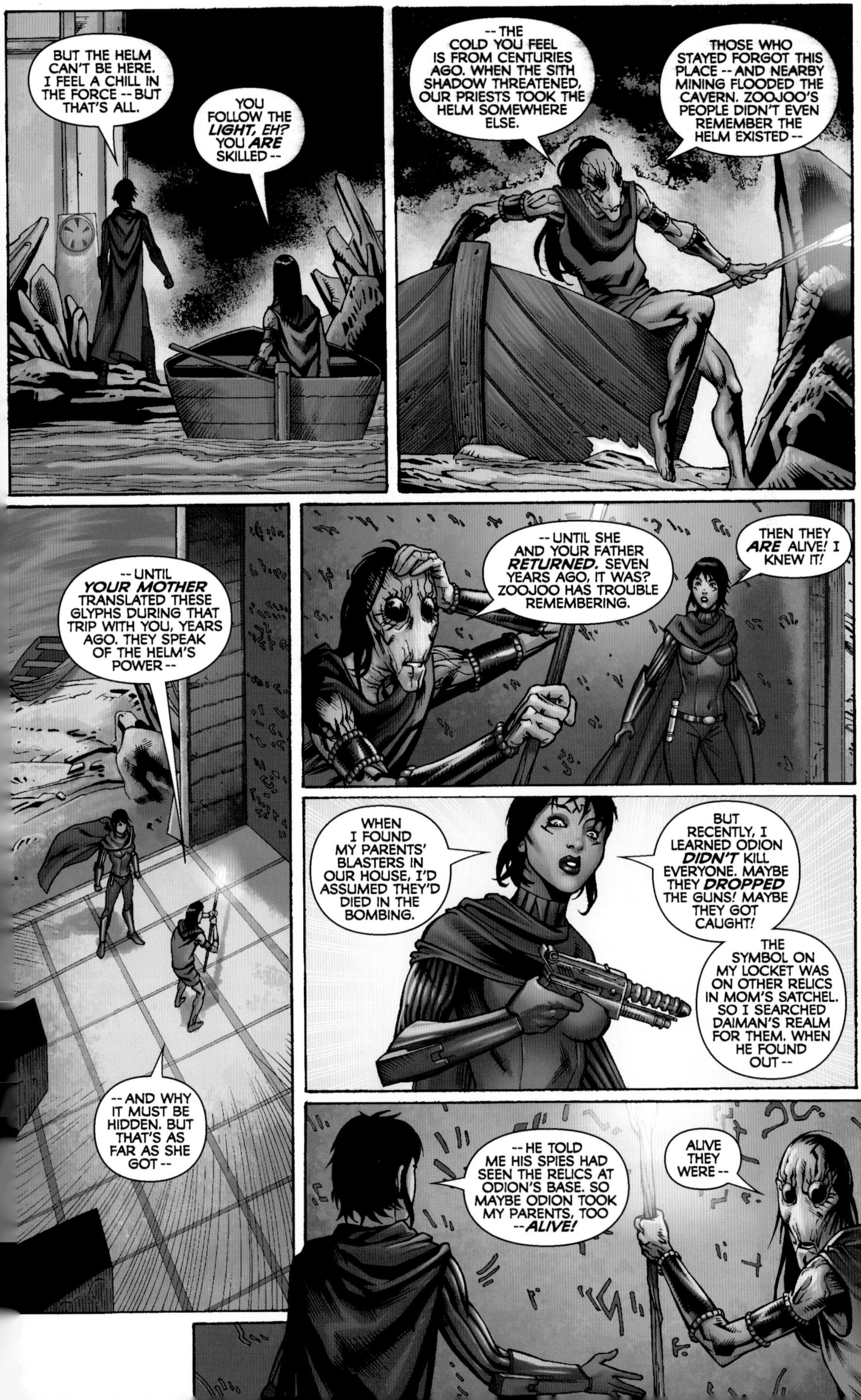

BUT THE HELM CAN'T BE HERE. I FEEL A CHILL IN THE FORCE -- BUT THAT'S ALL.
YOU FOLLOW THE LIGHT, EH? YOU ARE SKILLED --
-- THE COLD YOU FEEL IS FROM CENTURIES AGO. WHEN THE SITH SHADOW THREATENED, OUR PRIESTS TOOK THE HELM SOMEWHERE ELSE.
THOSE WHO STAYED FORGOT THIS PLACE -- AND NEARBY MINING FLOODED THE CAVERN. ZOOJOO'S PEOPLE DIDN'T EVEN REMEMBER THE HELM EXISTED --
-- UNTIL YOUR MOTHER TRANSLATED THESE GLYPHS DURING THAT TRIP WITH YOU, YEARS AGO. THEY SPEAK OF THE HELM'S POWER --
-- AND WHY IT MUST BE HIDDEN. BUT THAT'S AS FAR AS SHE GOT --
-- UNTIL SHE AND YOUR FATHER RETURNED. SEVEN YEARS AGO, IT WAS? ZOOJOO HAS TROUBLE REMEMBERING.
THEN THEY ARE ALIVE! I KNEW IT!
WHEN I FOUND MY PARENTS' BLASTERS IN OUR HOUSE, I'D ASSUMED THEY'D DIED IN THE BOMBING.
BUT RECENTLY, I LEARNED ODION DIDN'T KILL EVERYONE. MAYBE THEY DROPPED THE GUNS! MAYBE THEY GOT CAUGHT!
THE SYMBOL ON MY LOCKET WAS ON OTHER RELICS IN MOM'S SATCHEL. SO I SEARCHED DAIMAN'S REALM FOR THEM. WHEN HE FOUND OUT --
-- HE TOLD ME HIS SPIES HAD SEEN THE RELICS AT ODION'S BASE. SO MAYBE ODION TOOK MY PARENTS, TOO -- ALIVE!
ALIVE THEY WERE --

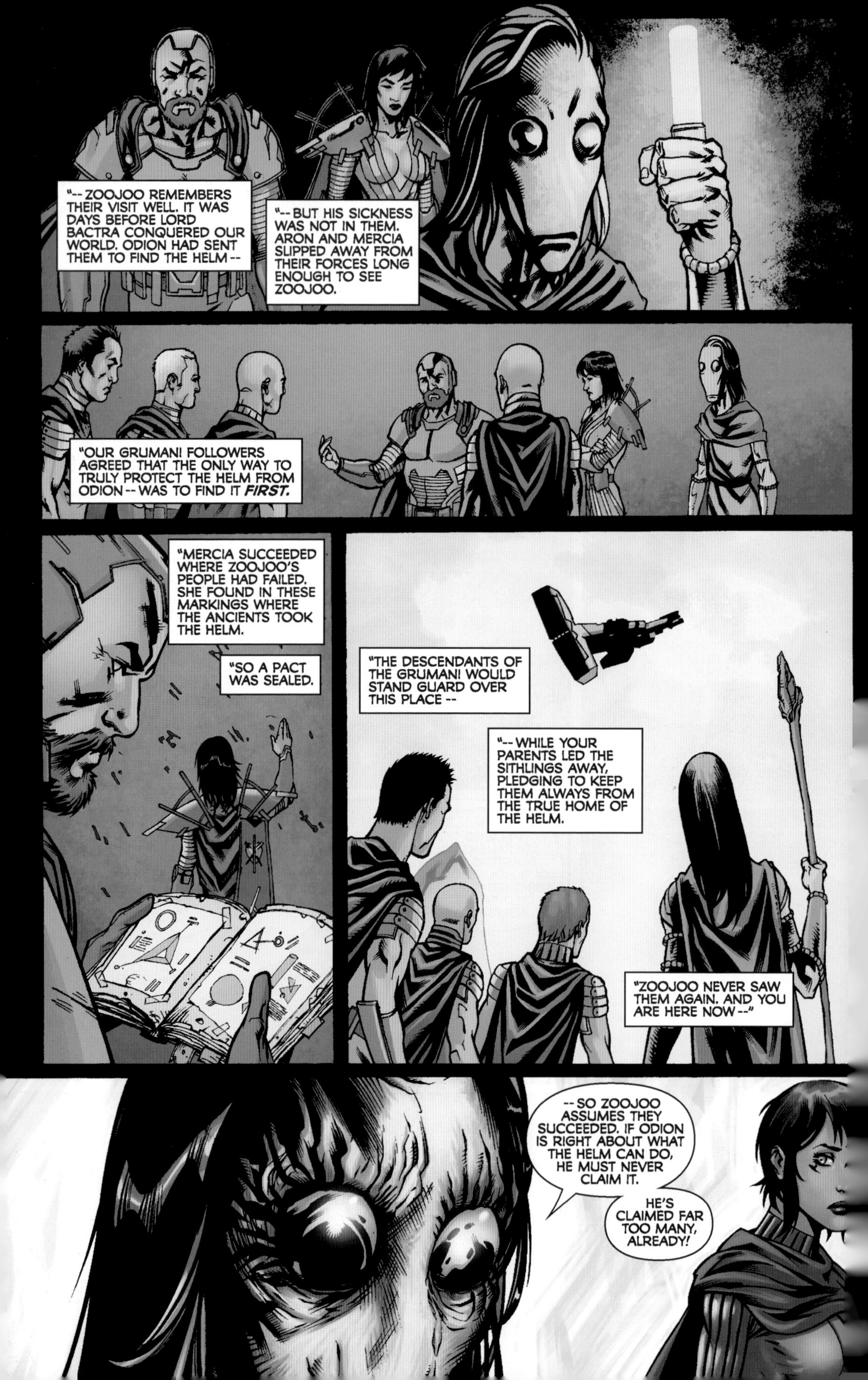
"-- ZOOJOO REMEMBERS THEIR VISIT WELL. IT WAS DAYS BEFORE LORD BACTRA CONQUERED OUR WORLD. ODION HAD SENT THEM TO FIND THE HELM --
"-- BUT HIS SICKNESS WAS NOT IN THEM. ARON AND MERCIA SLIPPED AWAY FROM THEIR FORCES LONG ENOUGH TO SEE ZOOJOO.
"OUR GRUMANI FOLLOWERS AGREED THAT THE ONLY WAY TO TRULY PROTECT THE HELM FROM ODION -- WAS TO FIND IT *FIRST.*
"MERCIA SUCCEEDED WHERE ZOOJOO'S PEOPLE HAD FAILED. SHE FOUND IN THESE MARKINGS WHERE THE ANCIENTS TOOK THE HELM.
"SO A PACT WAS SEALED.
"THE DESCENDANTS OF THE GRUMANI WOULD STAND GUARD OVER THIS PLACE --
"-- WHILE YOUR PARENTS LED THE SITHLINGS AWAY, PLEDGING TO KEEP THEM ALWAYS FROM THE TRUE HOME OF THE HELM.
"ZOOJOO NEVER SAW THEM AGAIN. AND YOU ARE HERE NOW --"
-- SO ZOOJOO ASSUMES THEY SUCCEEDED. IF ODION IS RIGHT ABOUT WHAT THE HELM CAN DO, HE MUST NEVER CLAIM IT.
HE'S CLAIMED FAR TOO MANY, ALREADY!

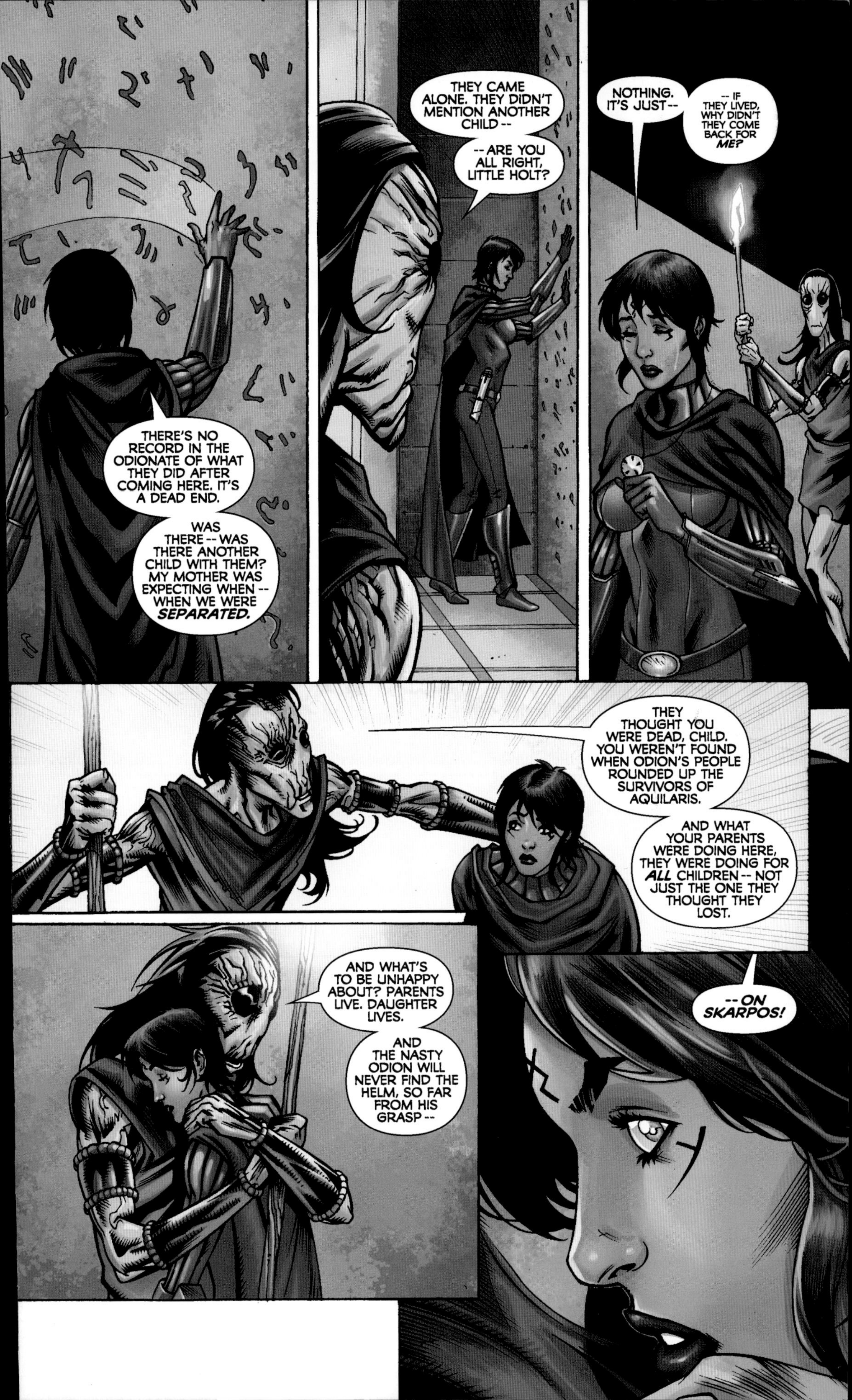
THERE'S NO RECORD IN THE ODIONATE OF WHAT THEY DID AFTER COMING HERE. IT'S A DEAD END.
WAS THERE -- WAS THERE ANOTHER CHILD WITH THEM? MY MOTHER WAS EXPECTING WHEN -- WHEN WE WERE *SEPARATED.*
THEY CAME ALONE. THEY DIDN'T MENTION ANOTHER CHILD --
-- ARE YOU ALL RIGHT, LITTLE HOLT?
NOTHING. IT'S JUST --
-- IF THEY LIVED, WHY DIDN'T THEY COME BACK FOR *ME?*
THEY THOUGHT YOU WERE DEAD, CHILD. YOU WEREN'T FOUND WHEN ODION'S PEOPLE ROUNDED UP THE SURVIVORS OF AQUILARIS.
AND WHAT YOUR PARENTS WERE DOING HERE, THEY WERE DOING FOR *ALL* CHILDREN -- NOT JUST THE ONE THEY THOUGHT THEY LOST.
AND WHAT'S TO BE UNHAPPY ABOUT? PARENTS LIVE. DAUGHTER LIVES.
AND THE NASTY ODION WILL NEVER FIND THE HELM, SO FAR FROM HIS GRASP --
-- ON SKARPOS!

SKARPOS? BUT ODION'S CONQUERING SKARPOS NOW!

I WAS JUST THERE THE OTHER DAY! ODION'S FIGHTING TO TAKE IT AWAY FROM *LORD MALAKITE!*

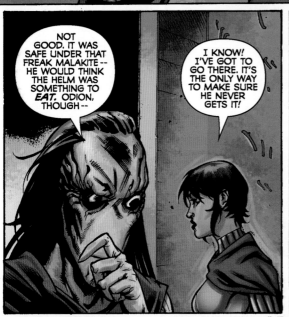

NOT GOOD. IT WAS SAFE UNDER THAT *FREAK* MALAKITE -- HE WOULD THINK THE HELM WAS SOMETHING TO *EAT.* ODION, THOUGH --

I KNOW! I'VE GOT TO GO THERE. IT'S THE ONLY WAY TO MAKE SURE HE NEVER GETS IT!

WHAT? THE PRIESTS WOULD'VE HIDDEN IT WELL, LITTLE HOLT. GOING BACK THERE WOULD JUST ATTRACT ODION'S ATTENTION!

HE'LL FIND IT ANYWAY, ZOOJOO -- LIKE HE'S FOUND THIS PLACE! HIS FORCES ARE CRAWLING OUTSIDE. I'VE GOT TO BEAT HIM TO IT!

AND DO WHAT?

NO. WAIT. ZOOJOO UNDERSTANDS. THIS ISN'T JUST ABOUT THE HELM --

-- YOU THINK YOU'LL FIND *YOUR PARENTS* THERE -- OR A CLUE TO WHERE THEY ARE. BUT THIS IS MORE IMPORTANT THAN WHAT YOU WANT!

ARON AND MERCIA HAD JUDGMENT, GIRL. THEY SET ASIDE WHA[T] THEY WANTED. WOU[LD] YOU GIVE ODION T[HE] HELM, JUST FOR A CHANCE AT --

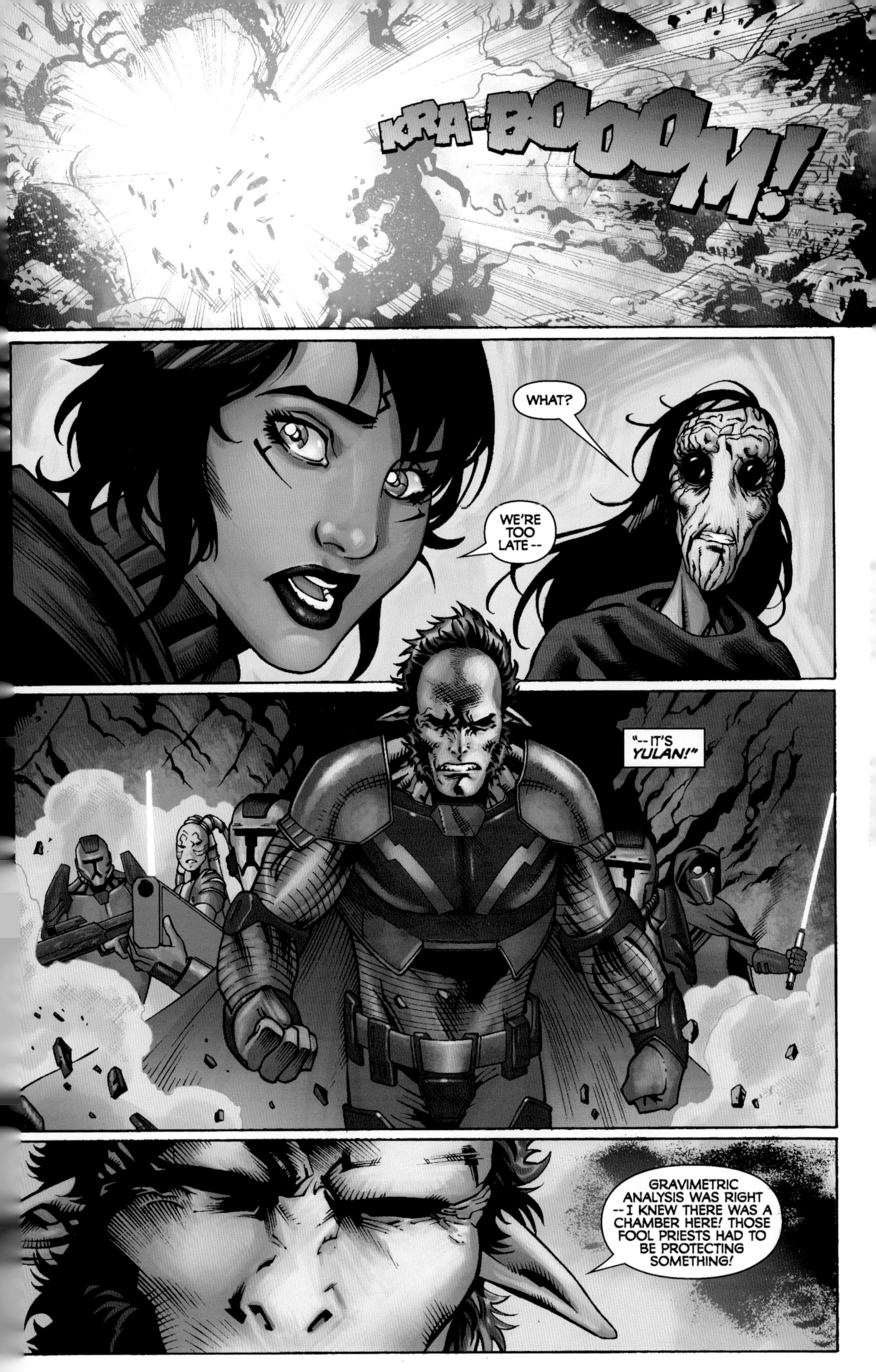
KRA-BOOOOM!
WHAT?
WE'RE TOO LATE --
"-- IT'S *YULAN!*"
GRAVIMETRIC ANALYSIS WAS RIGHT -- I KNEW THERE WAS A CHAMBER HERE! THOSE FOOL PRIESTS HAD TO BE PROTECTING SOMETHING!

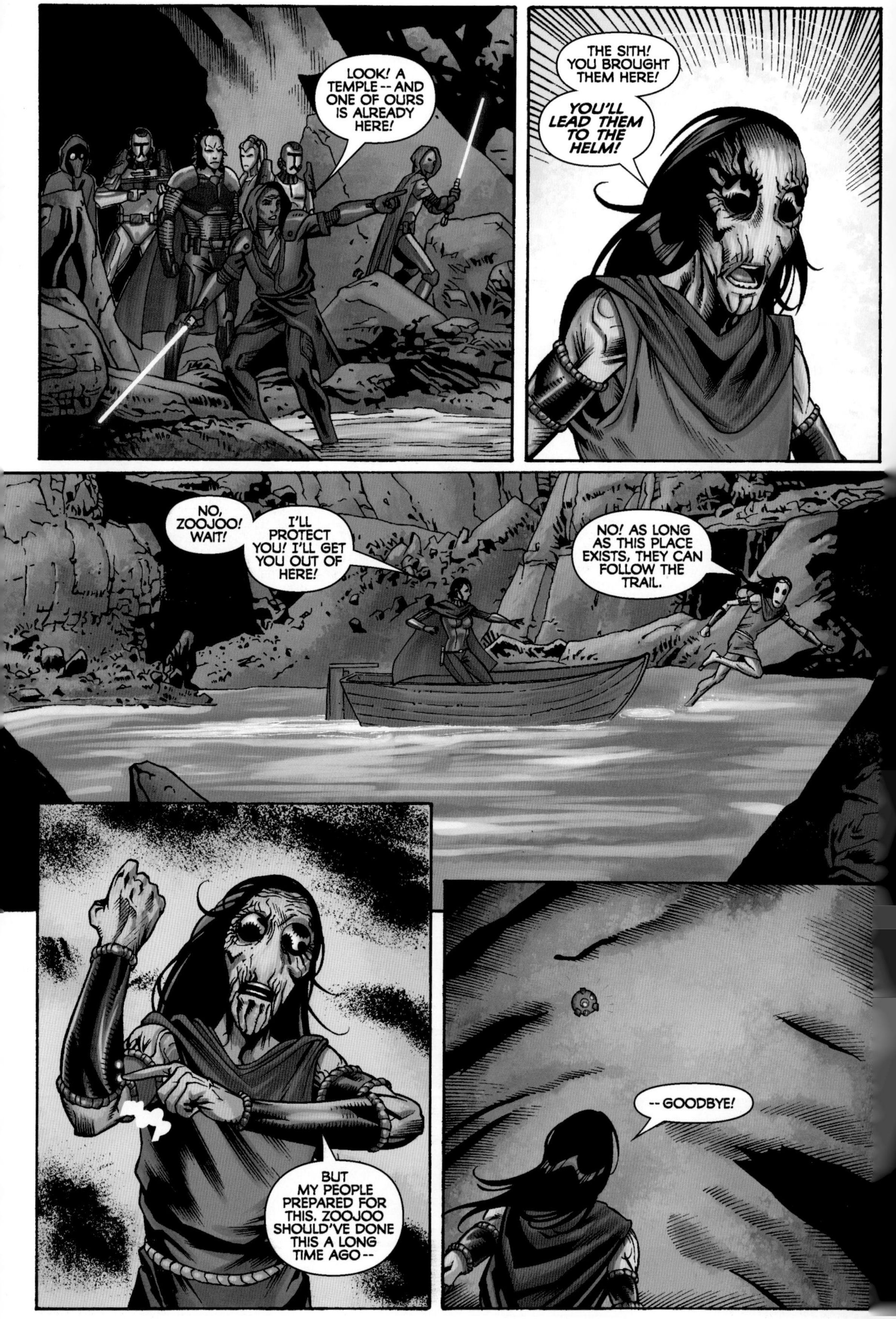
LOOK! A TEMPLE -- AND ONE OF OURS IS ALREADY HERE!
THE SITH! YOU BROUGHT THEM HERE!
YOU'LL LEAD THEM TO THE HELM!
NO, ZOOJOO! WAIT!
I'LL PROTECT YOU! I'LL GET YOU OUT OF HERE!
NO! AS LONG AS THIS PLACE EXISTS, THEY CAN FOLLOW THE TRAIL.
BUT MY PEOPLE PREPARED FOR THIS. ZOOJOO SHOULD'VE DONE THIS A LONG TIME AGO--
--GOODBYE!

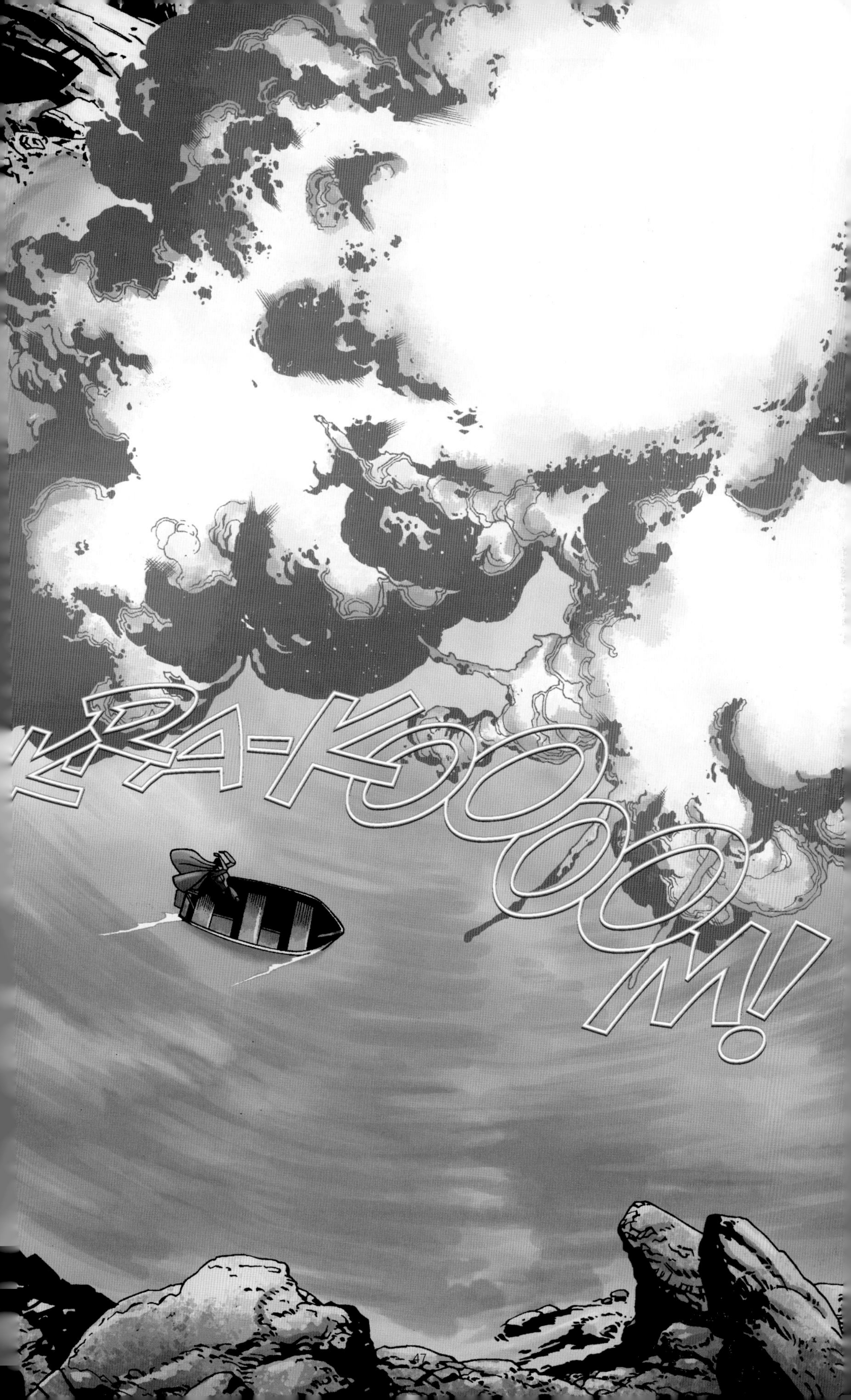
RA-KOOOOOM!

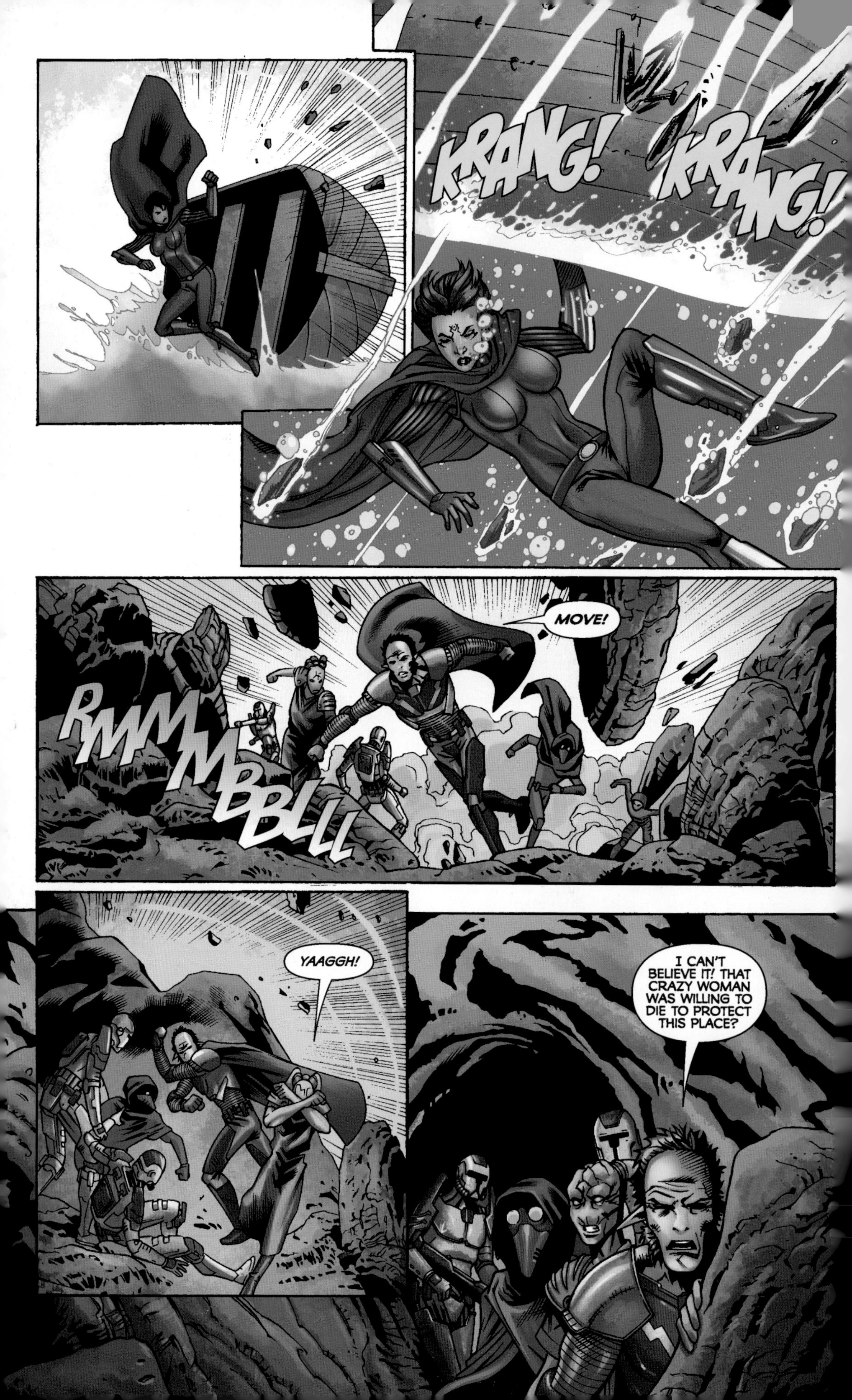
KRANG! KRANG!
MOVE!
RMMMBBLLL
YAAGGH!
I CAN'T BELIEVE IT! THAT CRAZY WOMAN WAS WILLING TO DIE TO PROTECT THIS PLACE?

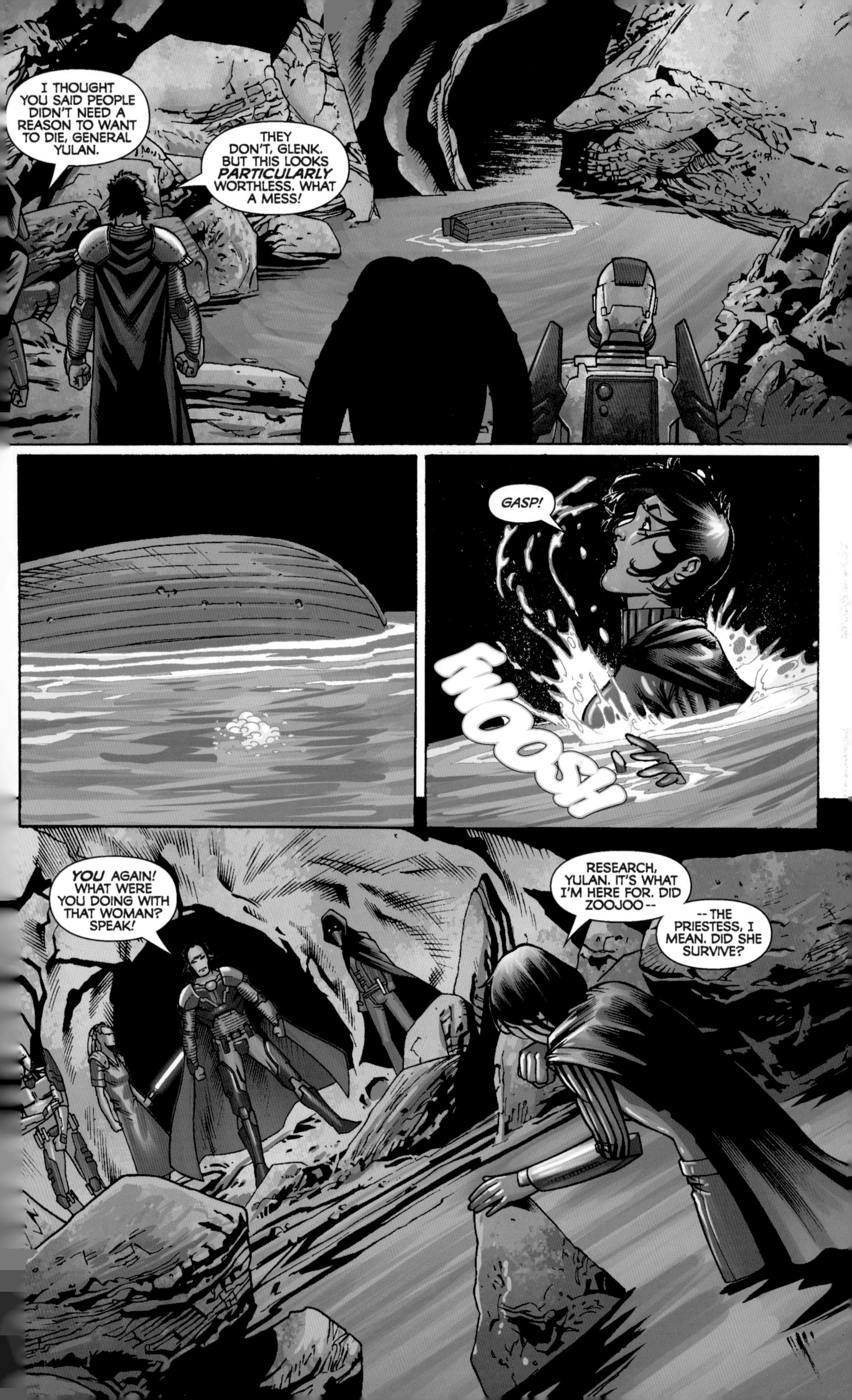
I THOUGHT YOU SAID PEOPLE DIDN'T NEED A REASON TO WANT TO DIE, GENERAL YULAN.
THEY DON'T, GLENK. BUT THIS LOOKS *PARTICULARLY* WORTHLESS. WHAT A MESS!
GASP!
KWOOOSH
YOU AGAIN! WHAT WERE YOU DOING WITH THAT WOMAN? SPEAK!
RESEARCH, YULAN. IT'S WHAT I'M HERE FOR. DID ZOOJOO--
--THE PRIESTESS, I MEAN. DID SHE SURVIVE?

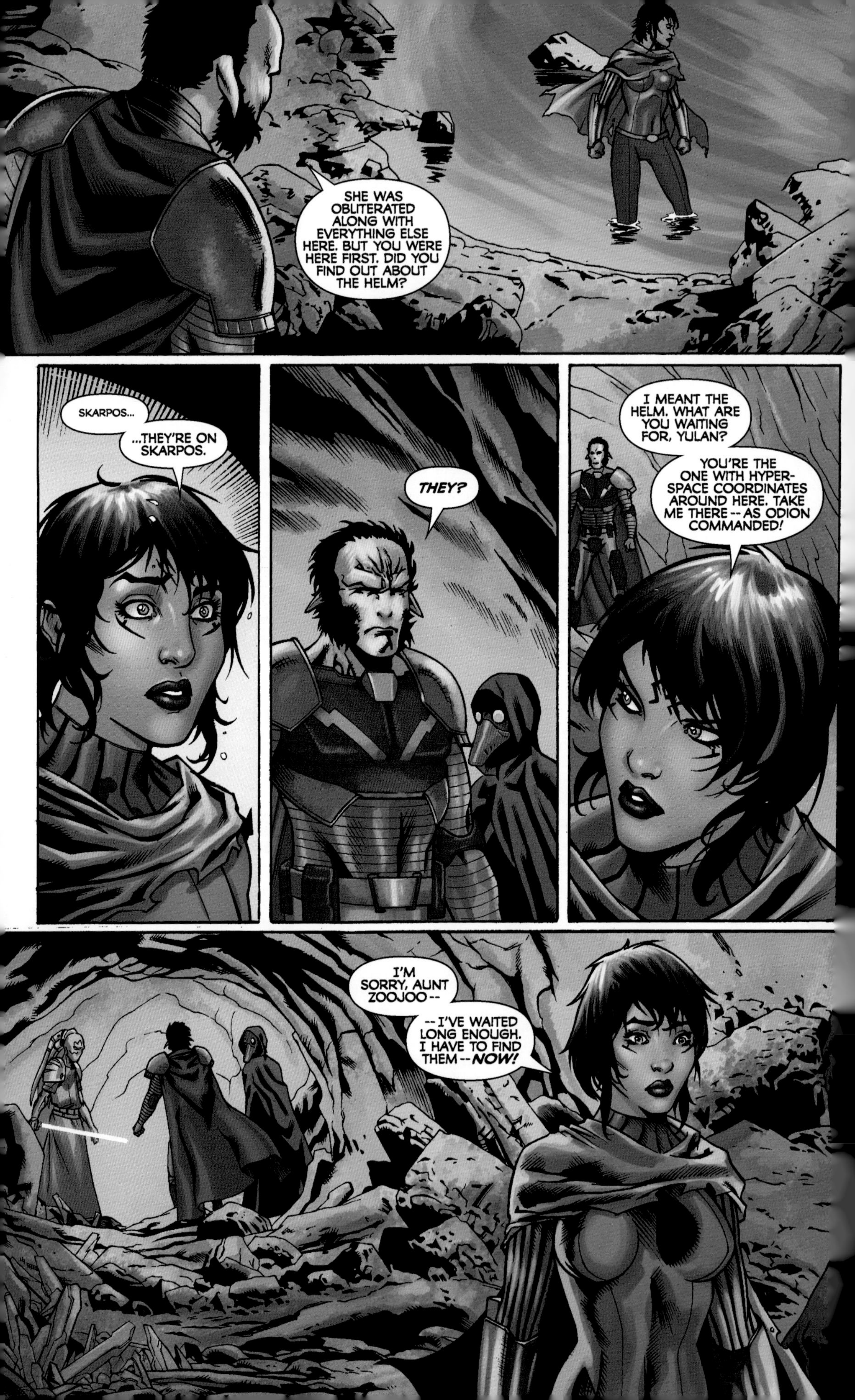
SHE WAS OBLITERATED ALONG WITH EVERYTHING ELSE HERE. BUT YOU WERE HERE FIRST. DID YOU FIND OUT ABOUT THE HELM?
SKARPOS...
...THEY'RE ON SKARPOS.
THEY?
I MEANT THE HELM. WHAT ARE YOU WAITING FOR, YULAN?
YOU'RE THE ONE WITH HYPER-SPACE COORDINATES AROUND HERE. TAKE ME THERE -- AS ODION COMMANDED!
I'M SORRY, AUNT ZOOJOO --
-- I'VE WAITED LONG ENOUGH. I HAVE TO FIND THEM -- NOW!

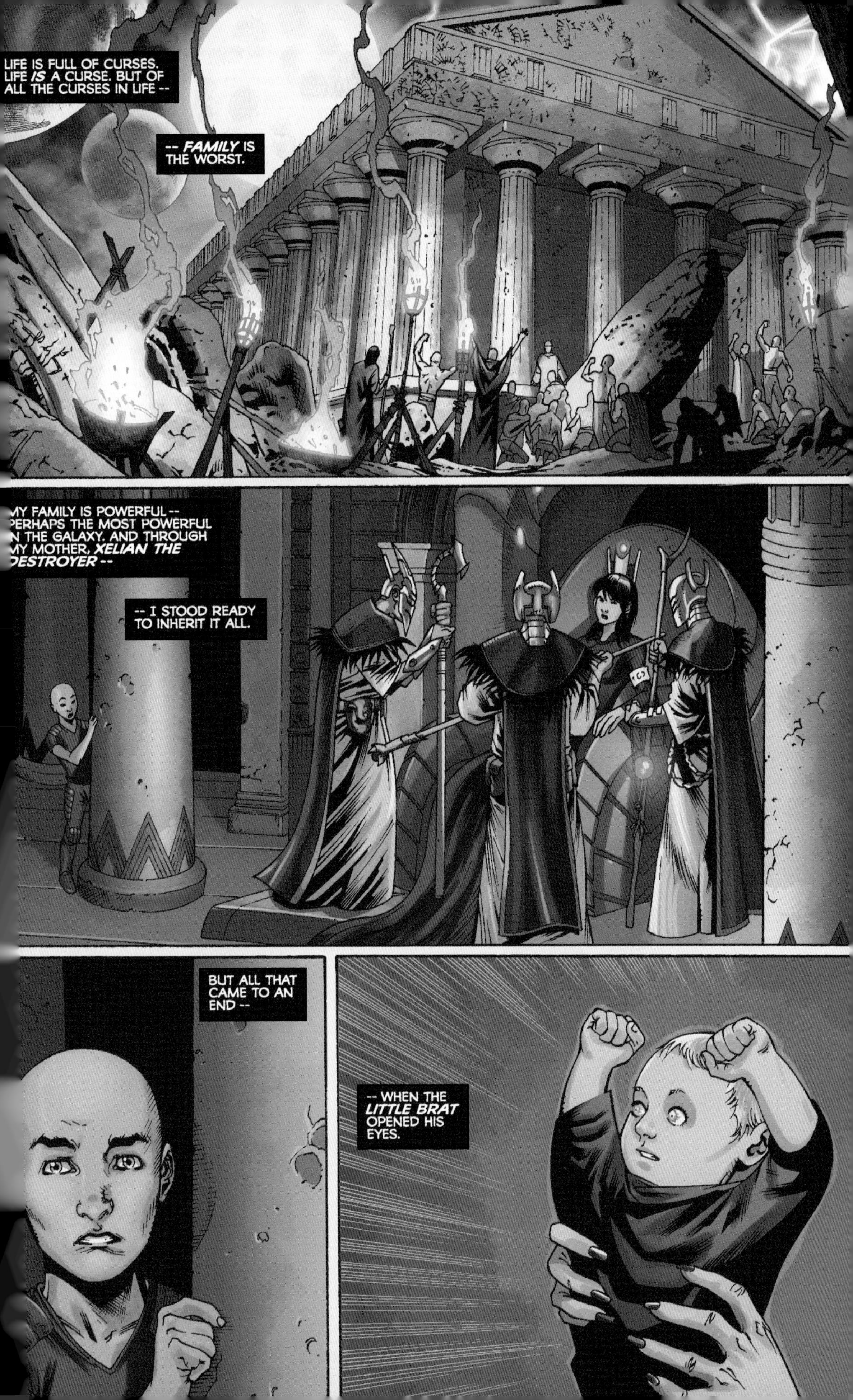
LIFE IS FULL OF CURSES. LIFE *IS* A CURSE. BUT OF ALL THE CURSES IN LIFE --
-- *FAMILY* IS THE WORST.
MY FAMILY IS POWERFUL -- PERHAPS THE MOST POWERFUL IN THE GALAXY. AND THROUGH MY MOTHER, *XELIAN THE DESTROYER* --
-- I STOOD READY TO INHERIT IT ALL.
BUT ALL THAT CAME TO AN END --
-- WHEN THE *LITTLE BRAT* OPENED HIS EYES.

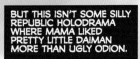

BUT THIS ISN'T SOME SILLY REPUBLIC HOLODRAMA WHERE MAMA LIKED PRETTY LITTLE DAIMAN MORE THAN UGLY ODION.

SO SHE FOUND ME REPULSIVE. WHAT DID IT MATTER? I WAS *SITH* --

-- AND I HAD A *GOAL*. MY GRANDMOTHER, VILIA, HAD PROMISED HER EXTENSIVE HOLDINGS TO THE HEIR THAT CONQUERED THE MOST.

IT'D BE OUR TURN ONE DAY. AND I WASN'T GOING TO LET THE LITTLE SNOT WIN.

EXCEPT -- HE ALREADY *HAD* WON. MY HEADACHES STARTED THE DAY HE WAS BORN.

SOON, IT WASN'T JUST HIM. AS MY FORCE TALENTS GREW, I BECAME HYPERSENSITIVE TO THE MERE EXISTENCE OF OTHERS. IT WAS DEBILITATING.

NO ONE COULD HELP. HIDING DIDN'T WORK. IN THE END, THERE WAS ONLY ONE SOLUTION --

-- *A SITH SOLUTION.* I LEARNED I COULD STRIKE OUT AGAINST THE PAIN --

-- BY SNUFFING OUT THE BRIGHT LIGHTS IN MY MIND, ONE BY ONE. EVERY DEATH PROVIDED RELIEF.

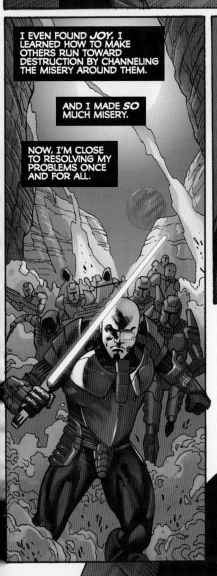

I EVEN FOUND *JOY.* I LEARNED HOW TO MAKE OTHERS RUN TOWARD DESTRUCTION BY CHANNELING THE MISERY AROUND THEM.

AND I MADE *SO* MUCH MISERY.

NOW, I'M CLOSE TO RESOLVING MY PROBLEMS ONCE AND FOR ALL.

NO NEWS FROM THE HUNTERS SEEKING THE *HELM OF IELDIS* ON SARRASSIA, LORD ODION. SHOULD I SEND A COURIER TO CHECK ON THEM?

DON'T BOTHER. I'M WAY AHEAD OF YOU.

IT'S CLOSE. I CAN *FEEL* IT. ALL THESE YEARS -- IT WON'T BE LONG NOW!

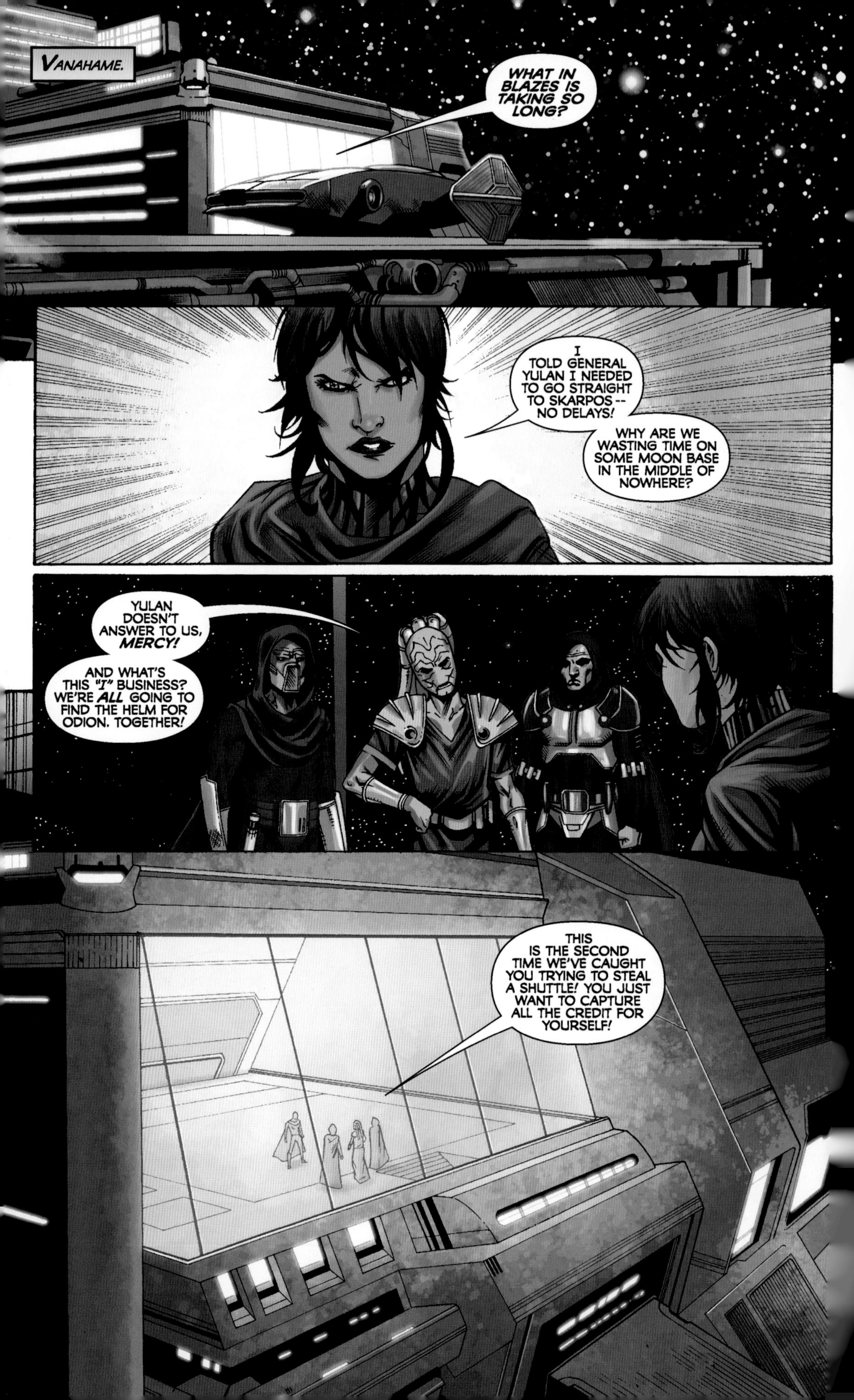
VANAHAME.
WHAT IN BLAZES IS TAKING SO LONG?
I TOLD GENERAL YULAN I NEEDED TO GO STRAIGHT TO SKARPOS -- NO DELAYS!
WHY ARE WE WASTING TIME ON SOME MOON BASE IN THE MIDDLE OF NOWHERE?
YULAN DOESN'T ANSWER TO US, MERCY!
AND WHAT'S THIS "I" BUSINESS? WE'RE ALL GOING TO FIND THE HELM FOR ODION. TOGETHER!
THIS IS THE SECOND TIME WE'VE CAUGHT YOU TRYING TO STEAL A SHUTTLE! YOU JUST WANT TO CAPTURE ALL THE CREDIT FOR YOURSELF!

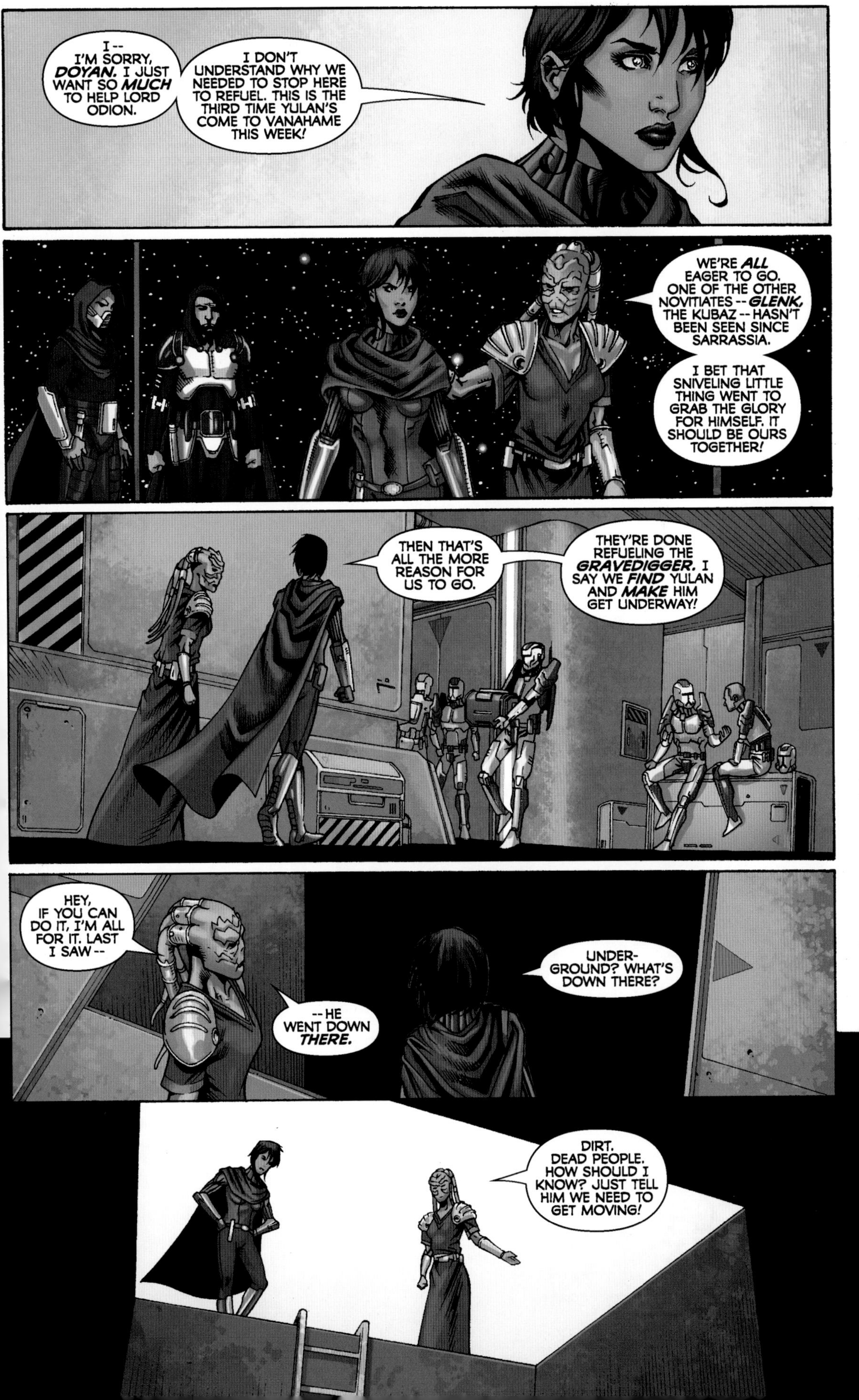
I -- I'M SORRY, DOYAN. I JUST WANT SO MUCH TO HELP LORD ODION.
I DON'T UNDERSTAND WHY WE NEEDED TO STOP HERE TO REFUEL. THIS IS THE THIRD TIME YULAN'S COME TO VANAHAME THIS WEEK!
WE'RE ALL EAGER TO GO. ONE OF THE OTHER NOVITIATES -- GLENK, THE KUBAZ -- HASN'T BEEN SEEN SINCE SARRASSIA.
I BET THAT SNIVELING LITTLE THING WENT TO GRAB THE GLORY FOR HIMSELF. IT SHOULD BE OURS TOGETHER!
THEN THAT'S ALL THE MORE REASON FOR US TO GO.
THEY'RE DONE REFUELING THE GRAVEDIGGER. I SAY WE FIND YULAN AND MAKE HIM GET UNDERWAY!
HEY, IF YOU CAN DO IT, I'M ALL FOR IT. LAST I SAW --
-- HE WENT DOWN THERE.
UNDER-GROUND? WHAT'S DOWN THERE?
DIRT. DEAD PEOPLE. HOW SHOULD I KNOW? JUST TELL HIM WE NEED TO GET MOVING!

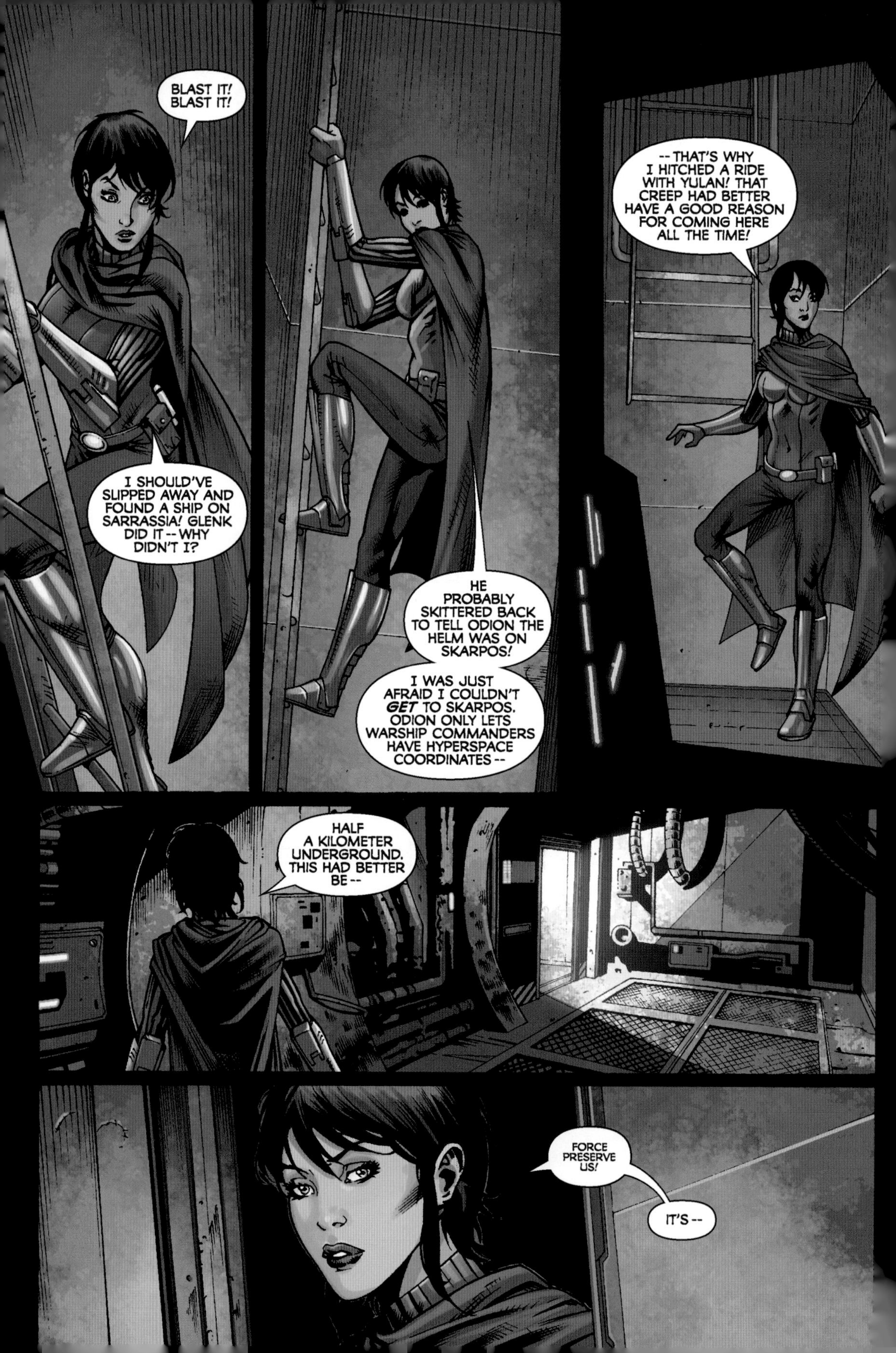
BLAST IT! BLAST IT!
I SHOULD'VE SLIPPED AWAY AND FOUND A SHIP ON SARRASSIA! GLENK DID IT -- WHY DIDN'T I?
HE PROBABLY SKITTERED BACK TO TELL ODION THE HELM WAS ON SKARPOS!
I WAS JUST AFRAID I COULDN'T *GET* TO SKARPOS. ODION ONLY LETS WARSHIP COMMANDERS HAVE HYPERSPACE COORDINATES --
-- THAT'S WHY I HITCHED A RIDE WITH YULAN! THAT CREEP HAD BETTER HAVE A GOOD REASON FOR COMING HERE ALL THE TIME!
HALF A KILOMETER UNDERGROUND. THIS HAD BETTER BE --
FORCE PRESERVE US!
IT'S --

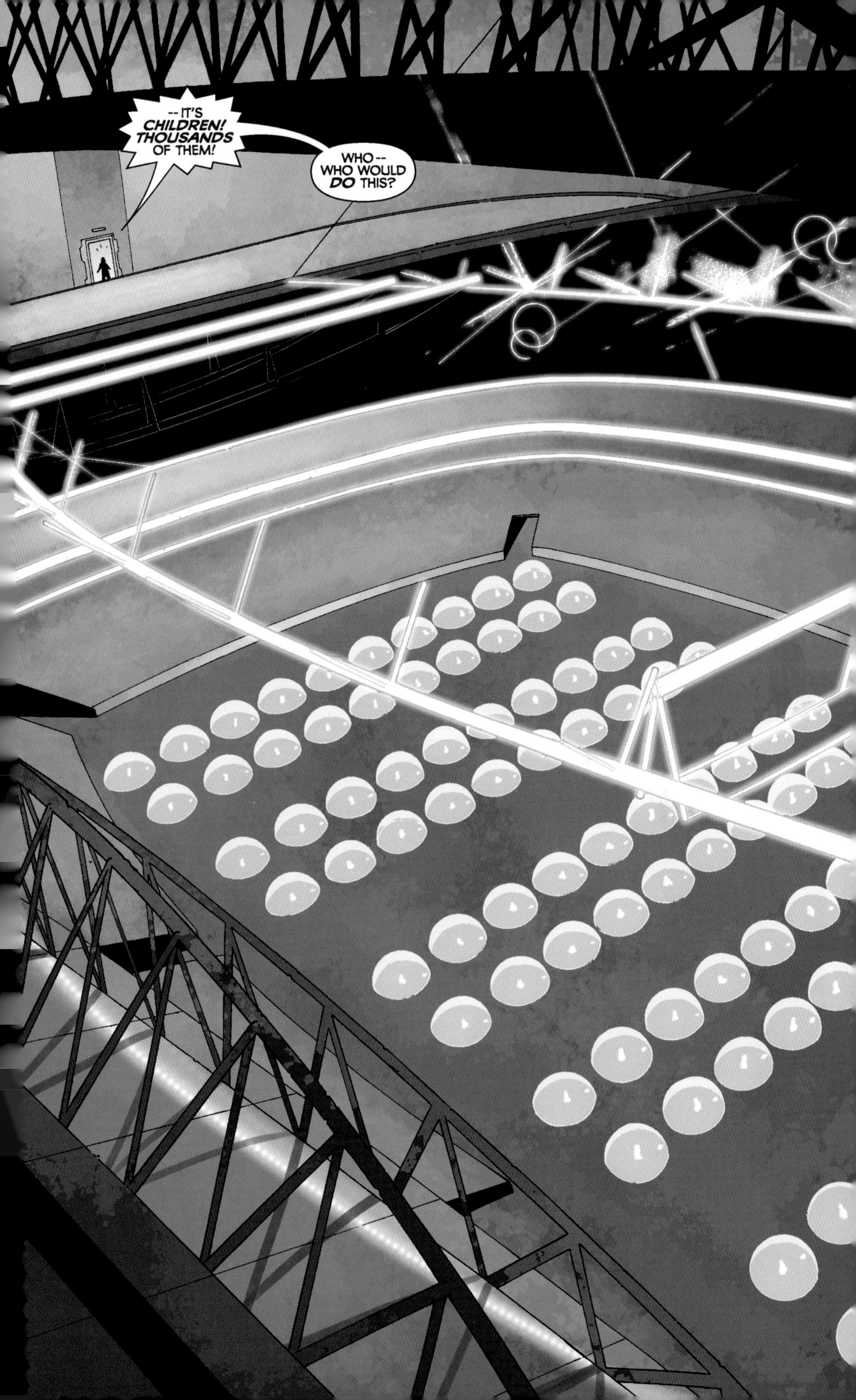
-- IT'S CHILDREN! THOUSANDS OF THEM!
WHO -- WHO WOULD DO THIS?

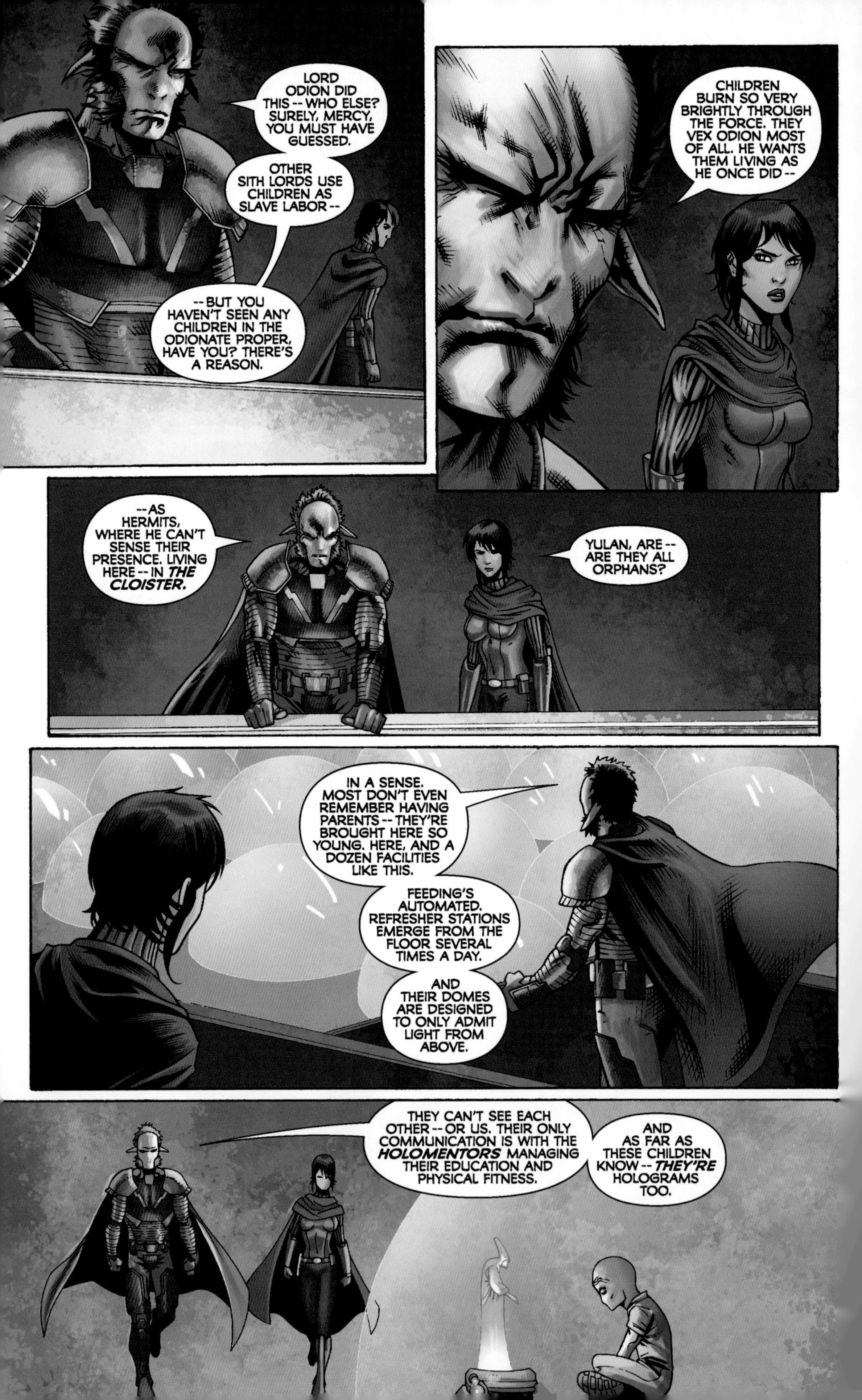
LORD ODION DID THIS -- WHO ELSE? SURELY, MERCY, YOU MUST HAVE GUESSED.
OTHER SITH LORDS USE CHILDREN AS SLAVE LABOR --
-- BUT YOU HAVEN'T SEEN ANY CHILDREN IN THE ODIONATE PROPER, HAVE YOU? THERE'S A REASON.
CHILDREN BURN SO VERY BRIGHTLY THROUGH THE FORCE. THEY VEX ODION MOST OF ALL. HE WANTS THEM LIVING AS HE ONCE DID --
-- AS HERMITS, WHERE HE CAN'T SENSE THEIR PRESENCE. LIVING HERE -- IN *THE CLOISTER.*
YULAN, ARE -- ARE THEY ALL ORPHANS?
IN A SENSE. MOST DON'T EVEN REMEMBER HAVING PARENTS -- THEY'RE BROUGHT HERE SO YOUNG. HERE, AND A DOZEN FACILITIES LIKE THIS.
FEEDING'S AUTOMATED. REFRESHER STATIONS EMERGE FROM THE FLOOR SEVERAL TIMES A DAY.
AND THEIR DOMES ARE DESIGNED TO ONLY ADMIT LIGHT FROM ABOVE.
THEY CAN'T SEE EACH OTHER -- OR US. THEIR ONLY COMMUNICATION IS WITH THE *HOLOMENTORS* MANAGING THEIR EDUCATION AND PHYSICAL FITNESS.
AND AS FAR AS THESE CHILDREN KNOW -- *THEY'RE* HOLOGRAMS TOO.

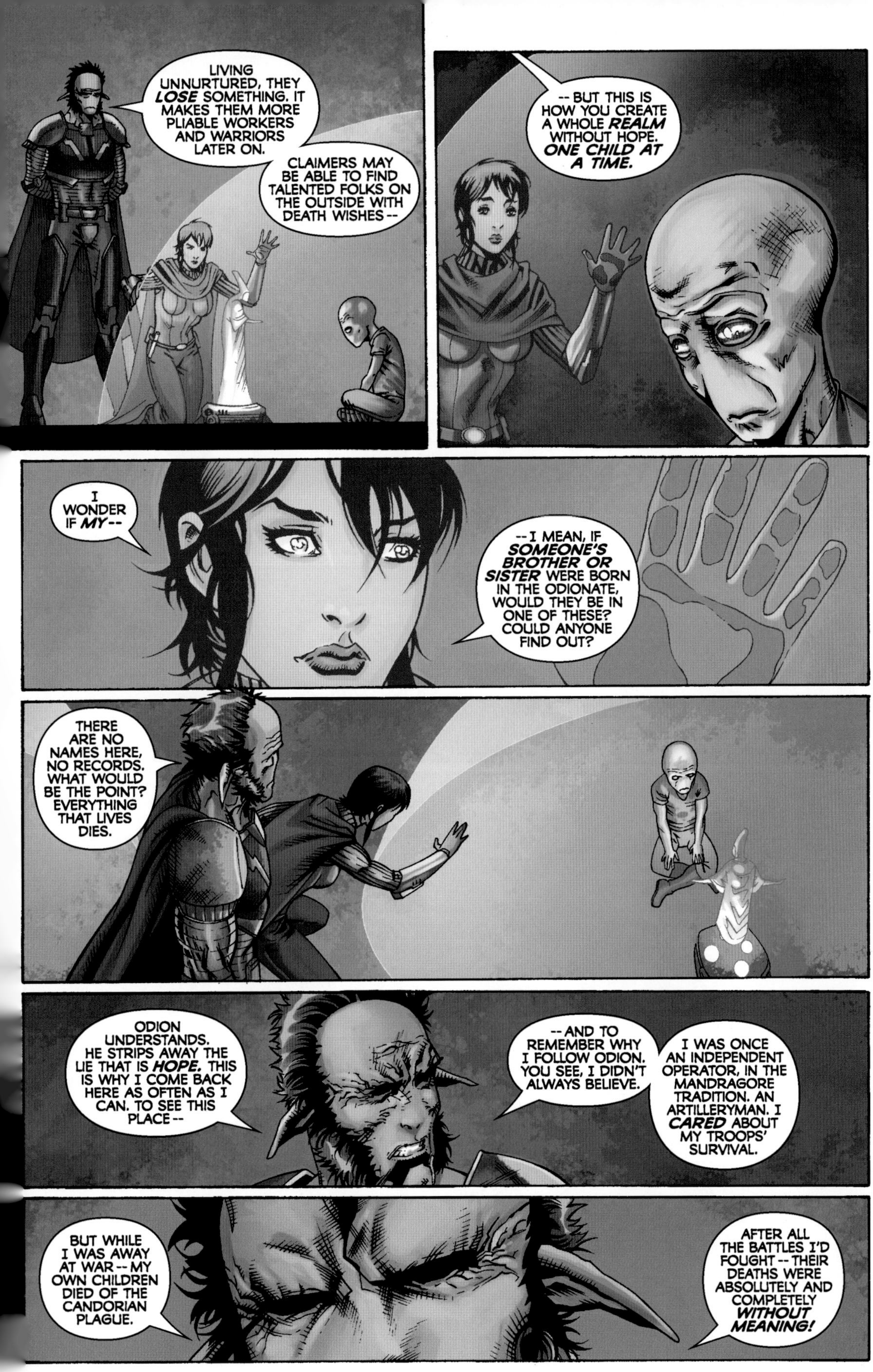
LIVING UNNURTURED, THEY *LOSE* SOMETHING. IT MAKES THEM MORE PLIABLE WORKERS AND WARRIORS LATER ON.
CLAIMERS MAY BE ABLE TO FIND TALENTED FOLKS ON THE OUTSIDE WITH DEATH WISHES --
-- BUT THIS IS HOW YOU CREATE A WHOLE *REALM* WITHOUT HOPE. *ONE CHILD AT A TIME.*
I WONDER IF *MY* --
-- I MEAN, IF *SOMEONE'S BROTHER OR SISTER* WERE BORN IN THE ODIONATE, WOULD THEY BE IN ONE OF THESE? COULD ANYONE FIND OUT?
THERE ARE NO NAMES HERE, NO RECORDS. WHAT WOULD BE THE POINT? EVERYTHING THAT LIVES DIES.
ODION UNDERSTANDS. HE STRIPS AWAY THE LIE THAT IS *HOPE.* THIS IS WHY I COME BACK HERE AS OFTEN AS I CAN. TO SEE THIS PLACE --
-- AND TO REMEMBER WHY I FOLLOW ODION. YOU SEE, I DIDN'T ALWAYS BELIEVE.
I WAS ONCE AN INDEPENDENT OPERATOR, IN THE MANDRAGORE TRADITION. AN ARTILLERYMAN. I *CARED* ABOUT MY TROOPS' SURVIVAL.
BUT WHILE I WAS AWAY AT WAR -- MY OWN CHILDREN DIED OF THE CANDORIAN PLAGUE.
AFTER ALL THE BATTLES I'D FOUGHT -- THEIR DEATHS WERE ABSOLUTELY AND COMPLETELY *WITHOUT MEANING!*

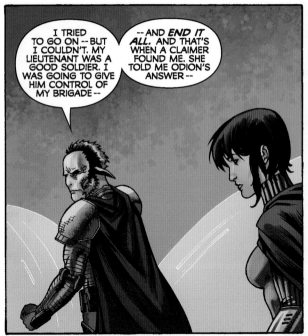

I TRIED TO GO ON -- BUT I COULDN'T. MY LIEUTENANT WAS A GOOD SOLDIER. I WAS GOING TO GIVE HIM CONTROL OF MY BRIGADE --

-- AND *END IT ALL.* AND THAT'S WHEN A CLAIMER FOUND ME. SHE TOLD ME ODION'S ANSWER --

-- TO *EMBRACE NOTHINGNESS.* DEATH *HAS* NO MEANING. AND WAR IS JUST A TOOL FOR SPEEDING THE KILLING ON BOTH SIDES.

YOU CAN'T CHANGE IT. YOU CAN JUST MAKE IT MORE EFFICIENT. AND THAT'S WHERE I COME IN.

YULAN -- SOME WOULD SAY THAT *ALL* LIFE IS SACRED. WHETHER IT'S THE ENEMY'S SOLDIERS OR YOUR OWN.

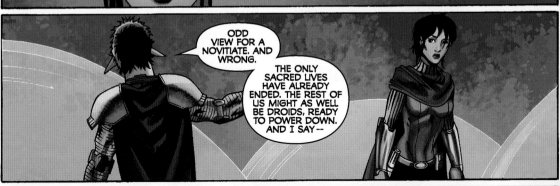

ODD VIEW FOR A NOVITIATE. AND WRONG.

THE ONLY SACRED LIVES HAVE ALREADY ENDED. THE REST OF US MIGHT AS WELL BE DROIDS, READY TO POWER DOWN. AND I SAY --

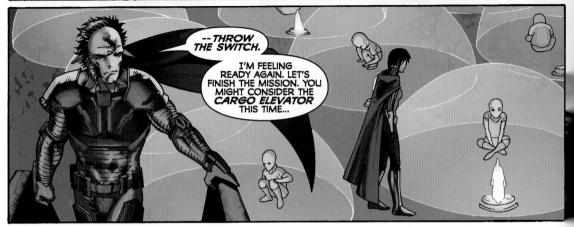

-- *THROW THE SWITCH.*

I'M FEELING READY AGAIN. LET'S FINISH THE MISSION. YOU MIGHT CONSIDER THE *CARGO ELEVATOR* THIS TIME...

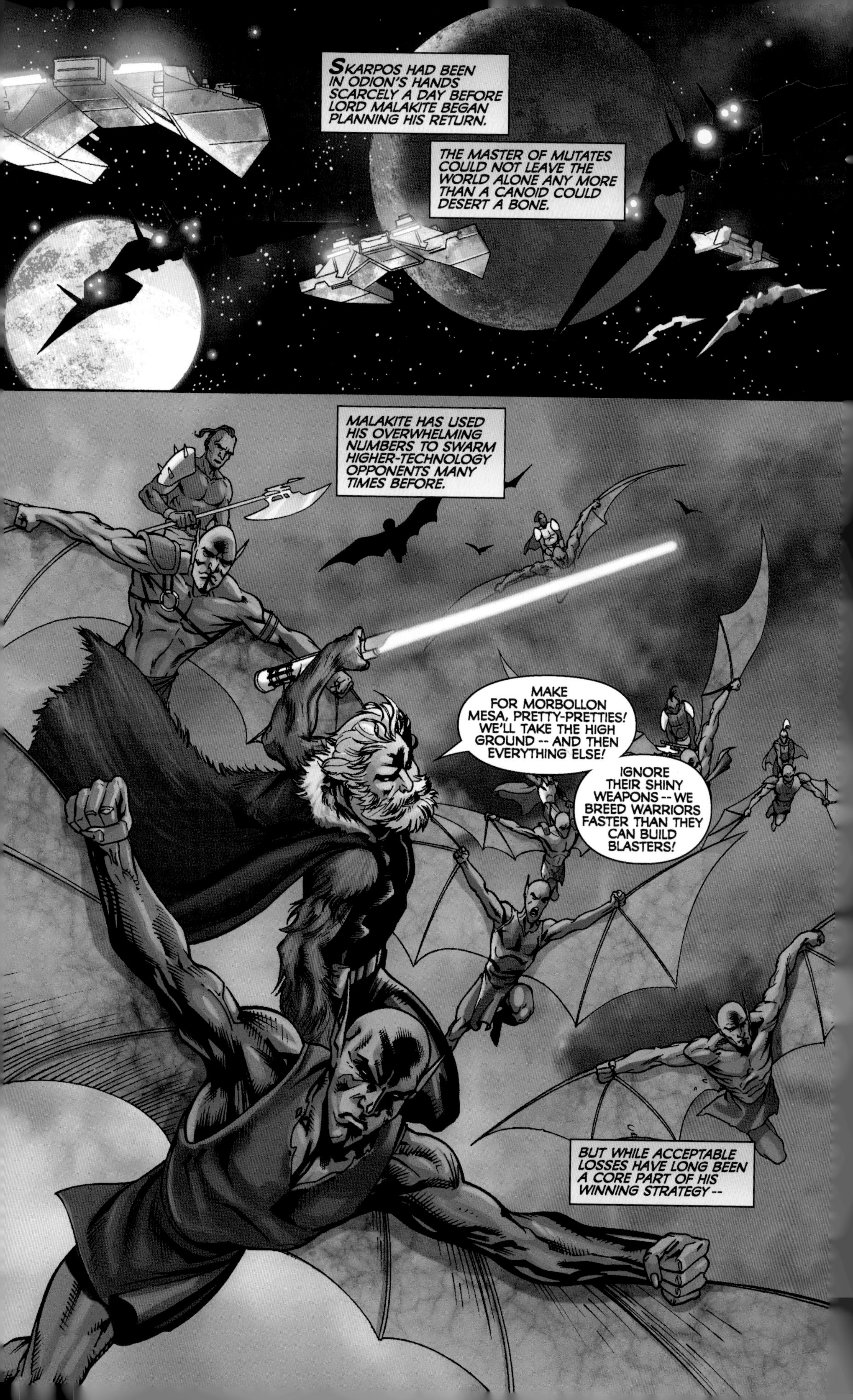
SKARPOS HAD BEEN IN ODION'S HANDS SCARCELY A DAY BEFORE LORD MALAKITE BEGAN PLANNING HIS RETURN.
THE MASTER OF MUTATES COULD NOT LEAVE THE WORLD ALONE ANY MORE THAN A CANOID COULD DESERT A BONE.
MALAKITE HAS USED HIS OVERWHELMING NUMBERS TO SWARM HIGHER-TECHNOLOGY OPPONENTS MANY TIMES BEFORE.
MAKE FOR MORBOLLON MESA, PRETTY-PRETTIES! WE'LL TAKE THE HIGH GROUND -- AND THEN EVERYTHING ELSE!
IGNORE THEIR SHINY WEAPONS -- WE BREED WARRIORS FASTER THAN THEY CAN BUILD BLASTERS!
BUT WHILE ACCEPTABLE LOSSES HAVE LONG BEEN A CORE PART OF HIS WINNING STRATEGY --

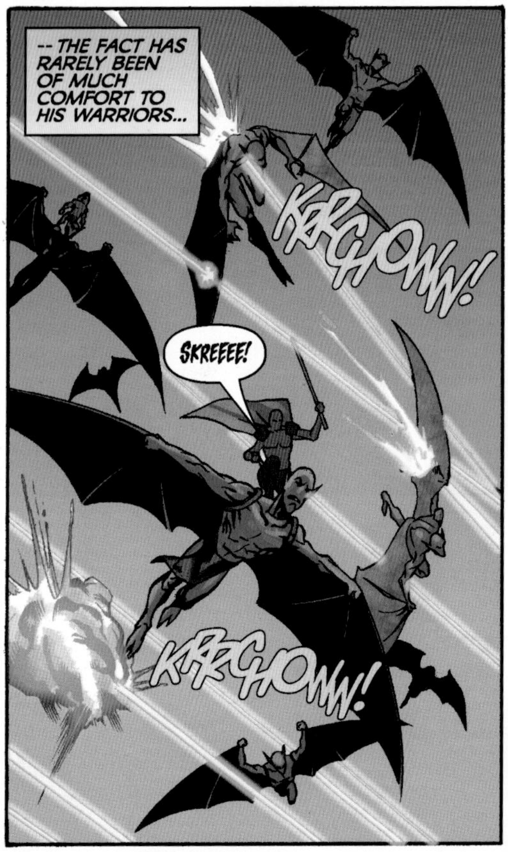
--THE FACT HAS RARELY BEEN OF MUCH COMFORT TO HIS WARRIORS...
KRRCHOWW!
SKREEEE!
KRRCHOWW!

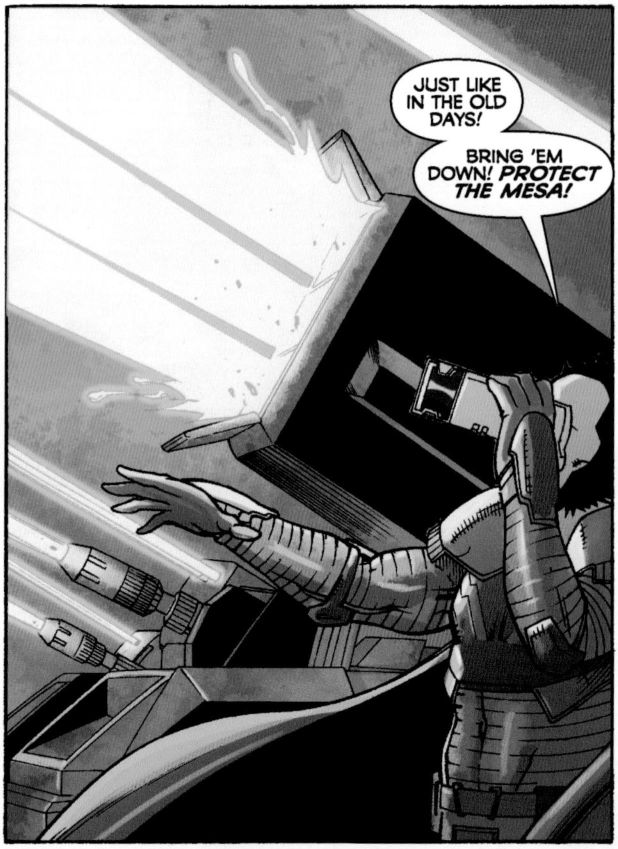
JUST LIKE IN THE OLD DAYS!
BRING 'EM DOWN! PROTECT THE MESA!

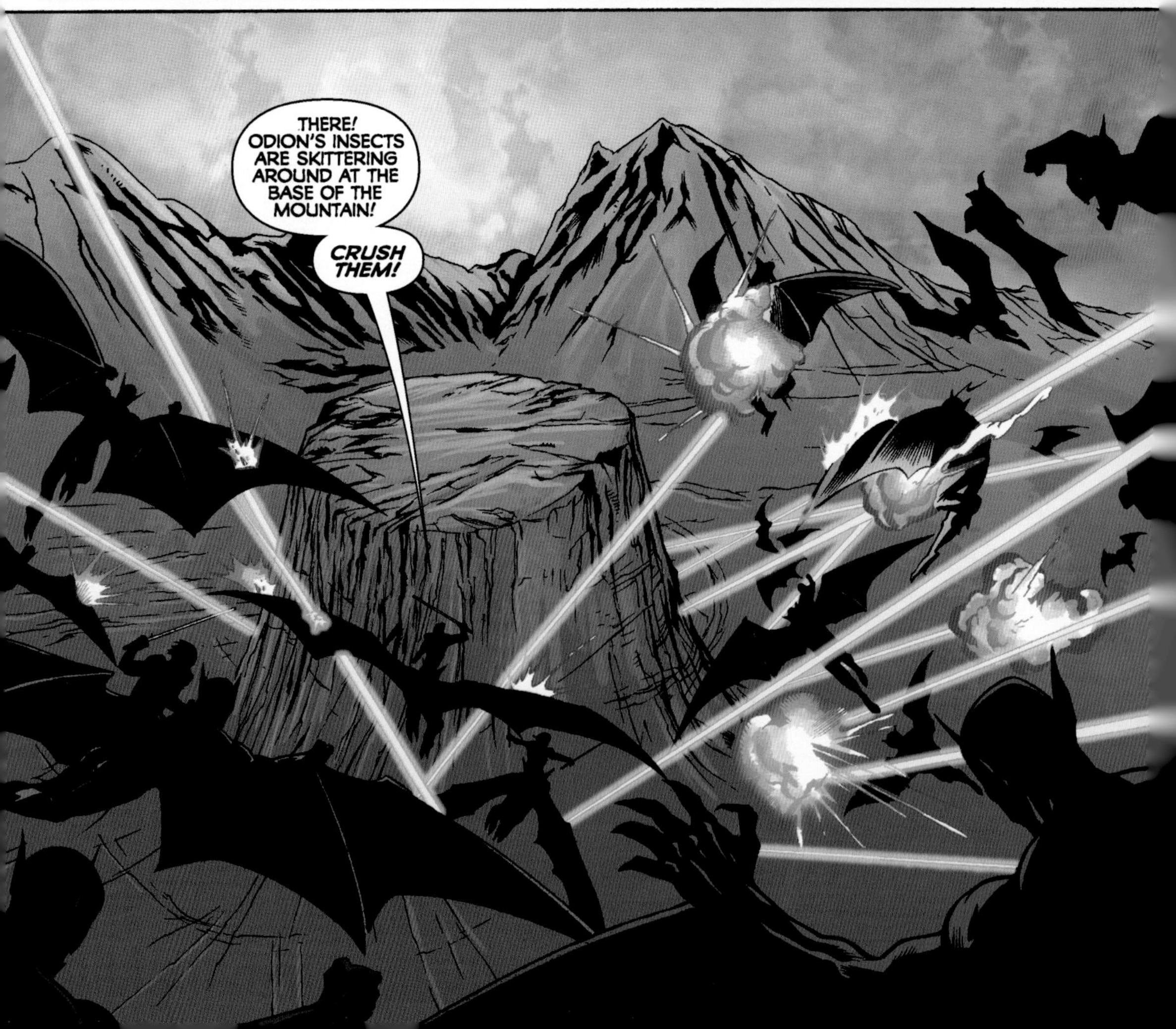
THERE! ODION'S INSECTS ARE SKITTERING AROUND AT THE BASE OF THE MOUNTAIN!
CRUSH THEM!

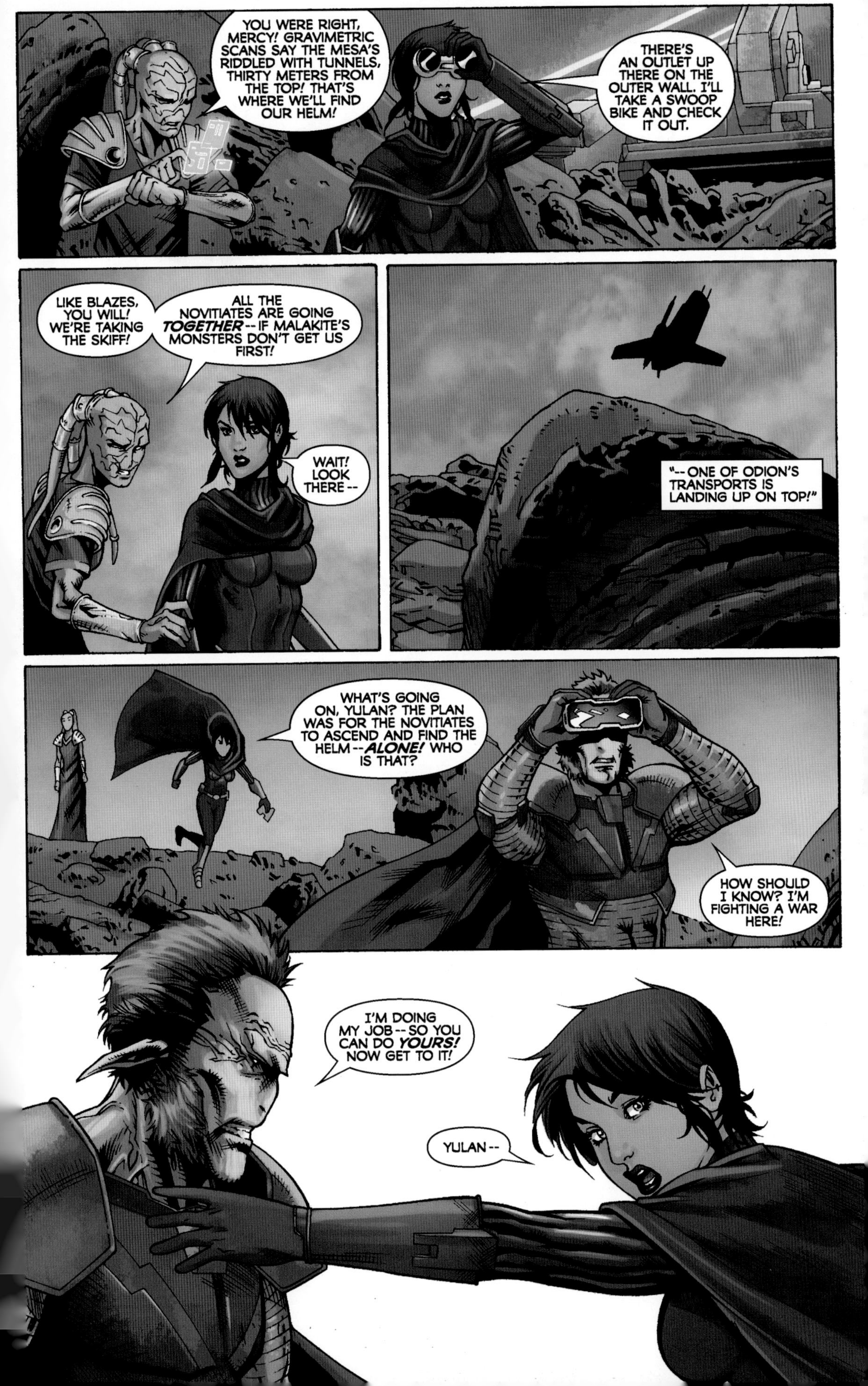
YOU WERE RIGHT, MERCY! GRAVIMETRIC SCANS SAY THE MESA'S RIDDLED WITH TUNNELS, THIRTY METERS FROM THE TOP! THAT'S WHERE WE'LL FIND OUR HELM!
THERE'S AN OUTLET UP THERE ON THE OUTER WALL. I'LL TAKE A SWOOP BIKE AND CHECK IT OUT.
LIKE BLAZES, YOU WILL! WE'RE TAKING THE SKIFF!
ALL THE NOVITIATES ARE GOING TOGETHER--IF MALAKITE'S MONSTERS DON'T GET US FIRST!
WAIT! LOOK THERE--
"--ONE OF ODION'S TRANSPORTS IS LANDING UP ON TOP!"
WHAT'S GOING ON, YULAN? THE PLAN WAS FOR THE NOVITIATES TO ASCEND AND FIND THE HELM--ALONE! WHO IS THAT?
HOW SHOULD I KNOW? I'M FIGHTING A WAR HERE!
I'M DOING MY JOB--SO YOU CAN DO YOURS! NOW GET TO IT!
YULAN--

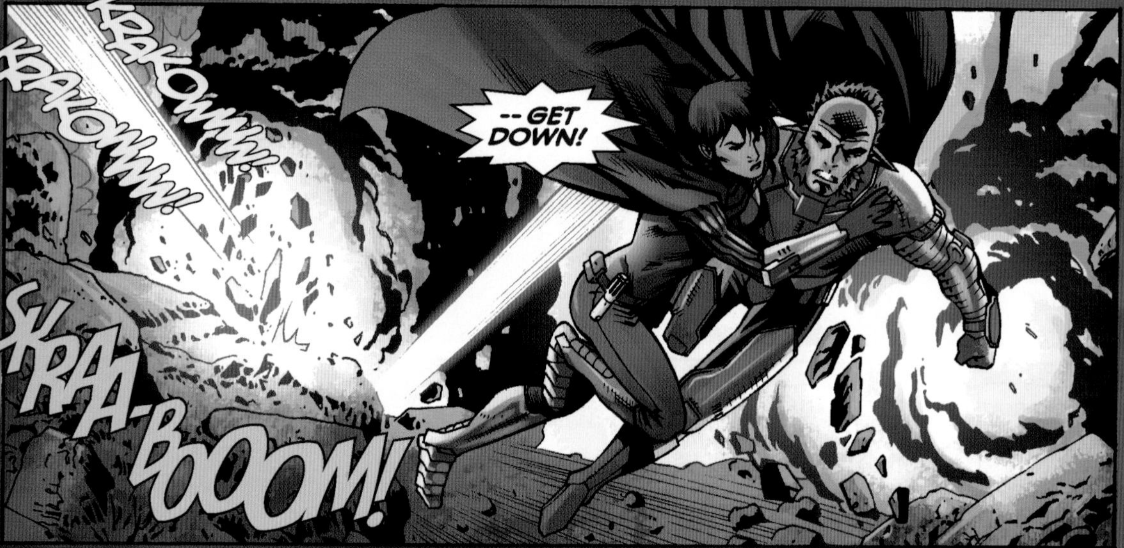
KRAKOWWW!
KRAKOWWW!
SKRAA-BOOOM!
-- GET DOWN!

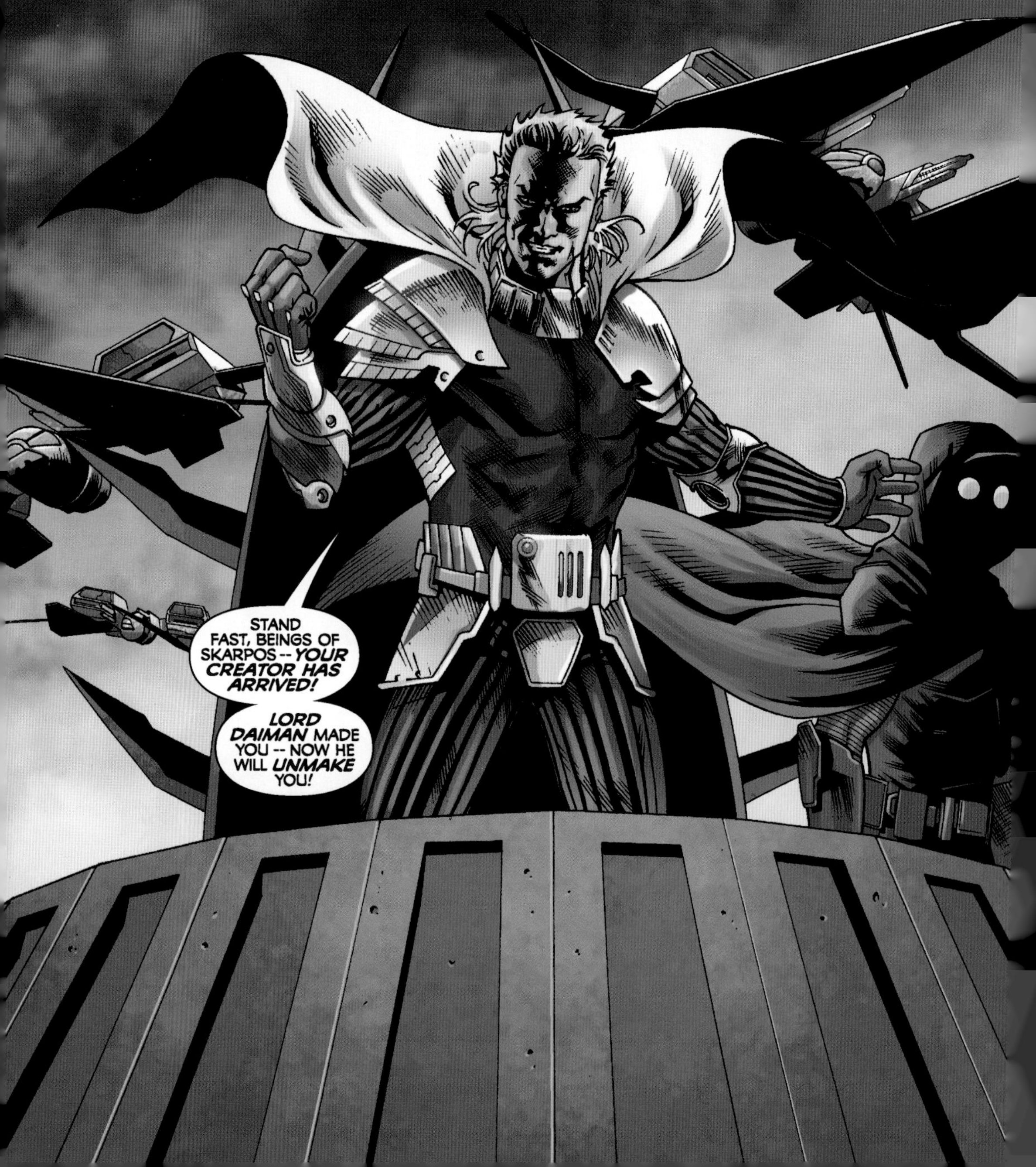
STAND FAST, BEINGS OF SKARPOS -- YOUR CREATOR HAS ARRIVED!
LORD DAIMAN MADE YOU -- NOW HE WILL UNMAKE YOU!

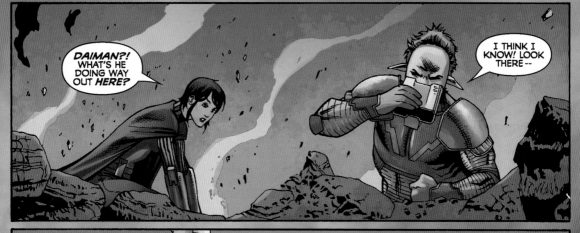

DAIMAN?! WHAT'S HE DOING WAY OUT *HERE*?

I THINK I KNOW! LOOK THERE--

"-- THAT'S THE NOVITIATE THAT WENT MISSING ON SARRASSIA-- *GLENK!* THE LITTLE TRAITOR WAS WORKING FOR DAIMAN!"

COMPLETE SURPRISE --JUST AS I EXPECTED! KERRA HOLT SHOULD HAVE KNOWN--

--I'D NEVER SEND HER ANYWHERE AS MY AGENT WITHOUT SENDING SOMEONE ELSE TO WATCH *HER*!

I EXIST TO SERVE, MY LORD!

ODION *WAS* AFTER THE HELM OF IELDIS, AS I SUSPECTED. AND THE SILLY JEDI HAS LED HIM STRAIGHT TO IT!

IT DOESN'T MATTER WHAT IT DOES. IF ODION WANTS IT -- I WANT IT, TOO!

CLEANSE THIS WORLD OF HIS FORCES! AND IF THAT ABOMINATION MALAKITE INTERFERES, TAKE HIM OUT, TOO!

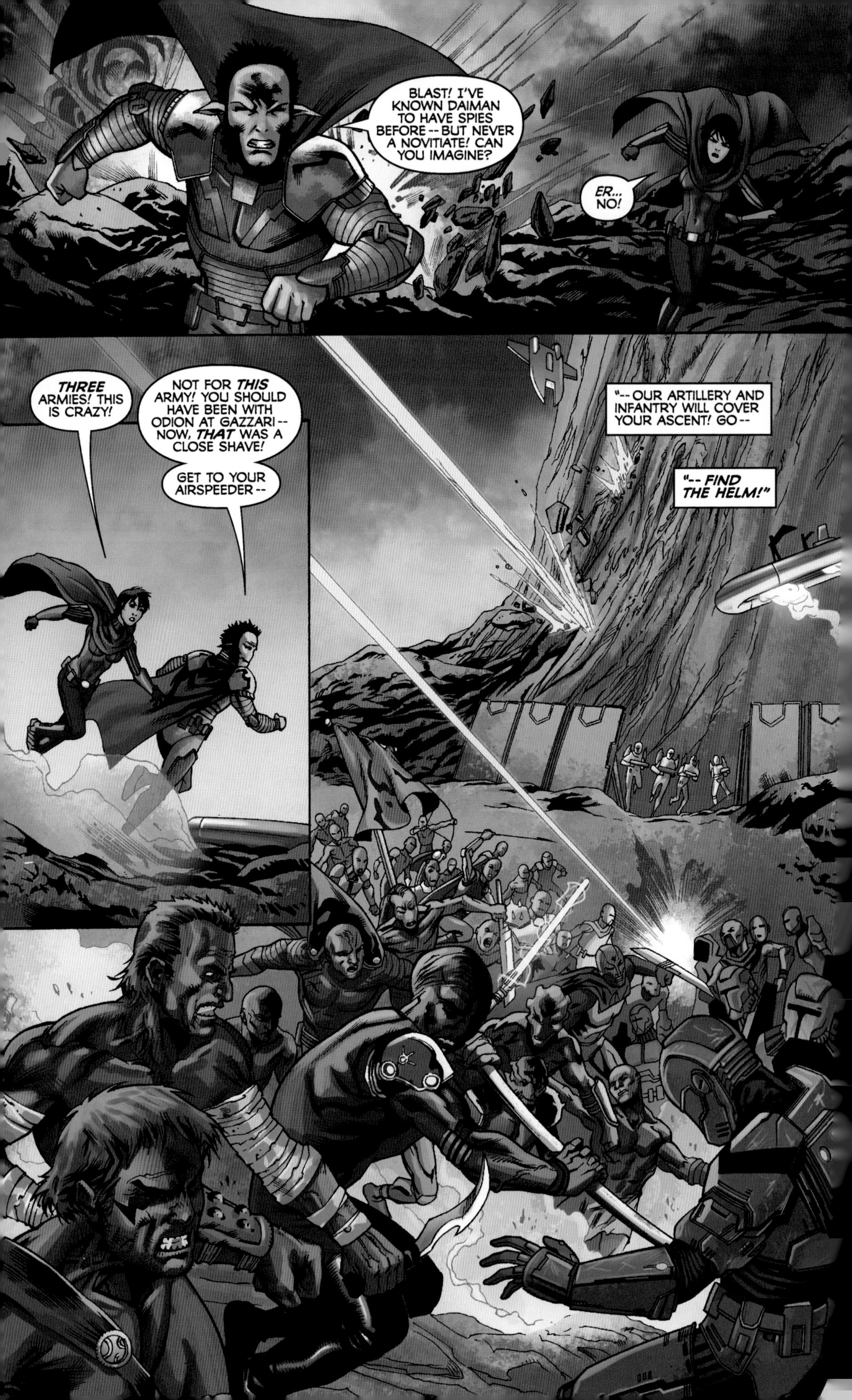
BLAST! I'VE KNOWN DAIMAN TO HAVE SPIES BEFORE -- BUT NEVER A NOVITIATE! CAN YOU IMAGINE?
ER... NO!
THREE ARMIES! THIS IS CRAZY!
NOT FOR THIS ARMY! YOU SHOULD HAVE BEEN WITH ODION AT GAZZARI -- NOW, THAT WAS A CLOSE SHAVE!
GET TO YOUR AIRSPEEDER --
"-- OUR ARTILLERY AND INFANTRY WILL COVER YOUR ASCENT! GO --
"-- FIND THE HELM!"

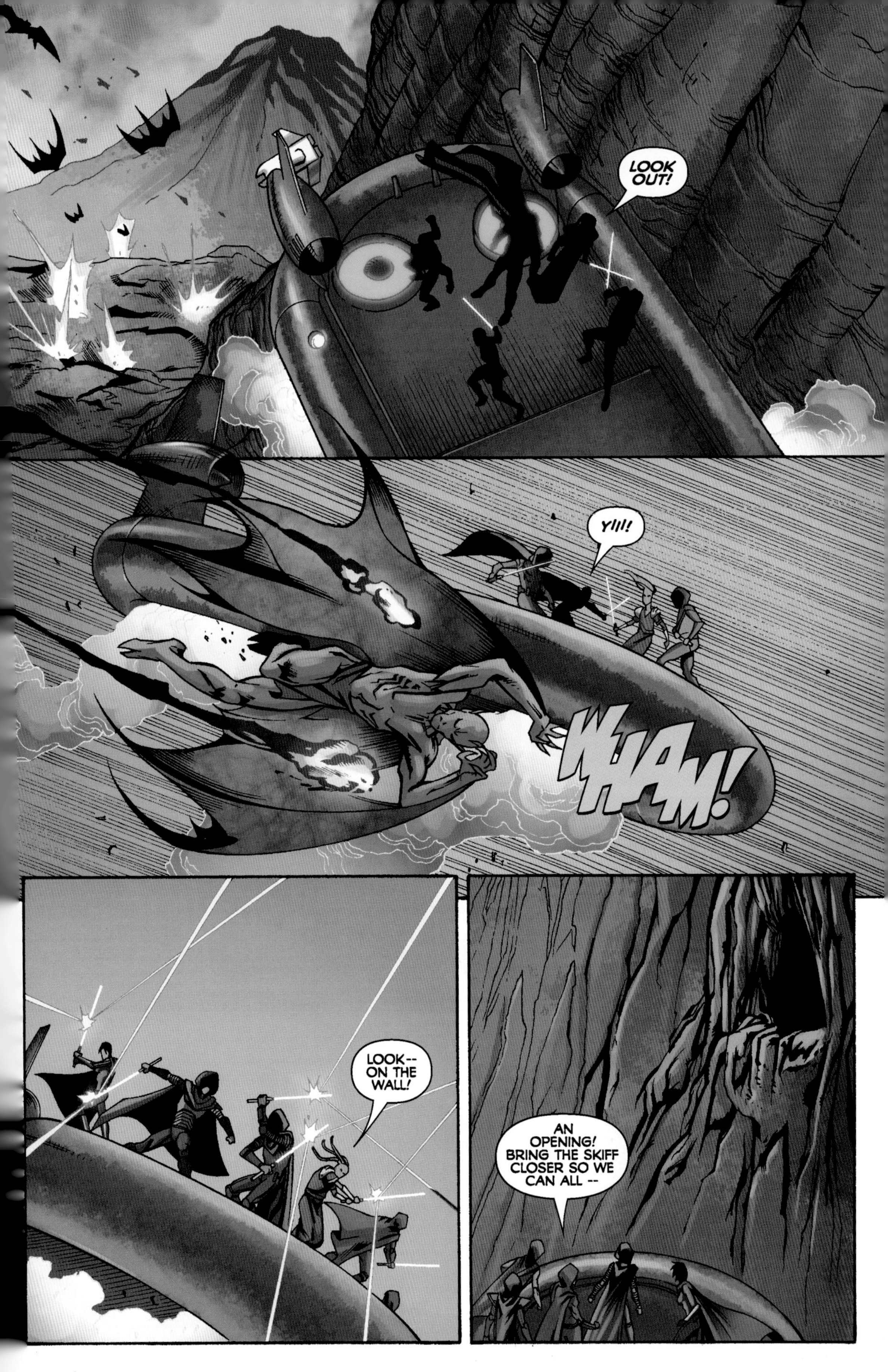
LOOK OUT!
YIII!
WHAM!
LOOK-- ON THE WALL!
AN OPENING! BRING THE SKIFF CLOSER SO WE CAN ALL --

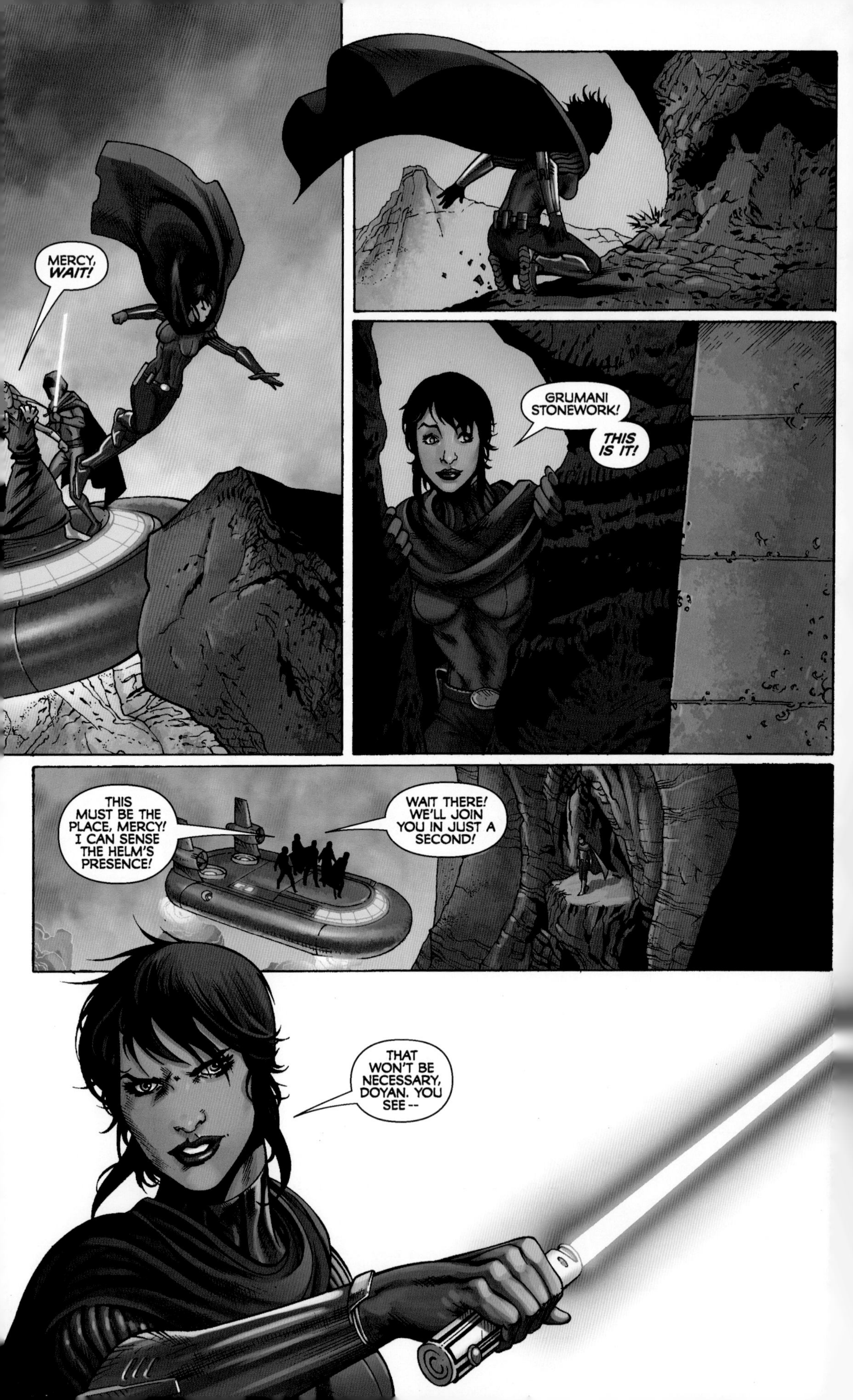
MERCY, WAIT!
GRUMANI STONEWORK!
THIS IS IT!
THIS MUST BE THE PLACE, MERCY! I CAN SENSE THE HELM'S PRESENCE!
WAIT THERE! WE'LL JOIN YOU IN JUST A SECOND!
THAT WON'T BE NECESSARY, DOYAN. YOU SEE --

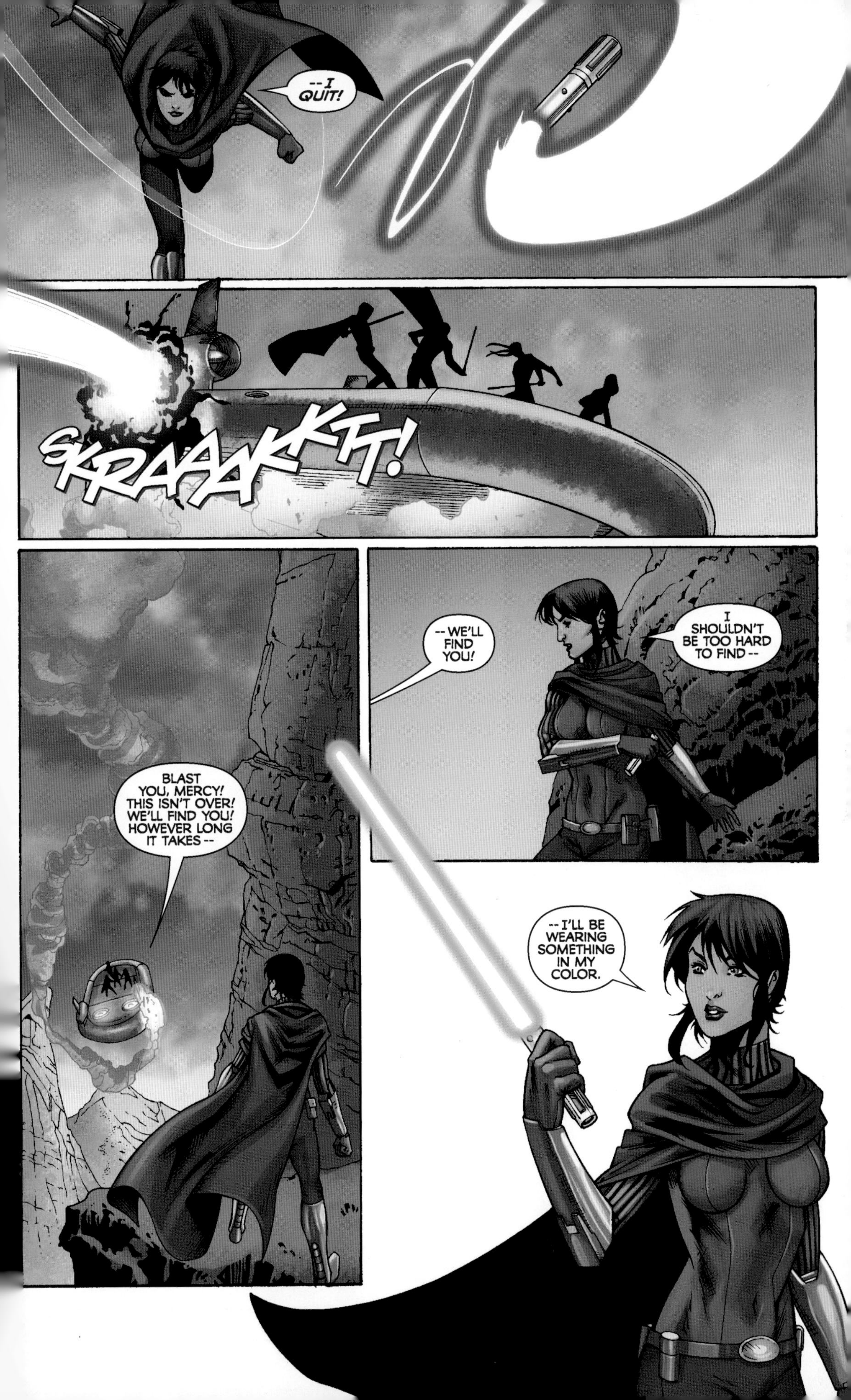
--I QUIT!
SKRAAAKKTT!
BLAST YOU, MERCY! THIS ISN'T OVER! WE'LL FIND YOU! HOWEVER LONG IT TAKES --
-- WE'LL FIND YOU!
I SHOULDN'T BE TOO HARD TO FIND --
-- I'LL BE WEARING SOMETHING IN MY COLOR.

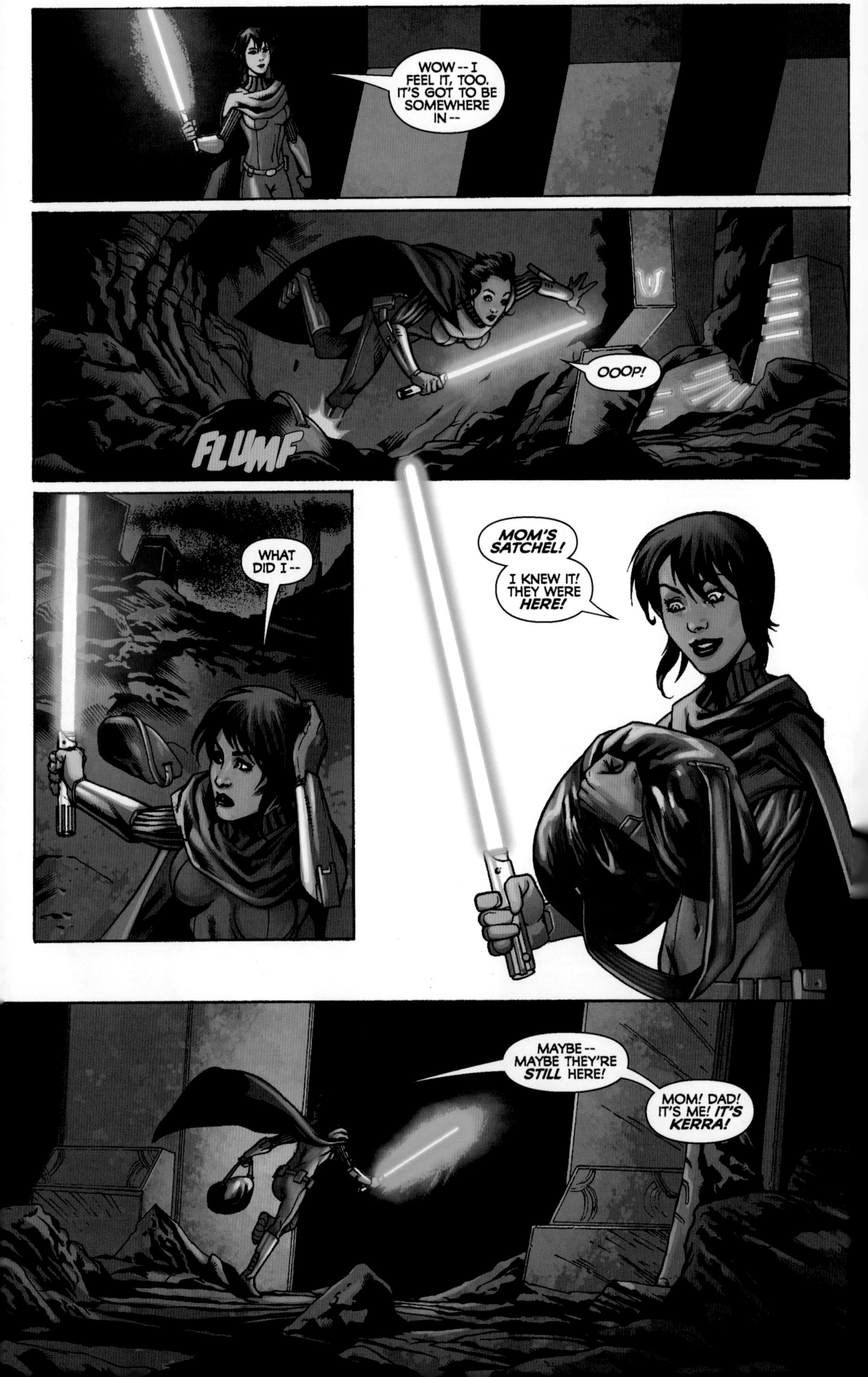
WOW -- I FEEL IT, TOO. IT'S GOT TO BE SOMEWHERE IN --
OOOP!
FLUMF
WHAT DID I --
MOM'S SATCHEL!
I KNEW IT! THEY WERE HERE!
MAYBE -- MAYBE THEY'RE STILL HERE!
MOM! DAD! IT'S ME! IT'S KERRA!

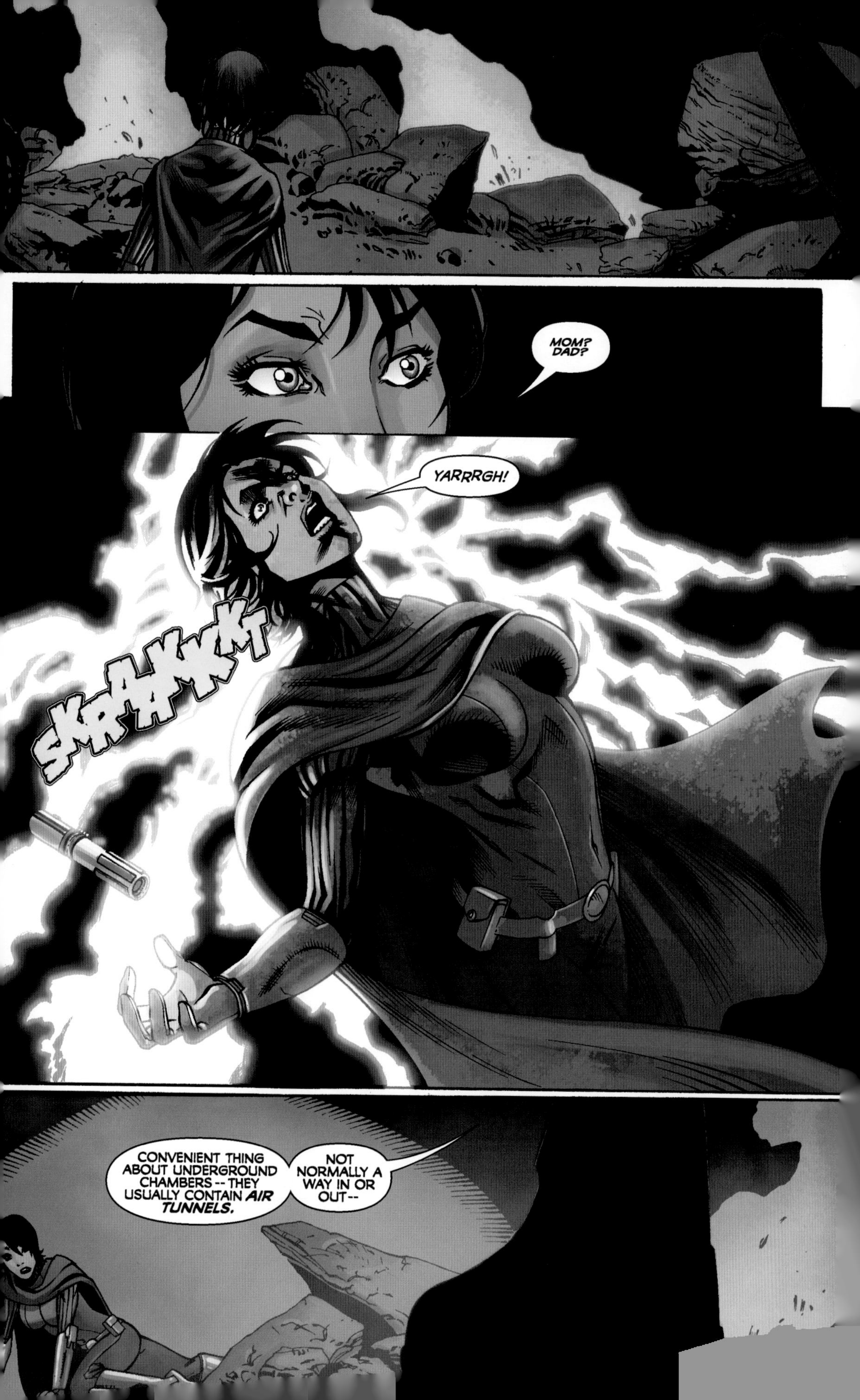
MOM?
DAD?
YARRRGH!
SKRAHKKKT
CONVENIENT THING ABOUT UNDERGROUND CHAMBERS -- THEY USUALLY CONTAIN *AIR TUNNELS.*
NOT NORMALLY A WAY IN OR OUT--

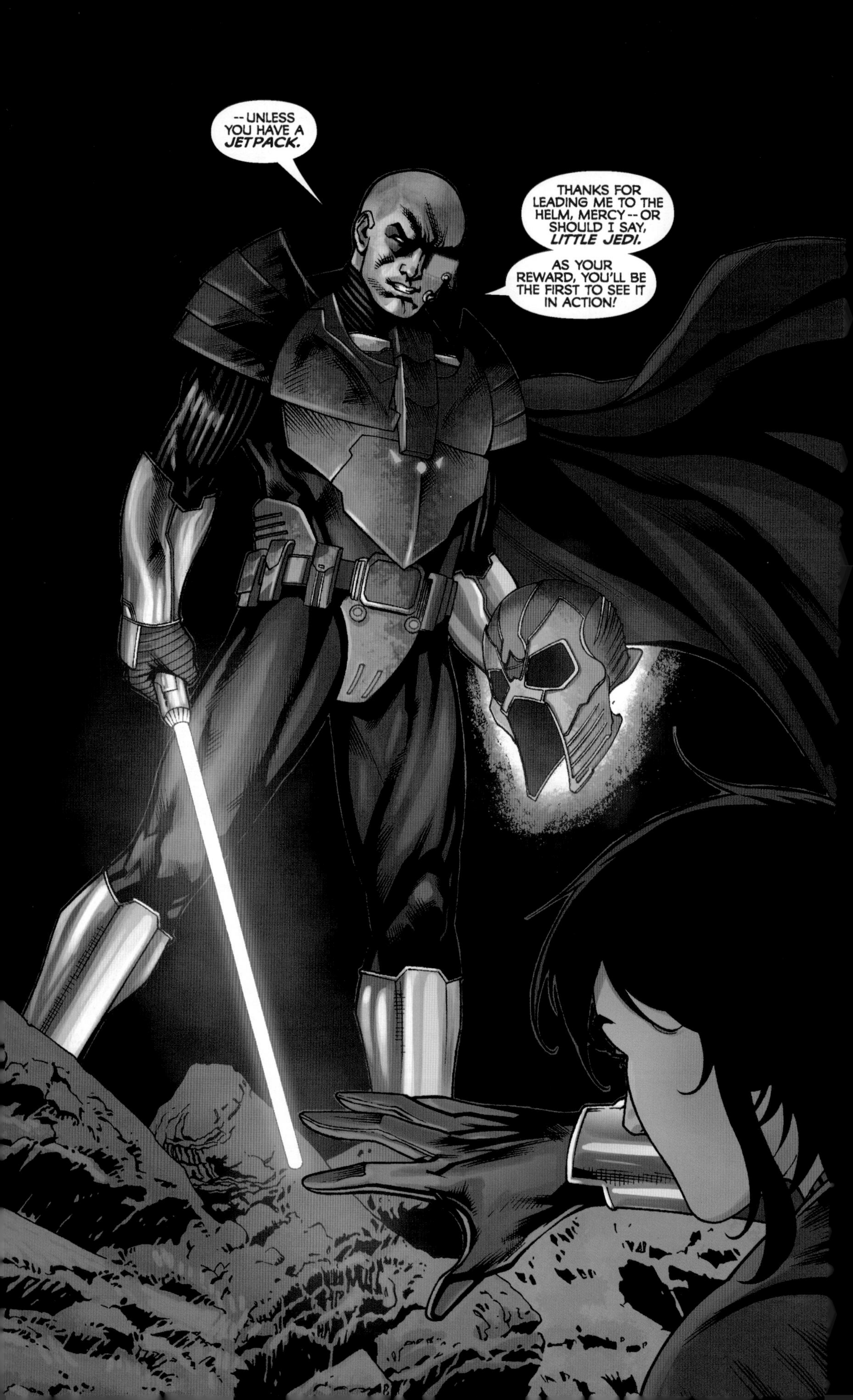
--UNLESS YOU HAVE A *JETPACK.*
THANKS FOR LEADING ME TO THE HELM, MERCY--OR SHOULD I SAY, *LITTLE JEDI.*
AS YOUR REWARD, YOU'LL BE THE FIRST TO SEE IT IN ACTION!

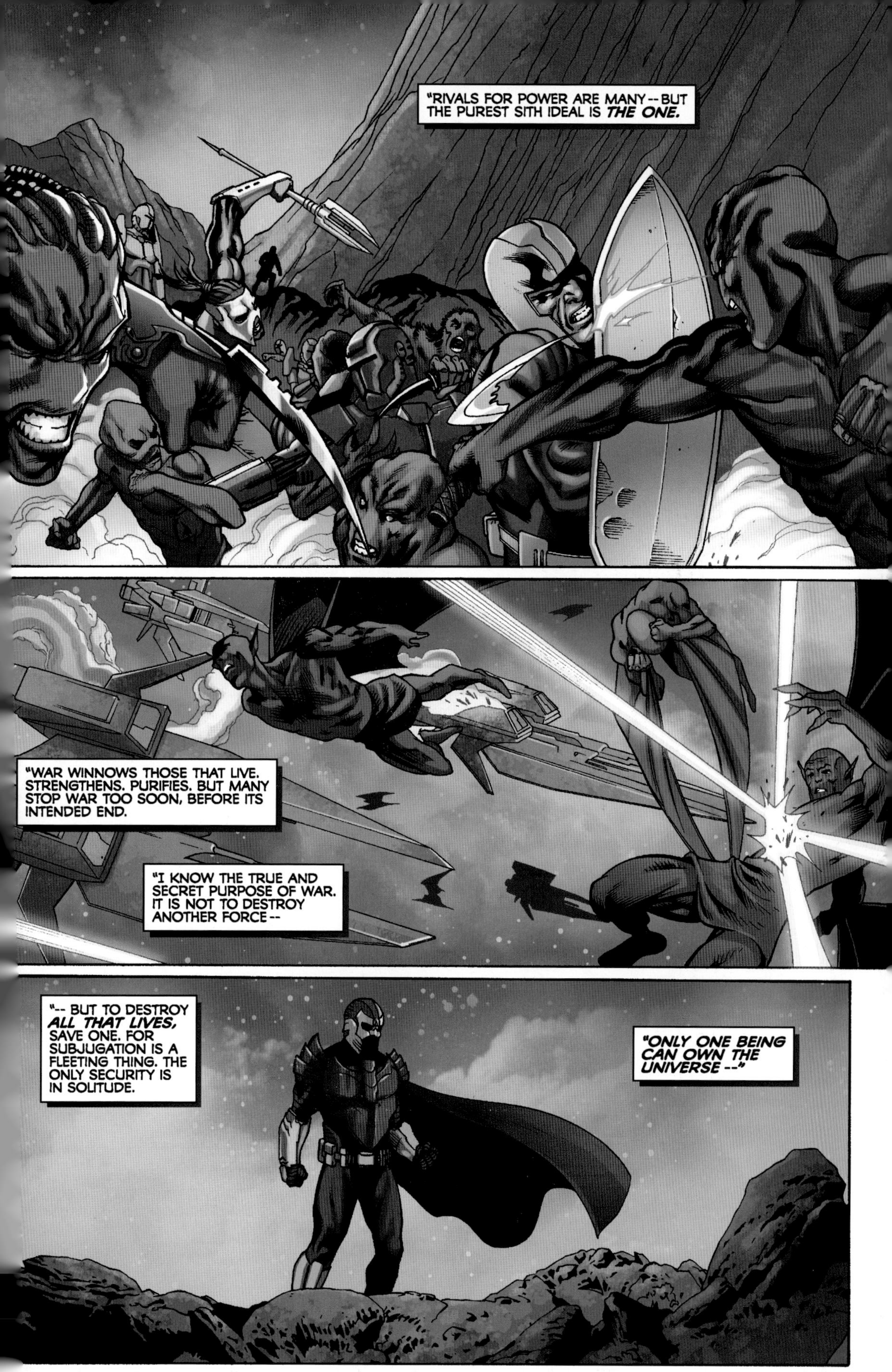
"RIVALS FOR POWER ARE MANY -- BUT THE PUREST SITH IDEAL IS ***THE ONE.***
"WAR WINNOWS THOSE THAT LIVE. STRENGTHENS. PURIFIES. BUT MANY STOP WAR TOO SOON, BEFORE ITS INTENDED END.
"I KNOW THE TRUE AND SECRET PURPOSE OF WAR. IT IS NOT TO DESTROY ANOTHER FORCE --
"-- BUT TO DESTROY ***ALL THAT LIVES,*** SAVE ONE. FOR SUBJUGATION IS A FLEETING THING. THE ONLY SECURITY IS IN SOLITUDE.
"ONLY ONE BEING CAN OWN THE UNIVERSE --"

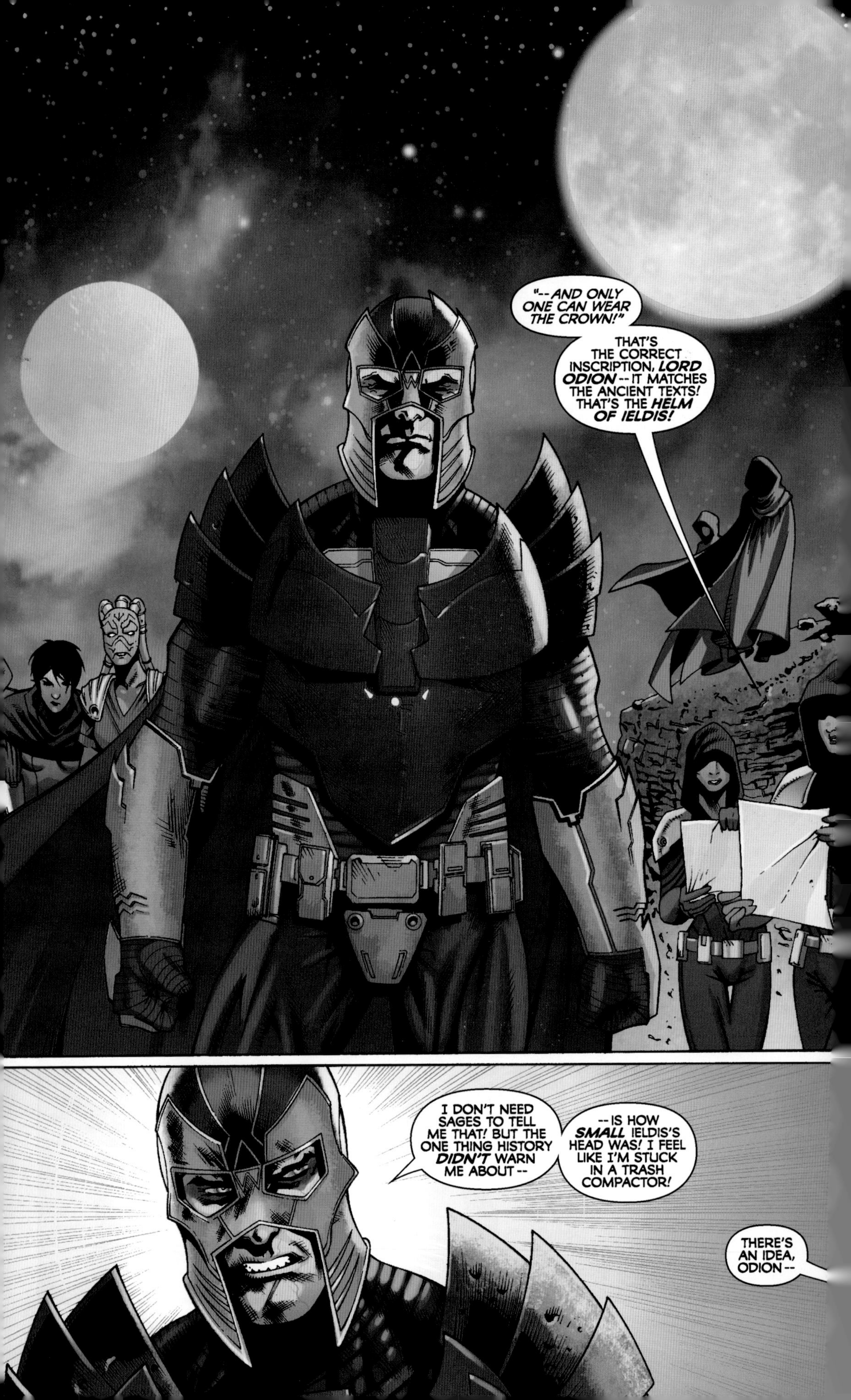
"-- AND ONLY ONE CAN WEAR THE CROWN!"
THAT'S THE CORRECT INSCRIPTION, LORD ODION -- IT MATCHES THE ANCIENT TEXTS! THAT'S THE HELM OF IELDIS!
I DON'T NEED SAGES TO TELL ME THAT! BUT THE ONE THING HISTORY DIDN'T WARN ME ABOUT --
-- IS HOW SMALL IELDIS'S HEAD WAS! I FEEL LIKE I'M STUCK IN A TRASH COMPACTOR!
THERE'S AN IDEA, ODION --

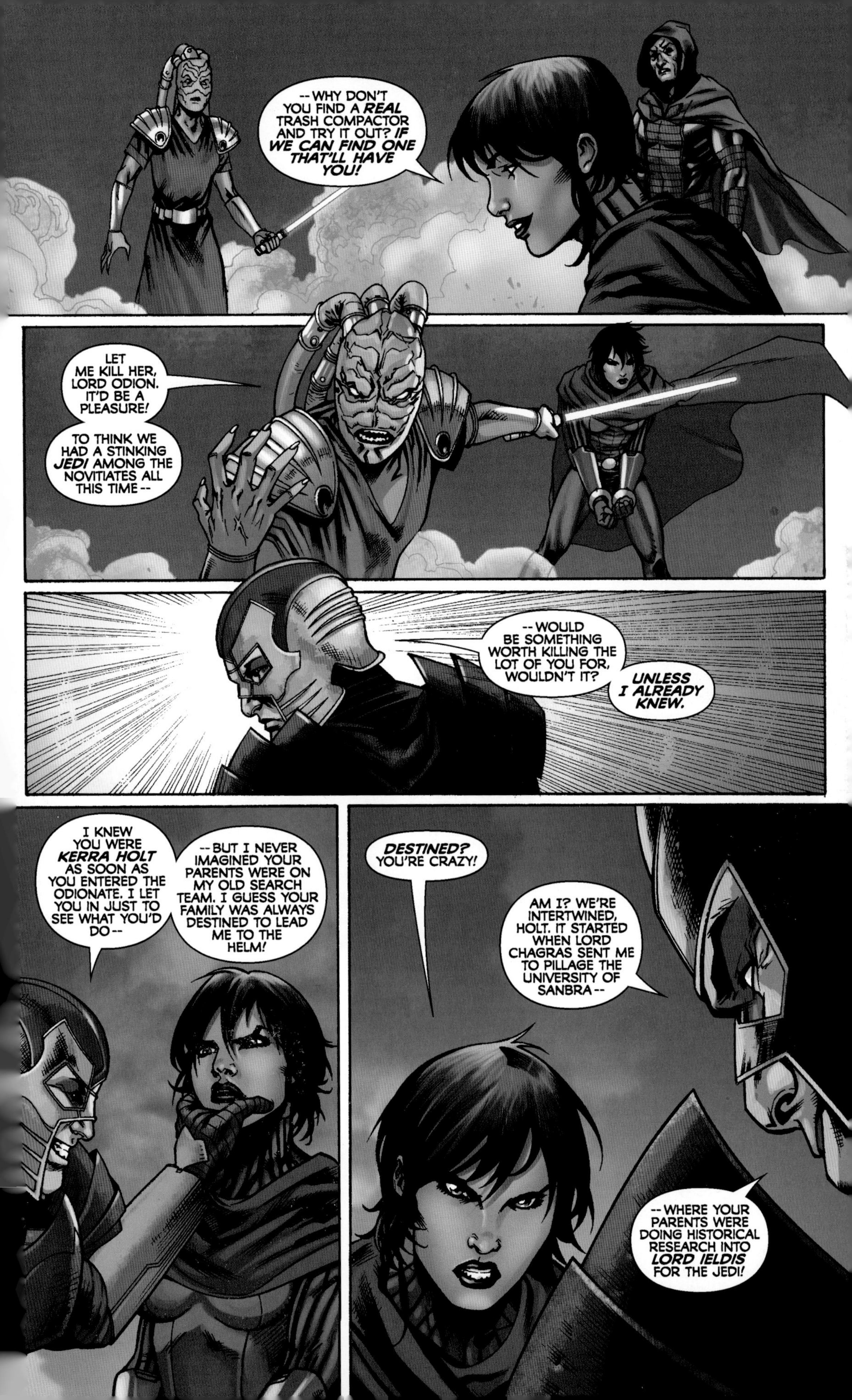

--WHY DON'T YOU FIND A *REAL* TRASH COMPACTOR AND TRY IT OUT? *IF WE CAN FIND ONE THAT'LL HAVE YOU!*
LET ME KILL HER, LORD ODION. IT'D BE A PLEASURE!
TO THINK WE HAD A STINKING *JEDI* AMONG THE NOVITIATES ALL THIS TIME--
--WOULD BE SOMETHING WORTH KILLING THE LOT OF YOU FOR, WOULDN'T IT?
UNLESS I ALREADY KNEW.
I KNEW YOU WERE *KERRA HOLT* AS SOON AS YOU ENTERED THE ODIONATE. I LET YOU IN JUST TO SEE WHAT YOU'D DO--
--BUT I NEVER IMAGINED YOUR PARENTS WERE ON MY OLD SEARCH TEAM. I GUESS YOUR FAMILY WAS ALWAYS DESTINED TO LEAD ME TO THE HELM!
DESTINED? YOU'RE CRAZY!
AM I? WE'RE INTERTWINED, HOLT. IT STARTED WHEN LORD CHAGRAS SENT ME TO PILLAGE THE UNIVERSITY OF SANBRA--
--WHERE YOUR PARENTS WERE DOING HISTORICAL RESEARCH INTO *LORD IELDIS* FOR THE JEDI!

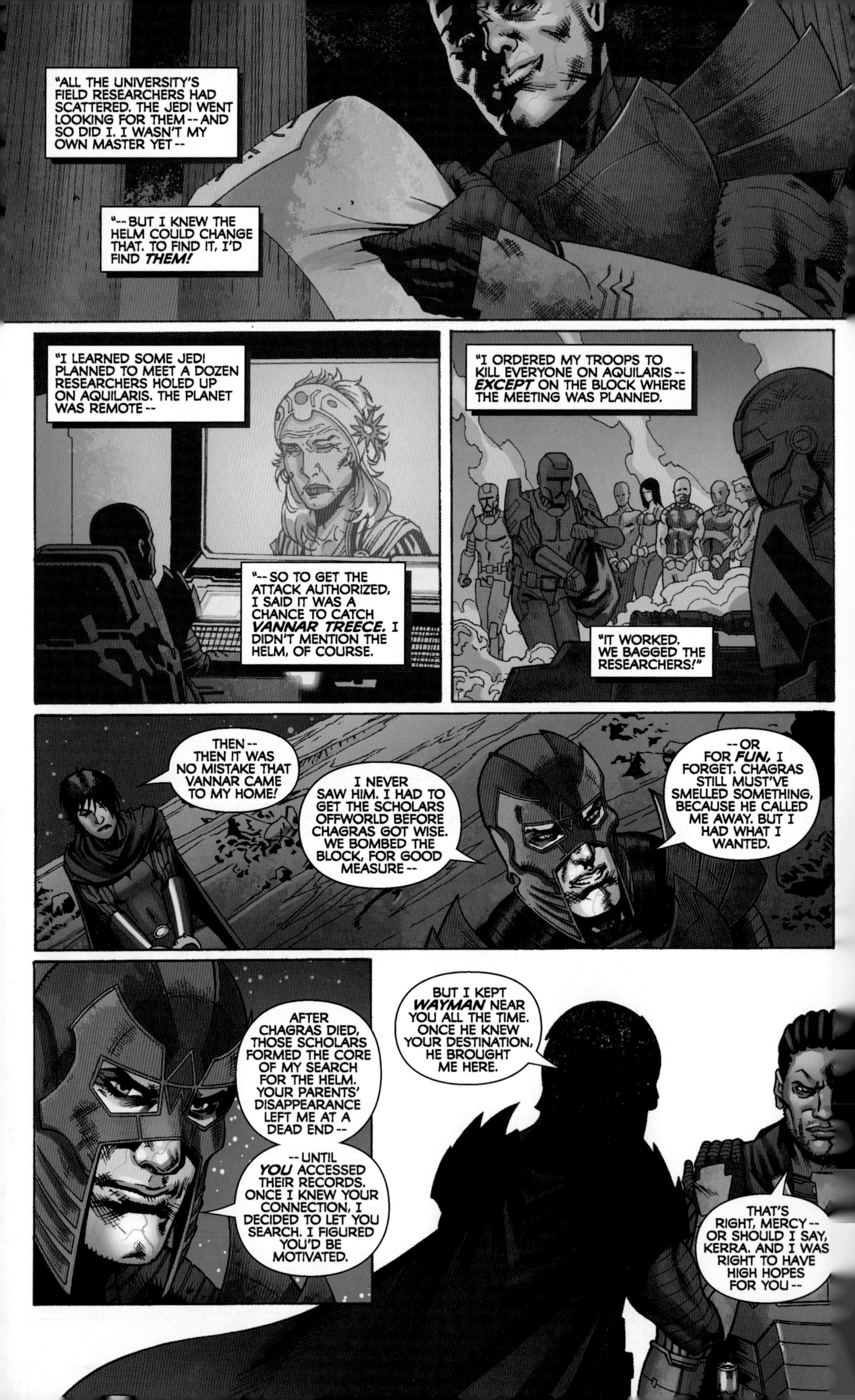
"ALL THE UNIVERSITY'S FIELD RESEARCHERS HAD SCATTERED. THE JEDI WENT LOOKING FOR THEM -- AND SO DID I. I WASN'T MY OWN MASTER YET --
"-- BUT I KNEW THE HELM COULD CHANGE THAT. TO FIND IT, I'D FIND ***THEM!***
"I LEARNED SOME JEDI PLANNED TO MEET A DOZEN RESEARCHERS HOLED UP ON AQUILARIS. THE PLANET WAS REMOTE --
"-- SO TO GET THE ATTACK AUTHORIZED, I SAID IT WAS A CHANCE TO CATCH ***VANNAR TREECE.*** I DIDN'T MENTION THE HELM, OF COURSE.
"I ORDERED MY TROOPS TO KILL EVERYONE ON AQUILARIS -- ***EXCEPT*** ON THE BLOCK WHERE THE MEETING WAS PLANNED.
"IT WORKED. WE BAGGED THE RESEARCHERS!"
THEN -- THEN IT WAS NO MISTAKE THAT VANNAR CAME TO MY HOME!
I NEVER SAW HIM. I HAD TO GET THE SCHOLARS OFFWORLD BEFORE CHAGRAS GOT WISE. WE BOMBED THE BLOCK, FOR GOOD MEASURE --
-- OR FOR ***FUN,*** I FORGET. CHAGRAS STILL MUST'VE SMELLED SOMETHING, BECAUSE HE CALLED ME AWAY. BUT I HAD WHAT I WANTED.
AFTER CHAGRAS DIED, THOSE SCHOLARS FORMED THE CORE OF MY SEARCH FOR THE HELM. YOUR PARENTS' DISAPPEARANCE LEFT ME AT A DEAD END --
-- UNTIL ***YOU*** ACCESSED THEIR RECORDS. ONCE I KNEW YOUR CONNECTION, I DECIDED TO LET YOU SEARCH. I FIGURED YOU'D BE MOTIVATED.
BUT I KEPT ***WAYMAN*** NEAR YOU ALL THE TIME. ONCE HE KNEW YOUR DESTINATION, HE BROUGHT ME HERE.
THAT'S RIGHT, MERCY -- OR SHOULD I SAY, KERRA. AND I WAS RIGHT TO HAVE HIGH HOPES FOR YOU --

"-- YOU LED US TO THE EXACT PLACE! ODION SENSED THE HELM'S LOCATION INSTANTLY. PART OF THE CHAMBER CEILING HAD COLLAPSED --

"-- BUT NO ROCK CAN CRUSH THE WORK OF IELDIS. YULAN BROUGHT UP SOME SOLDIERS FROM THE BATTLE TO SEARCH THE REST."

ANYTHING ELSE DOWN THERE, YULAN? AN OPERATOR'S GUIDE? I FEEL LIKE A FOOL WITH THIS THING ON! IT DOESN'T DO ANYTHING!

IT'S A MESS DOWN THERE, MY LORD. SOMEONE BROUGHT THAT CEILING DOWN WITH A DEMOLITION CHARGE --

-- *FROM INSIDE.* ALL WE'VE FOUND ARE SOME CAMPING SUPPLIES -- AND TWO HUMAN SKELETONS, CRUSHED UNDER THE ROCK.

THEY MUST'VE BEEN INSIDE DURING THE EXPLOSION. YOU CAN'T TELL MUCH ABOUT THEM NOW --

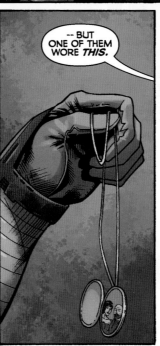

-- BUT ONE OF THEM WORE *THIS.*

NO!

77

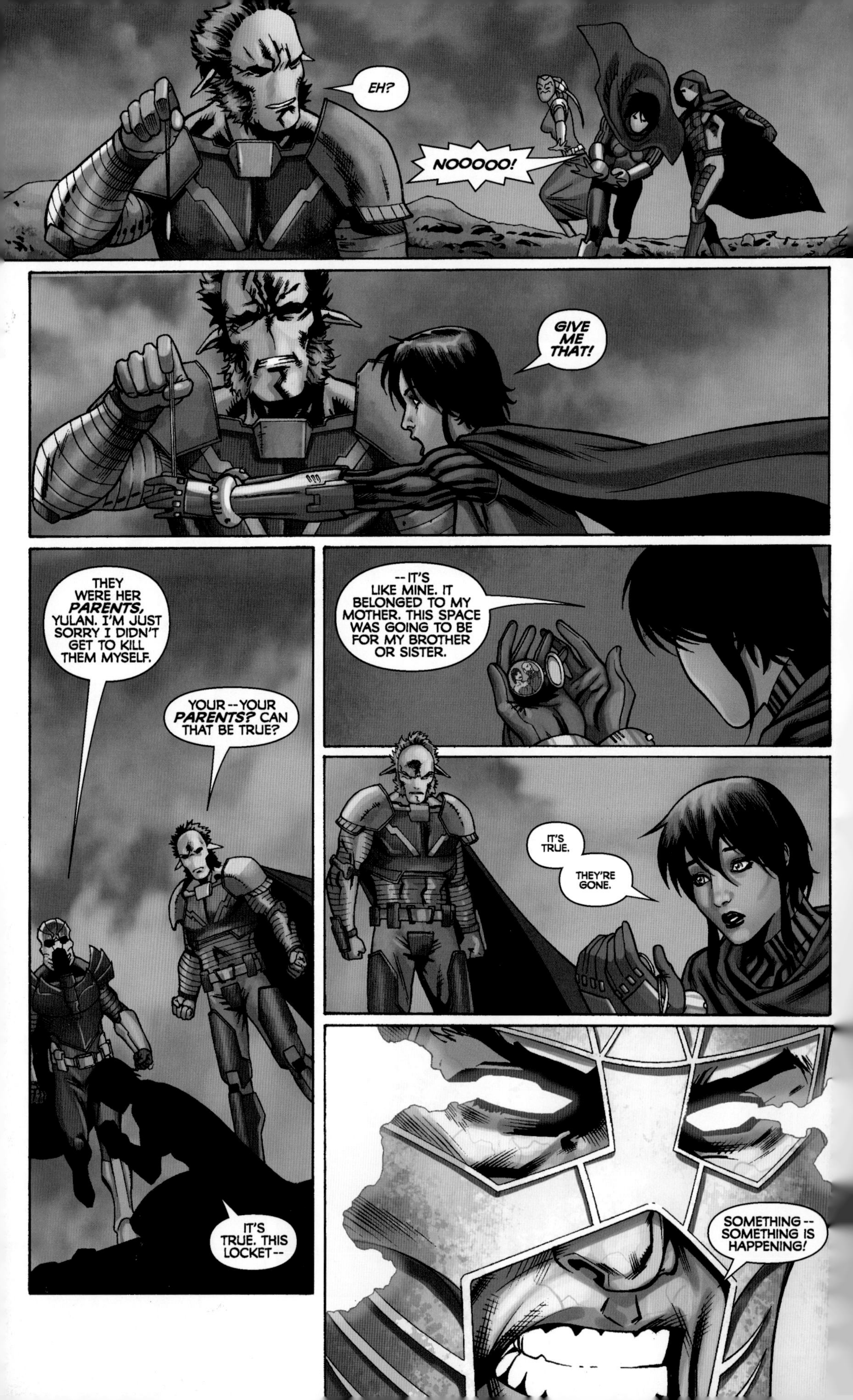
EH?
NOOOOO!
GIVE ME THAT!
THEY WERE HER PARENTS, YULAN. I'M JUST SORRY I DIDN'T GET TO KILL THEM MYSELF.
YOUR--YOUR PARENTS? CAN THAT BE TRUE?
IT'S TRUE. THIS LOCKET--
--IT'S LIKE MINE. IT BELONGED TO MY MOTHER. THIS SPACE WAS GOING TO BE FOR MY BROTHER OR SISTER.
IT'S TRUE.
THEY'RE GONE.
SOMETHING--SOMETHING IS HAPPENING!

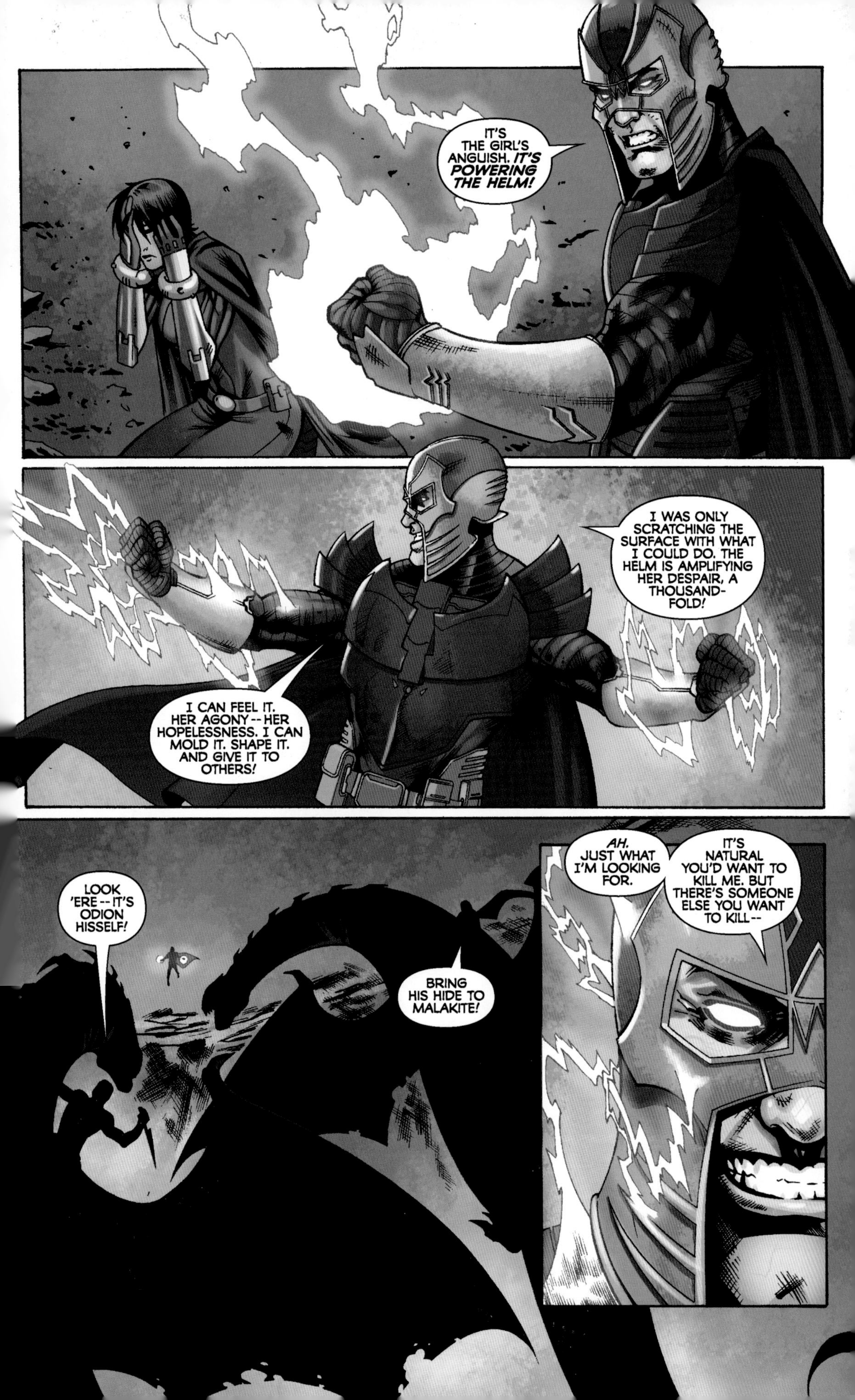
IT'S THE GIRL'S ANGUISH. IT'S POWERING THE HELM!
I WAS ONLY SCRATCHING THE SURFACE WITH WHAT I COULD DO. THE HELM IS AMPLIFYING HER DESPAIR, A THOUSAND-FOLD!
I CAN FEEL IT. HER AGONY--HER HOPELESSNESS. I CAN MOLD IT. SHAPE IT. AND GIVE IT TO OTHERS!
LOOK 'ERE--IT'S ODION HISSELF!
BRING HIS HIDE TO MALAKITE!
AH. JUST WHAT I'M LOOKING FOR.
IT'S NATURAL YOU'D WANT TO KILL ME. BUT THERE'S SOMEONE ELSE YOU WANT TO KILL--

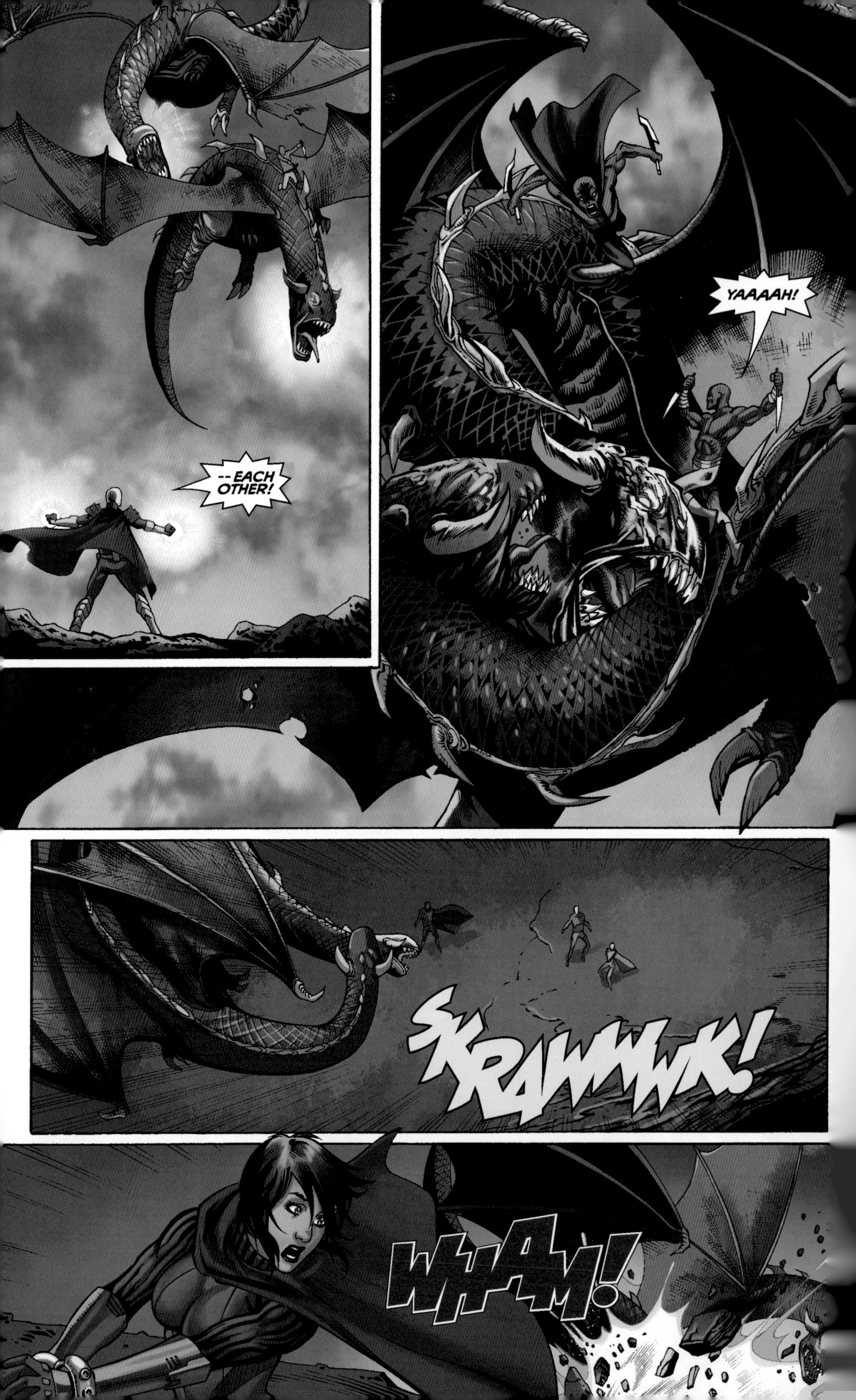

--EACH OTHER!
YAAAAH!
SKRAWWWK!
WHAM!

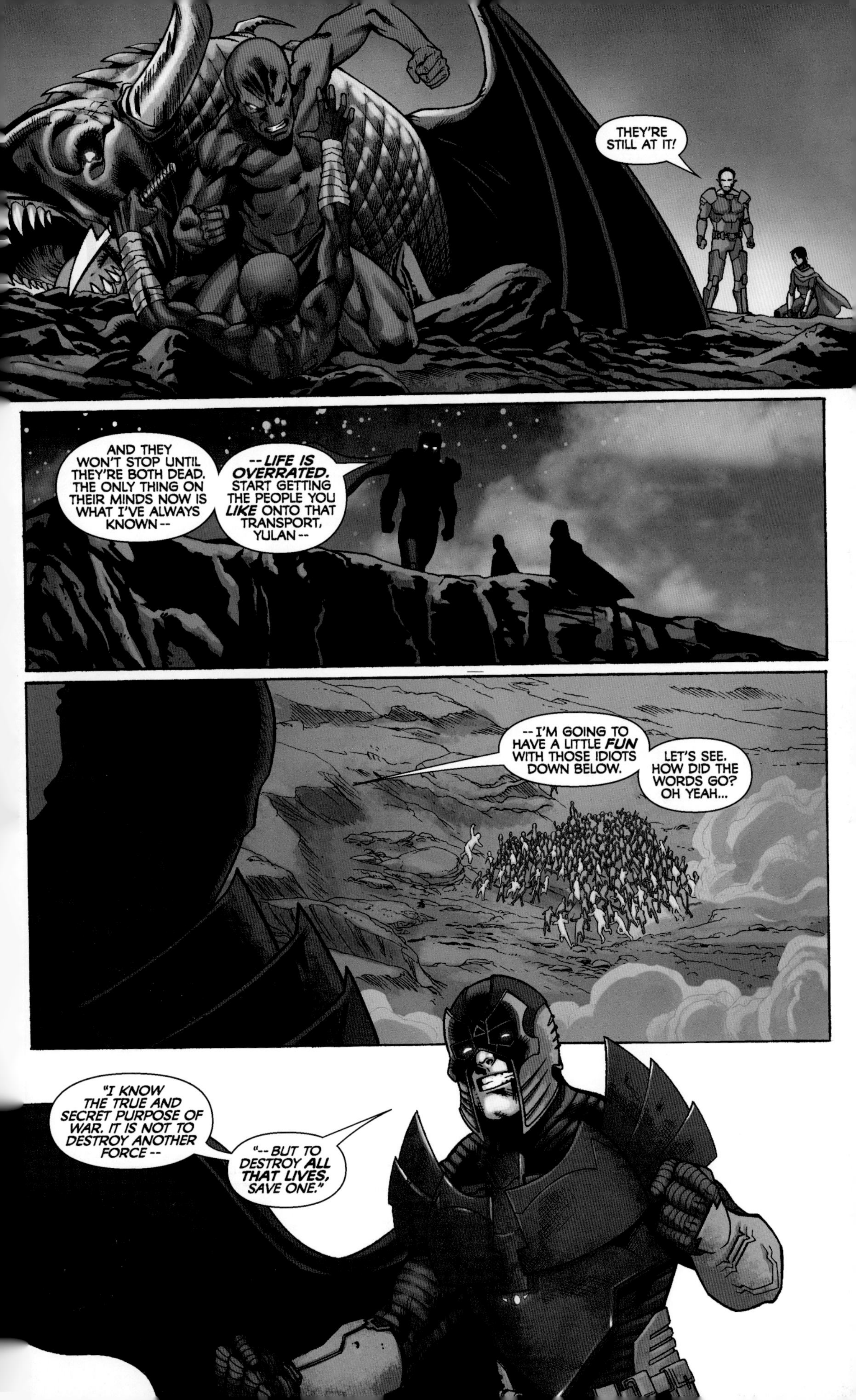
THEY'RE STILL AT IT!
AND THEY WON'T STOP UNTIL THEY'RE BOTH DEAD. THE ONLY THING ON THEIR MINDS NOW IS WHAT I'VE ALWAYS KNOWN--
--LIFE IS OVERRATED. START GETTING THE PEOPLE YOU LIKE ONTO THAT TRANSPORT, YULAN--
--I'M GOING TO HAVE A LITTLE FUN WITH THOSE IDIOTS DOWN BELOW.
LET'S SEE. HOW DID THE WORDS GO? OH YEAH...
"I KNOW THE TRUE AND SECRET PURPOSE OF WAR. IT IS NOT TO DESTROY ANOTHER FORCE--
"--BUT TO DESTROY ALL THAT LIVES, SAVE ONE."

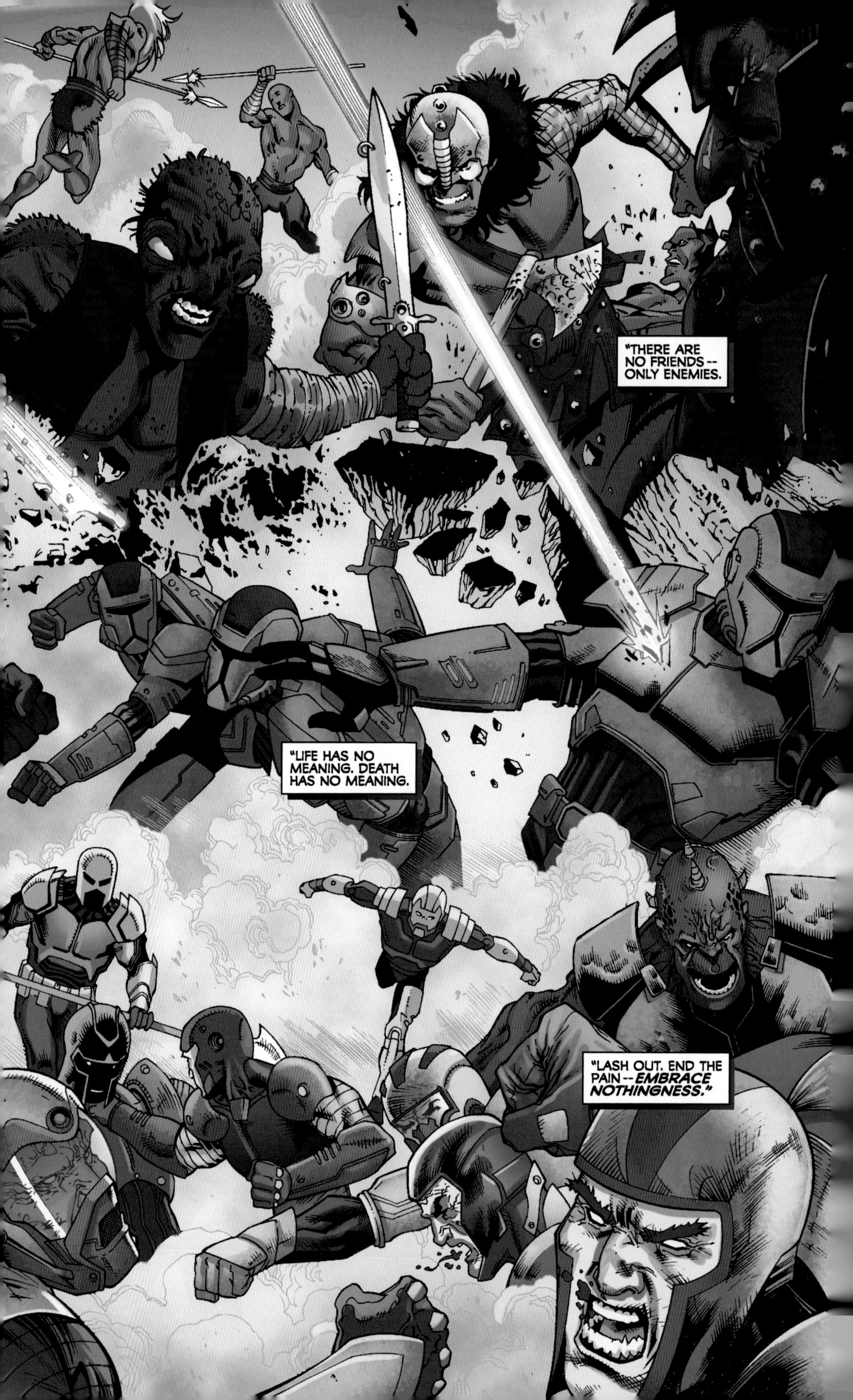
"THERE ARE NO FRIENDS -- ONLY ENEMIES.
"LIFE HAS NO MEANING. DEATH HAS NO MEANING.
"LASH OUT. END THE PAIN -- *EMBRACE NOTHINGNESS.*"

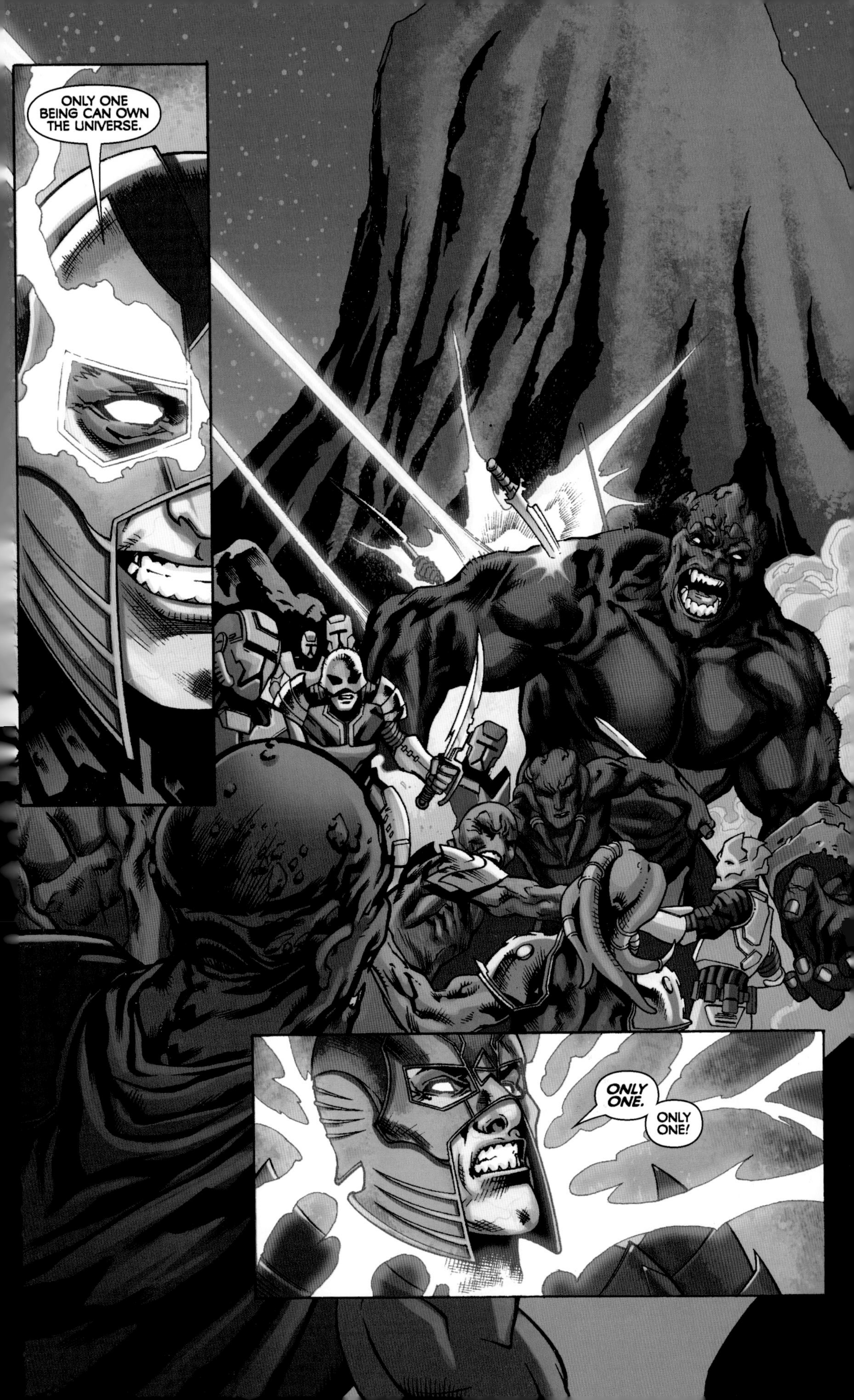
ONLY ONE BEING CAN OWN THE UNIVERSE.
ONLY ONE.
ONLY ONE!

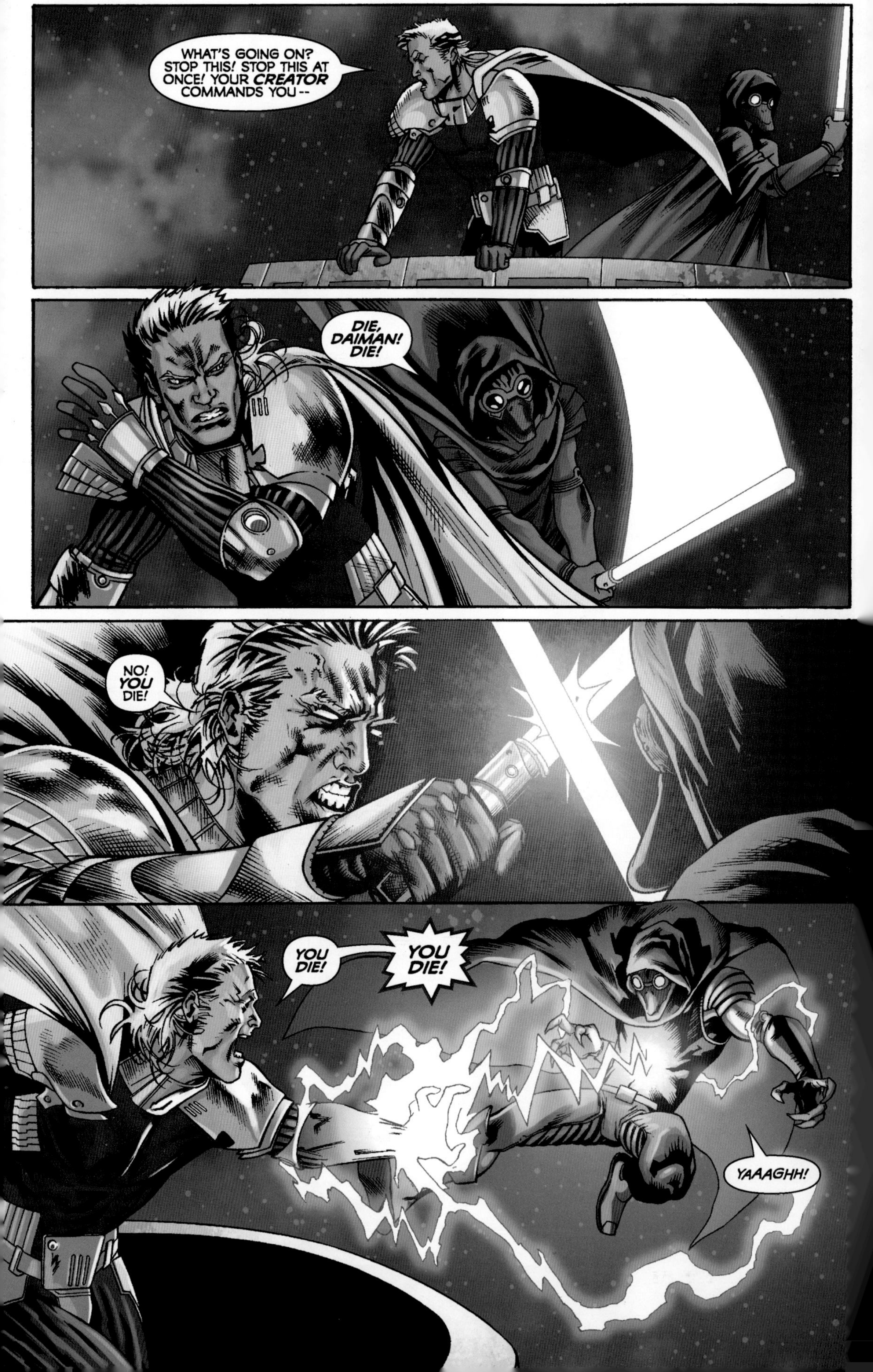
WHAT'S GOING ON? STOP THIS! STOP THIS AT ONCE! YOUR CREATOR COMMANDS YOU--
DIE, DAIMAN! DIE!
NO! YOU DIE!
YOU DIE!
YOU DIE!
YAAAGHH!

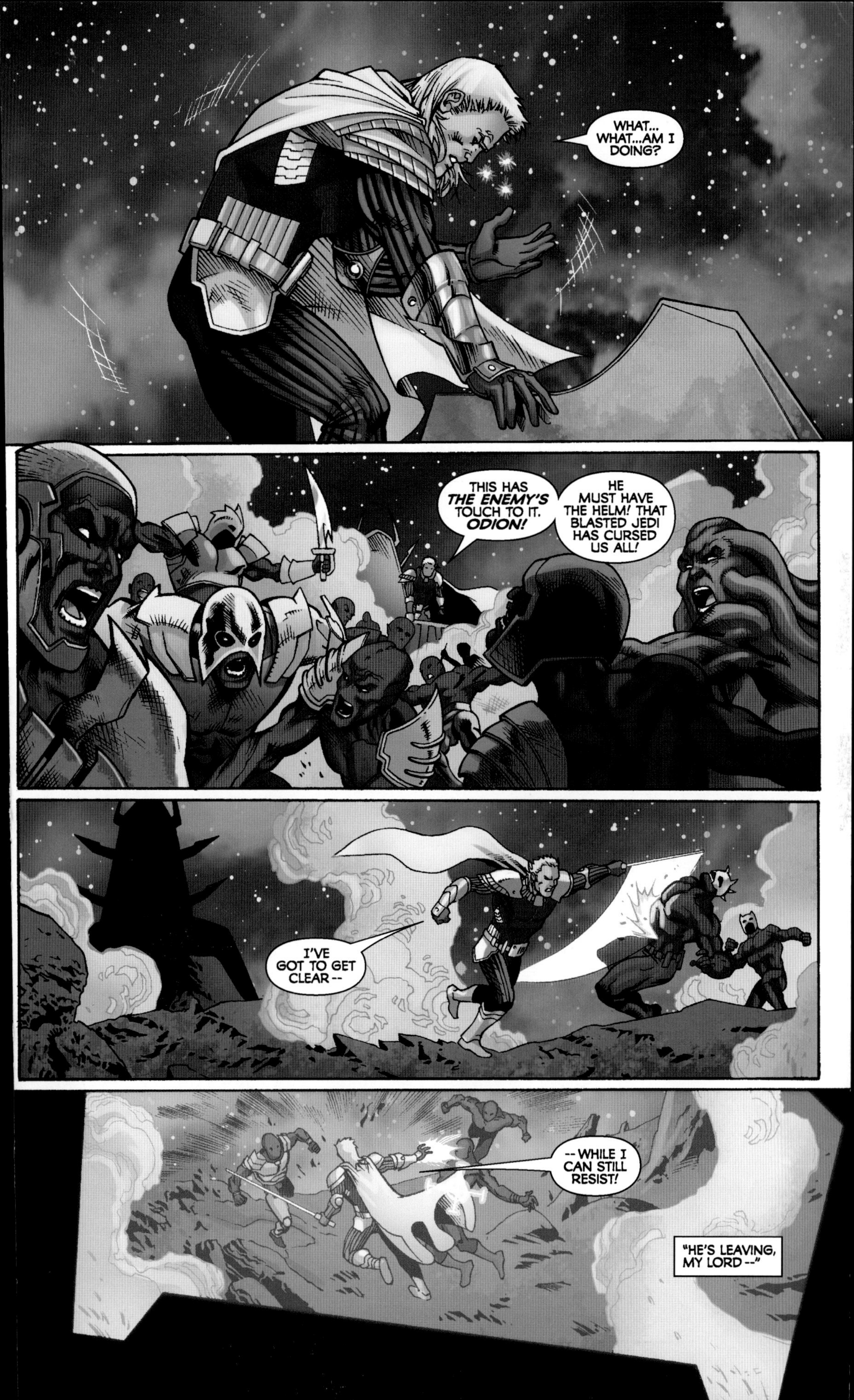
WHAT... WHAT...AM I DOING?
THIS HAS *THE ENEMY'S* TOUCH TO IT. ***ODION!***
HE MUST HAVE THE HELM! THAT BLASTED JEDI HAS CURSED US ALL!
I'VE GOT TO GET CLEAR --
-- WHILE I CAN STILL RESIST!
"HE'S LEAVING, MY LORD --"

-- AND MALAKITE HAS FLED, AS WELL.

WHO CARES ABOUT THEM?

DO YOU SEE IT, JEDI? DO YOU SEE IT?

YOU SAW WHAT I COULD DO ON MY *OWN* ON JUBALENE. I HAD TO USE THE MISERY OF A WHOLE WORLD TO DRIVE THOSE DUROS TO DESTRUCTION.

THE HELM -- IT'S A MORE EFFICIENT CONVERTER. YOUR DESPAIR ALONE DROVE THREE ARMIES MAD!

THAT'S RIGHT, LITTLE JEDI -- YOU MADE IT POSSIBLE.

THIS IS JUST THE BEGINNING. AND I WANT YOU TO SEE IT ALL!

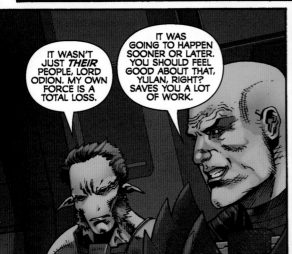

IT WASN'T JUST *THEIR* PEOPLE, LORD ODION. MY OWN FORCE IS A TOTAL LOSS.

IT WAS GOING TO HAPPEN SOONER OR LATER. YOU SHOULD FEEL GOOD ABOUT THAT, YULAN, RIGHT? SAVES YOU A LOT OF WORK.

LOCK THE GIRL UP. I HAVE A *NEW DESTINATION* IN MIND...

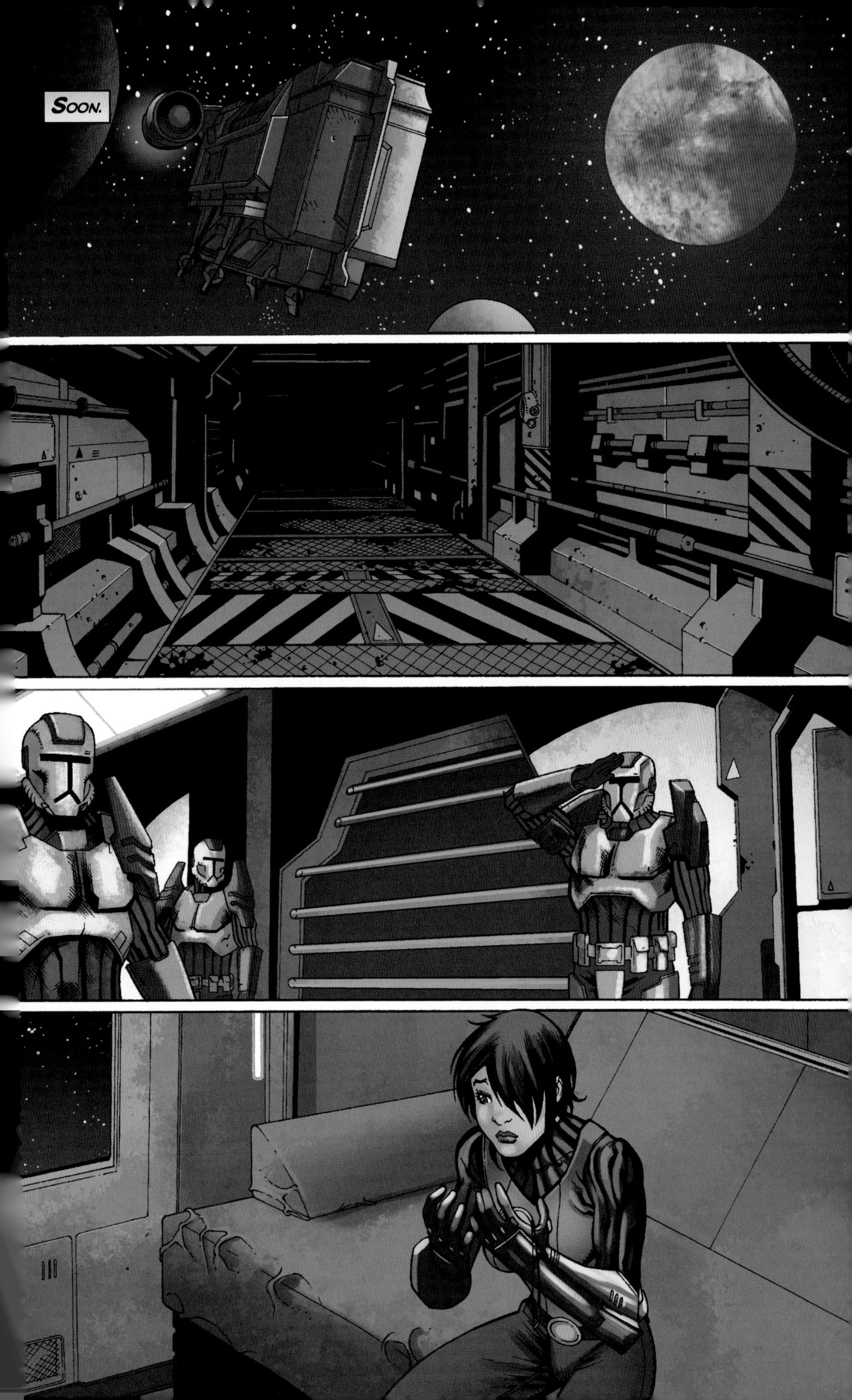
SOON.

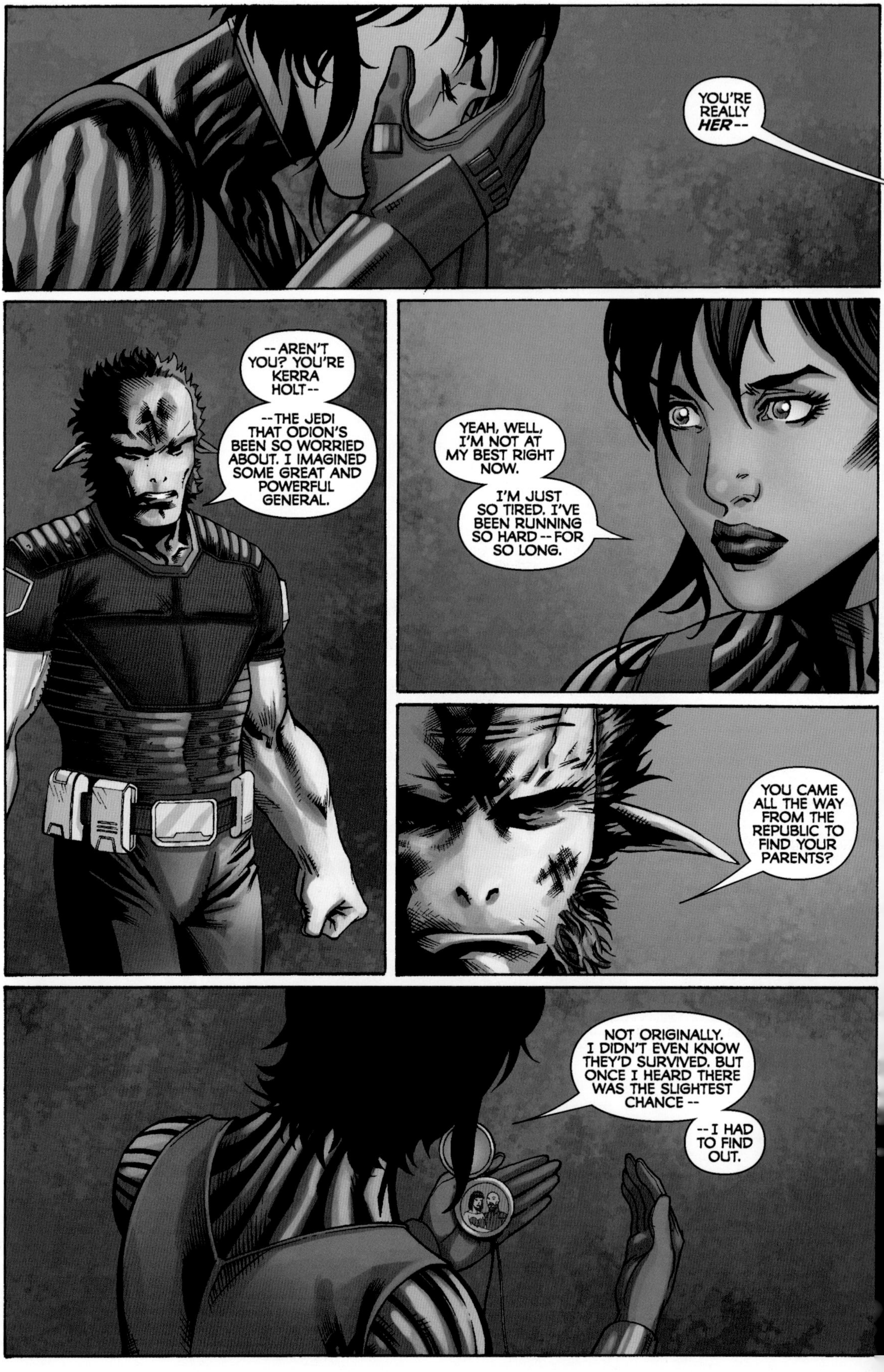
YOU'RE REALLY HER--
--AREN'T YOU? YOU'RE KERRA HOLT--
--THE JEDI THAT ODION'S BEEN SO WORRIED ABOUT. I IMAGINED SOME GREAT AND POWERFUL GENERAL.
YEAH, WELL, I'M NOT AT MY BEST RIGHT NOW.
I'M JUST SO TIRED. I'VE BEEN RUNNING SO HARD--FOR SO LONG.
YOU CAME ALL THE WAY FROM THE REPUBLIC TO FIND YOUR PARENTS?
NOT ORIGINALLY. I DIDN'T EVEN KNOW THEY'D SURVIVED. BUT ONCE I HEARD THERE WAS THE SLIGHTEST CHANCE--
--I HAD TO FIND OUT.

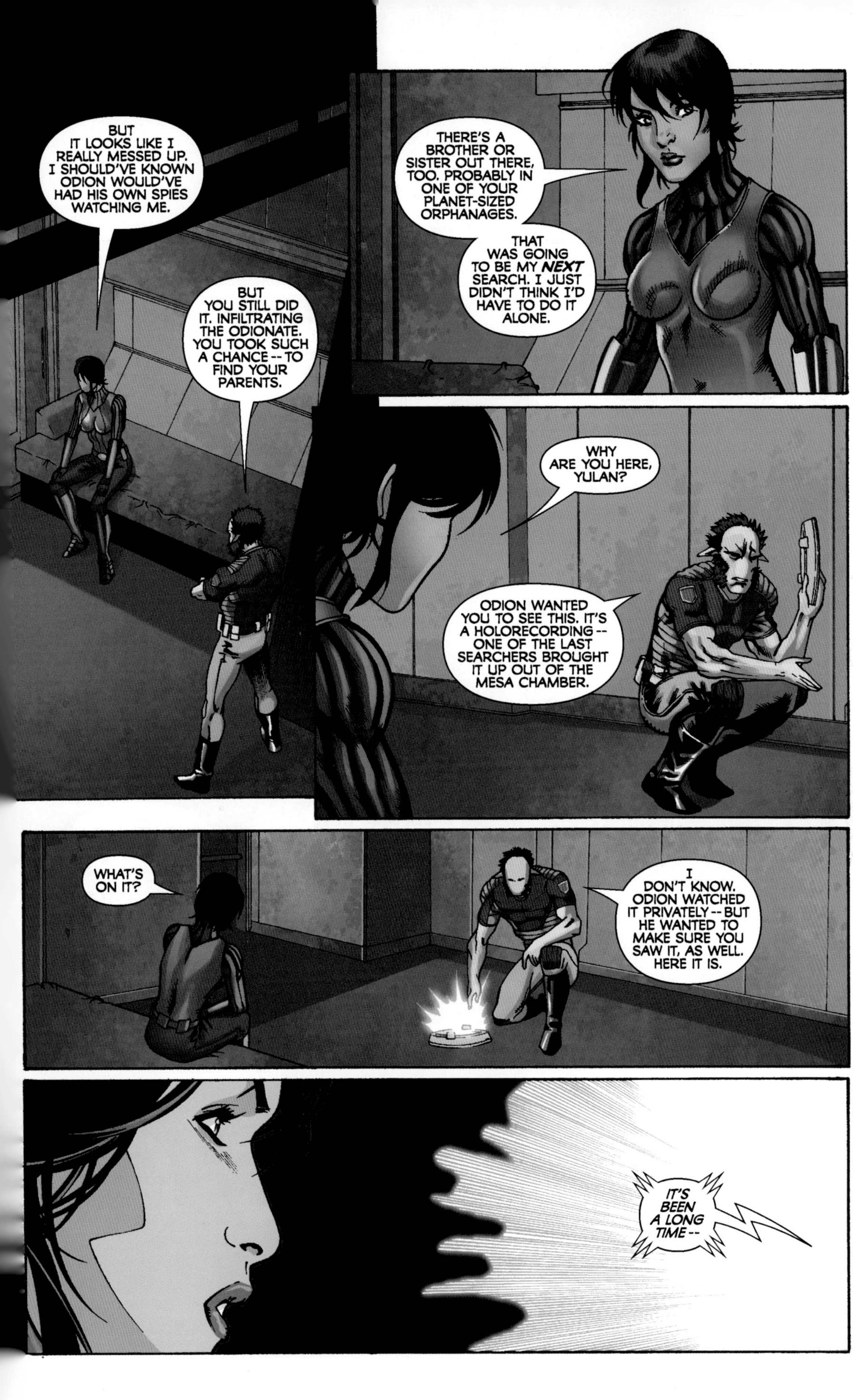
BUT IT LOOKS LIKE I REALLY MESSED UP. I SHOULD'VE KNOWN ODION WOULD'VE HAD HIS OWN SPIES WATCHING ME.
BUT YOU STILL DID IT. INFILTRATING THE ODIONATE. YOU TOOK SUCH A CHANCE -- TO FIND YOUR PARENTS.
THERE'S A BROTHER OR SISTER OUT THERE, TOO. PROBABLY IN ONE OF YOUR PLANET-SIZED ORPHANAGES.
THAT WAS GOING TO BE MY *NEXT* SEARCH. I JUST DIDN'T THINK I'D HAVE TO DO IT ALONE.
WHY ARE YOU HERE, YULAN?
ODION WANTED YOU TO SEE THIS. IT'S A HOLORECORDING -- ONE OF THE LAST SEARCHERS BROUGHT IT UP OUT OF THE MESA CHAMBER.
WHAT'S ON IT?
I DON'T KNOW. ODION WATCHED IT PRIVATELY -- BUT HE WANTED TO MAKE SURE YOU SAW IT, AS WELL. HERE IT IS.
IT'S BEEN A LONG TIME --

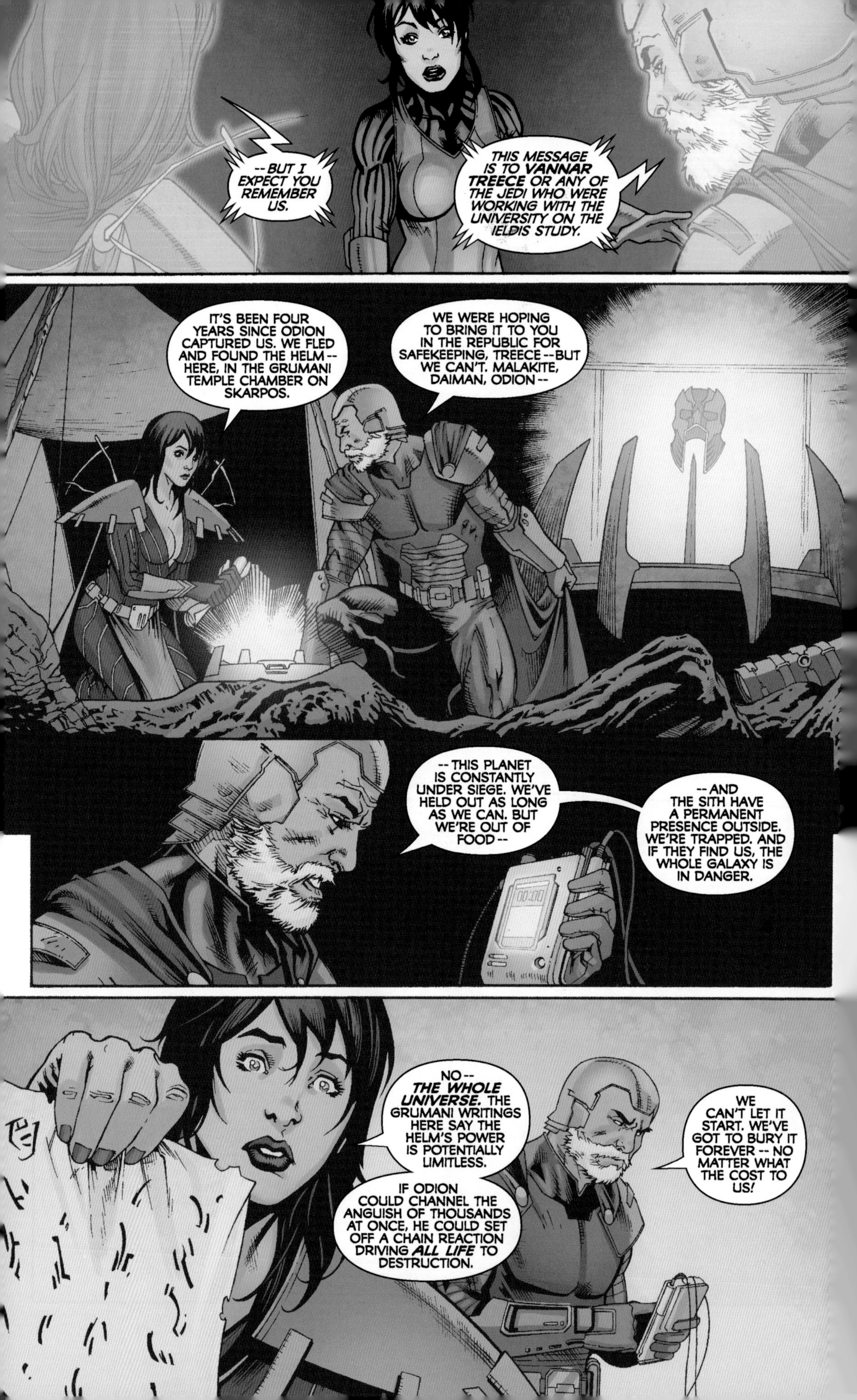

--BUT I EXPECT YOU REMEMBER US.
THIS MESSAGE IS TO **VANNAR TREECE** OR ANY OF THE JEDI WHO WERE WORKING WITH THE UNIVERSITY ON THE IELDIS STUDY.
IT'S BEEN FOUR YEARS SINCE ODION CAPTURED US. WE FLED AND FOUND THE HELM--HERE, IN THE GRUMANI TEMPLE CHAMBER ON SKARPOS.
WE WERE HOPING TO BRING IT TO YOU IN THE REPUBLIC FOR SAFEKEEPING, TREECE--BUT WE CAN'T. MALAKITE, DAIMAN, ODION--
--THIS PLANET IS CONSTANTLY UNDER SIEGE. WE'VE HELD OUT AS LONG AS WE CAN. BUT WE'RE OUT OF FOOD--
--AND THE SITH HAVE A PERMANENT PRESENCE OUTSIDE. WE'RE TRAPPED. AND IF THEY FIND US, THE WHOLE GALAXY IS IN DANGER.
NO--***THE WHOLE UNIVERSE.*** THE GRUMANI WRITINGS HERE SAY THE HELM'S POWER IS POTENTIALLY LIMITLESS.
IF ODION COULD CHANNEL THE ANGUISH OF THOUSANDS AT ONCE, HE COULD SET OFF A CHAIN REACTION DRIVING ***ALL LIFE*** TO DESTRUCTION.
WE CAN'T LET IT START. WE'VE GOT TO BURY IT FOREVER--NO MATTER WHAT THE COST TO US!

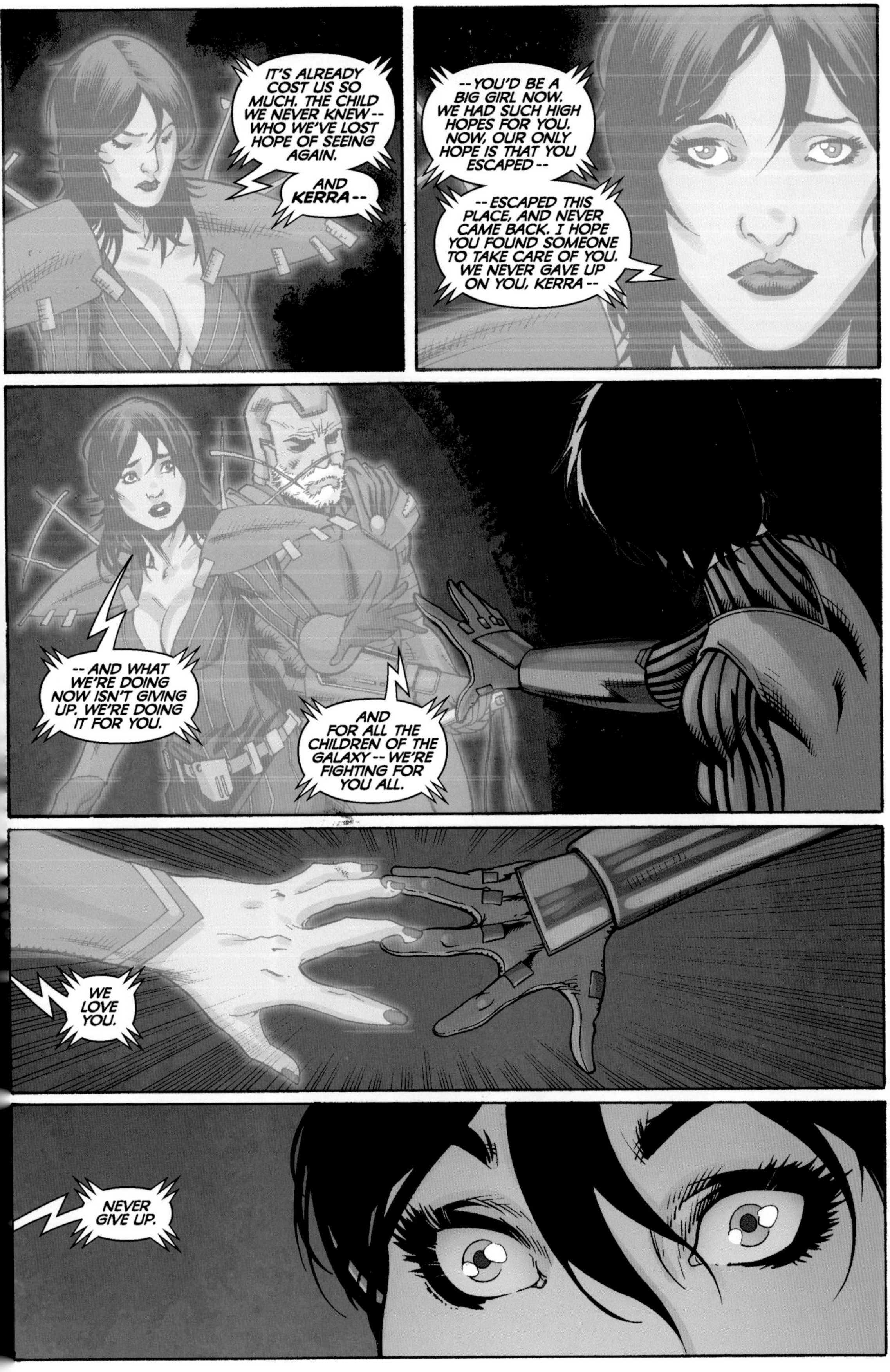
IT'S ALREADY COST US SO MUCH. THE CHILD WE NEVER KNEW -- WHO WE'VE LOST HOPE OF SEEING AGAIN.
AND KERRA --
-- YOU'D BE A BIG GIRL NOW. WE HAD SUCH HIGH HOPES FOR YOU. NOW, OUR ONLY HOPE IS THAT YOU ESCAPED --
-- ESCAPED THIS PLACE, AND NEVER CAME BACK. I HOPE YOU FOUND SOMEONE TO TAKE CARE OF YOU. WE NEVER GAVE UP ON YOU, KERRA --
-- AND WHAT WE'RE DOING NOW ISN'T GIVING UP. WE'RE DOING IT FOR YOU.
AND FOR ALL THE CHILDREN OF THE GALAXY -- WE'RE FIGHTING FOR YOU ALL.
WE LOVE YOU.
NEVER GIVE UP.

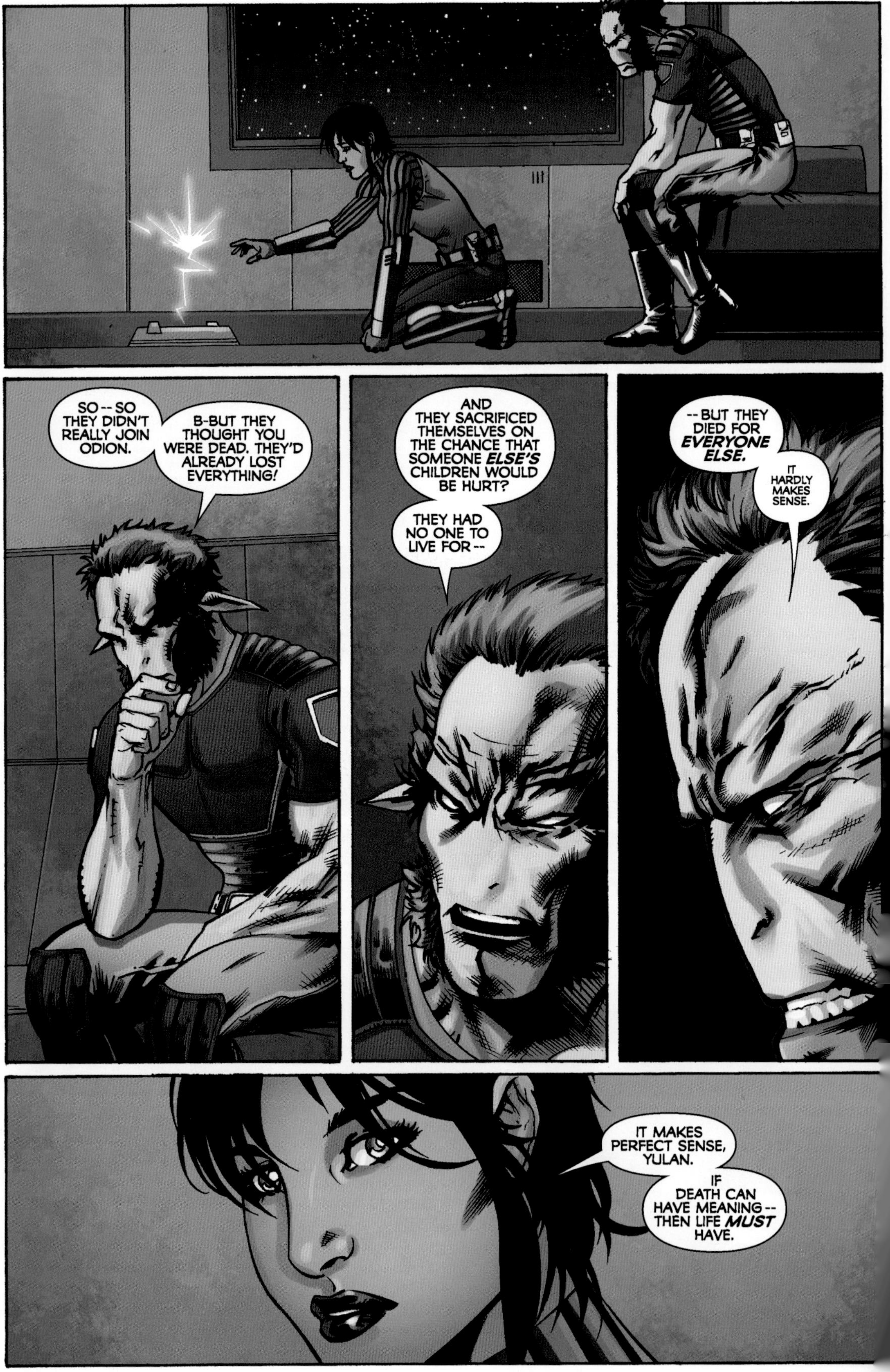
SO -- SO THEY DIDN'T REALLY JOIN ODION.
B-BUT THEY THOUGHT YOU WERE DEAD. THEY'D ALREADY LOST EVERYTHING!
AND THEY SACRIFICED THEMSELVES ON THE CHANCE THAT SOMEONE ELSE'S CHILDREN WOULD BE HURT?
THEY HAD NO ONE TO LIVE FOR --
-- BUT THEY DIED FOR EVERYONE ELSE.
IT HARDLY MAKES SENSE.
IT MAKES PERFECT SENSE, YULAN.
IF DEATH CAN HAVE MEANING -- THEN LIFE MUST HAVE.

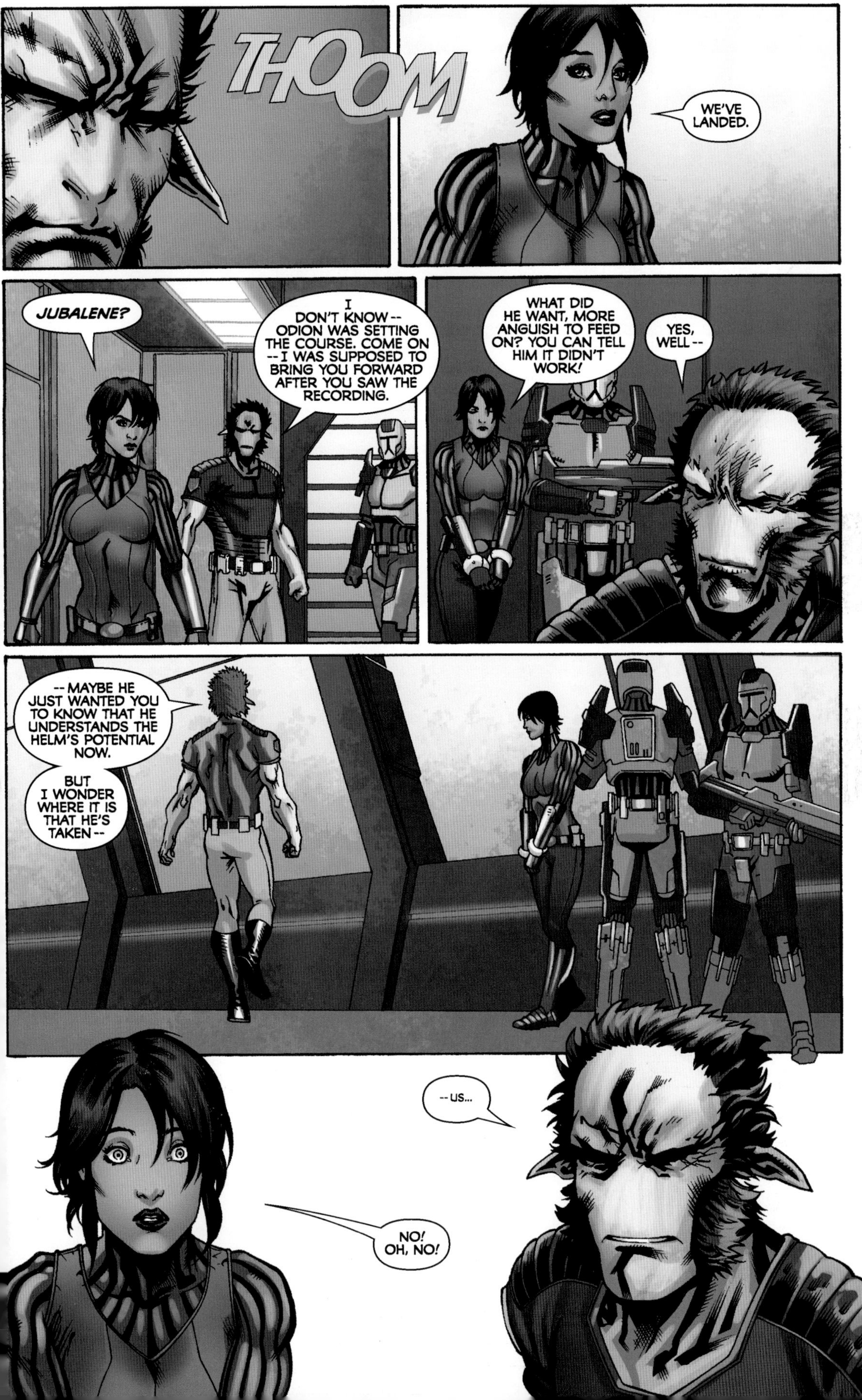
THOOM
WE'VE LANDED.
JUBALENE?
I DON'T KNOW -- ODION WAS SETTING THE COURSE. COME ON -- I WAS SUPPOSED TO BRING YOU FORWARD AFTER YOU SAW THE RECORDING.
WHAT DID HE WANT, MORE ANGUISH TO FEED ON? YOU CAN TELL HIM IT DIDN'T WORK!
YES, WELL --
-- MAYBE HE JUST WANTED YOU TO KNOW THAT HE UNDERSTANDS THE HELM'S POTENTIAL NOW.
BUT I WONDER WHERE IT IS THAT HE'S TAKEN --
-- US...
NO! OH, NO!

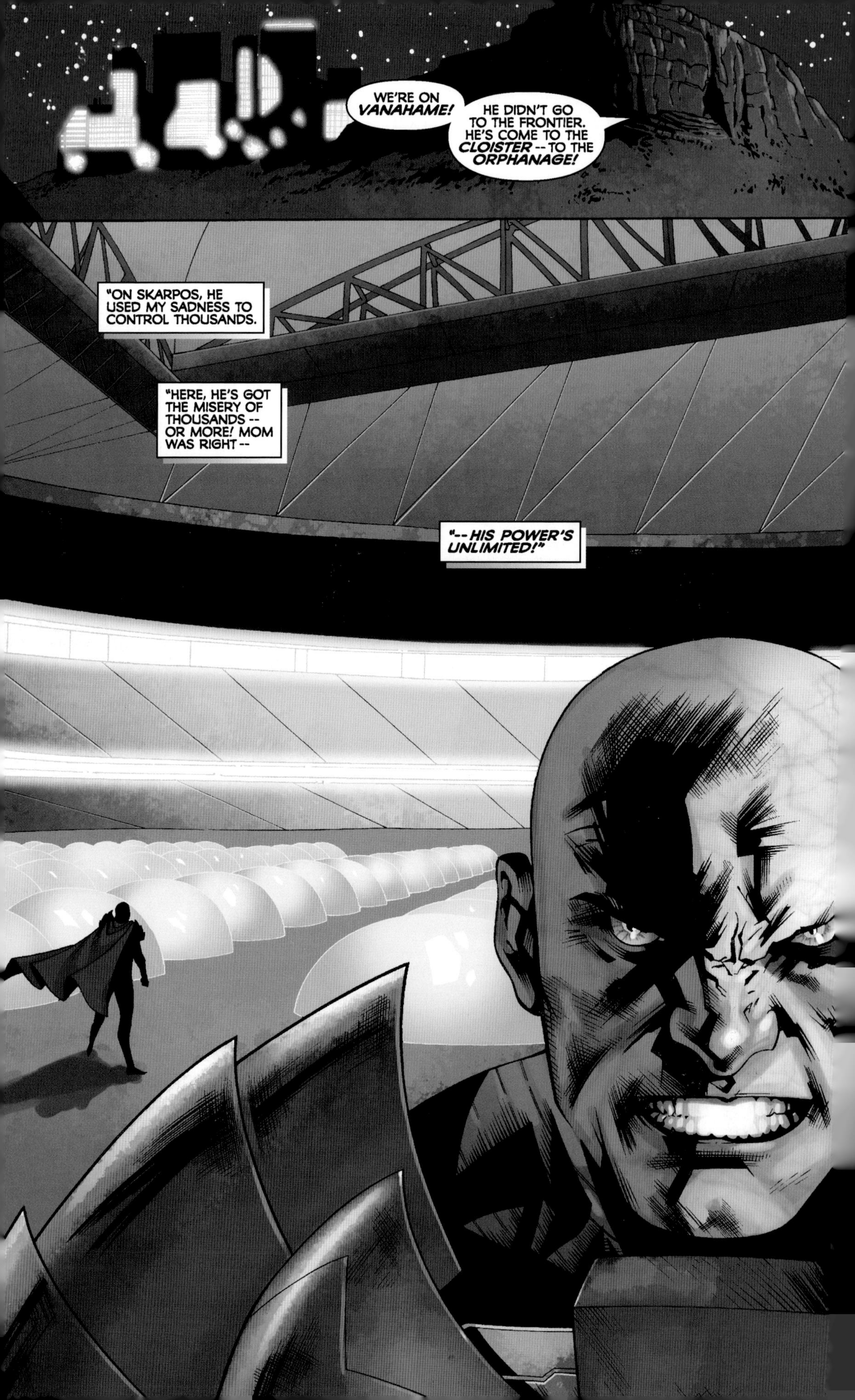
WE'RE ON *VANAHAME!*
HE DIDN'T GO TO THE FRONTIER. HE'S COME TO THE *CLOISTER* -- TO THE *ORPHANAGE!*
"ON SKARPOS, HE USED MY SADNESS TO CONTROL THOUSANDS.
"HERE, HE'S GOT THE MISERY OF THOUSANDS -- OR MORE! MOM WAS RIGHT --
"-- *HIS POWER'S UNLIMITED!"*

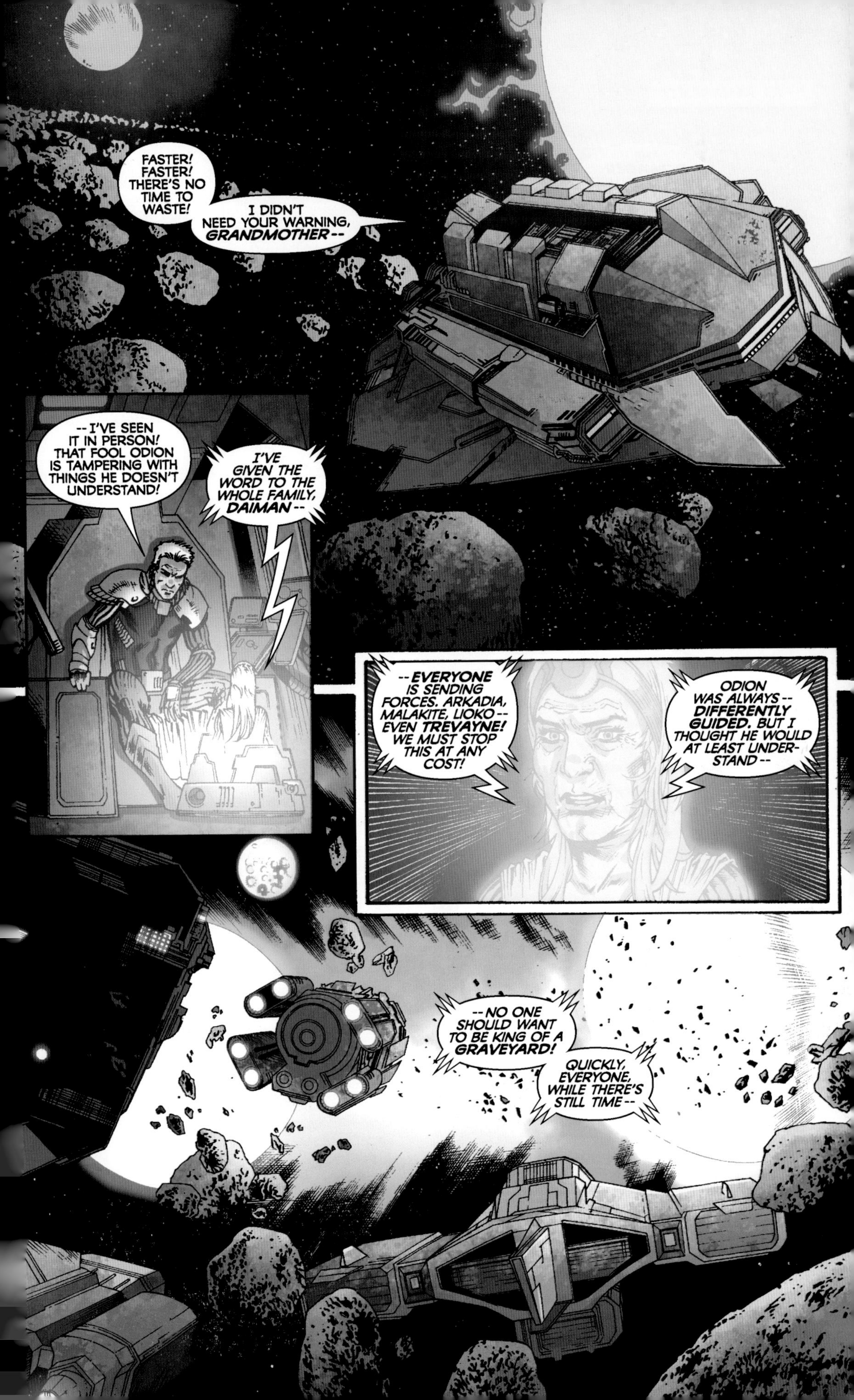
FASTER! FASTER! THERE'S NO TIME TO WASTE!
I DIDN'T NEED YOUR WARNING, GRANDMOTHER --
-- I'VE SEEN IT IN PERSON! THAT FOOL ODION IS TAMPERING WITH THINGS HE DOESN'T UNDERSTAND!
I'VE GIVEN THE WORD TO THE WHOLE FAMILY, DAIMAN --
-- EVERYONE IS SENDING FORCES. ARKADIA, MALAKITE, LIOKO -- EVEN TREVAYNE! WE MUST STOP THIS AT ANY COST!
ODION WAS ALWAYS -- DIFFERENTLY GUIDED. BUT I THOUGHT HE WOULD AT LEAST UNDER-STAND --
-- NO ONE SHOULD WANT TO BE KING OF A GRAVEYARD!
QUICKLY, EVERYONE, WHILE THERE'S STILL TIME --

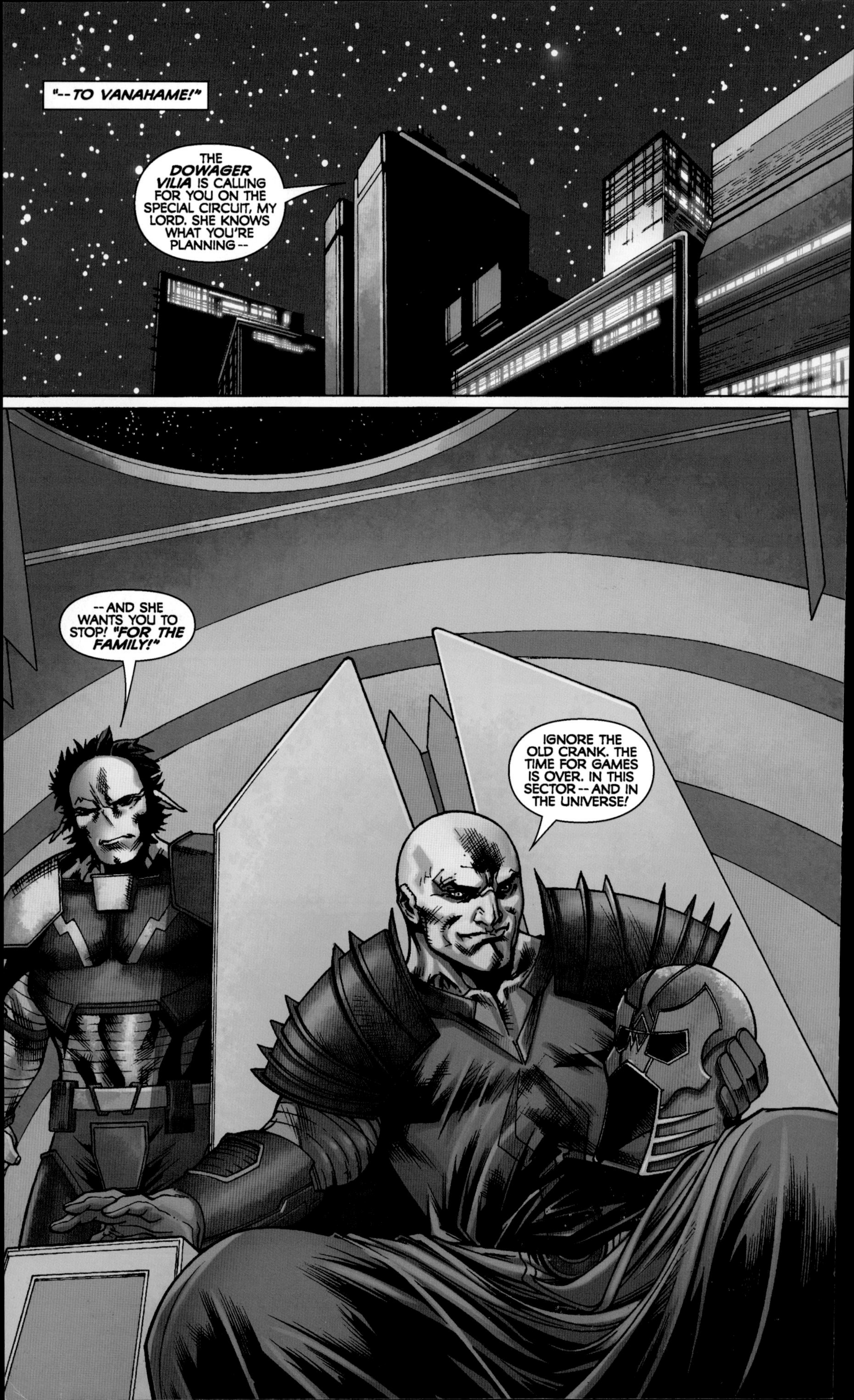

"--TO VANAHAME!"
THE ***DOWAGER VILIA*** IS CALLING FOR YOU ON THE SPECIAL CIRCUIT, MY LORD. SHE KNOWS WHAT YOU'RE PLANNING--
--AND SHE WANTS YOU TO STOP! ***"FOR THE FAMILY!"***
IGNORE THE OLD CRANK. THE TIME FOR GAMES IS OVER. IN THIS SECTOR--AND IN THE UNIVERSE!

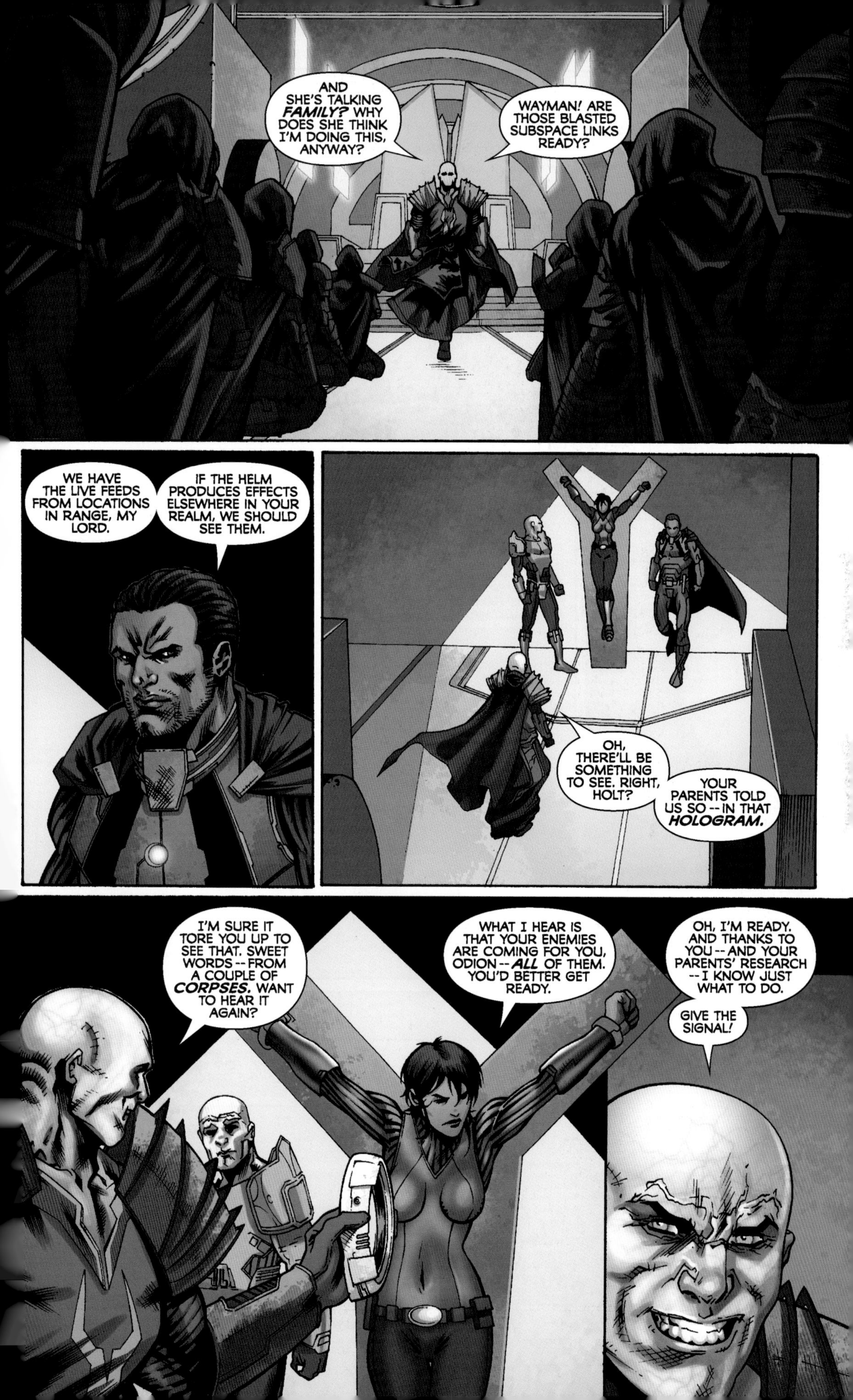
AND SHE'S TALKING *FAMILY?* WHY DOES SHE THINK I'M DOING THIS, ANYWAY?
WAYMAN! ARE THOSE BLASTED SUBSPACE LINKS READY?
WE HAVE THE LIVE FEEDS FROM LOCATIONS IN RANGE, MY LORD.
IF THE HELM PRODUCES EFFECTS ELSEWHERE IN YOUR REALM, WE SHOULD SEE THEM.
OH, THERE'LL BE SOMETHING TO SEE. RIGHT, HOLT?
YOUR PARENTS TOLD US SO -- IN THAT *HOLOGRAM.*
I'M SURE IT TORE YOU UP TO SEE THAT. SWEET WORDS -- FROM A COUPLE OF *CORPSES.* WANT TO HEAR IT AGAIN?
WHAT I HEAR IS THAT YOUR ENEMIES ARE COMING FOR YOU, ODION -- *ALL* OF THEM. YOU'D BETTER GET READY.
OH, I'M READY. AND THANKS TO YOU -- AND YOUR PARENTS' RESEARCH -- I KNOW JUST WHAT TO DO.
GIVE THE SIGNAL!

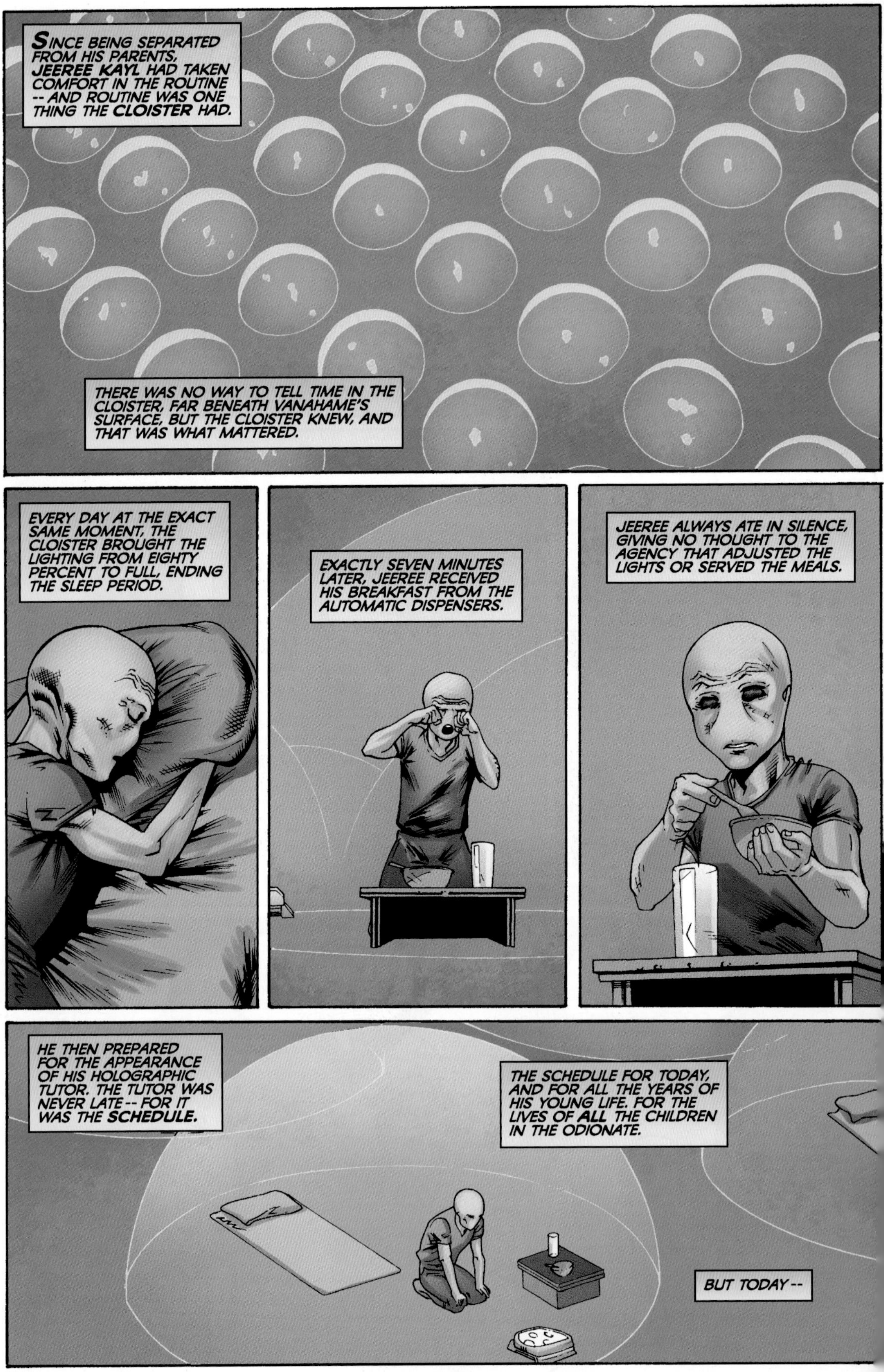
SINCE BEING SEPARATED FROM HIS PARENTS, JEEREE KAYL HAD TAKEN COMFORT IN THE ROUTINE -- AND ROUTINE WAS ONE THING THE CLOISTER HAD.
THERE WAS NO WAY TO TELL TIME IN THE CLOISTER, FAR BENEATH VANAHAME'S SURFACE, BUT THE CLOISTER KNEW, AND THAT WAS WHAT MATTERED.
EVERY DAY AT THE EXACT SAME MOMENT, THE CLOISTER BROUGHT THE LIGHTING FROM EIGHTY PERCENT TO FULL, ENDING THE SLEEP PERIOD.
EXACTLY SEVEN MINUTES LATER, JEEREE RECEIVED HIS BREAKFAST FROM THE AUTOMATIC DISPENSERS.
JEEREE ALWAYS ATE IN SILENCE, GIVING NO THOUGHT TO THE AGENCY THAT ADJUSTED THE LIGHTS OR SERVED THE MEALS.
HE THEN PREPARED FOR THE APPEARANCE OF HIS HOLOGRAPHIC TUTOR. THE TUTOR WAS NEVER LATE -- FOR IT WAS THE SCHEDULE.
THE SCHEDULE FOR TODAY, AND FOR ALL THE YEARS OF HIS YOUNG LIFE. FOR THE LIVES OF ALL THE CHILDREN IN THE ODIONATE.
BUT TODAY --

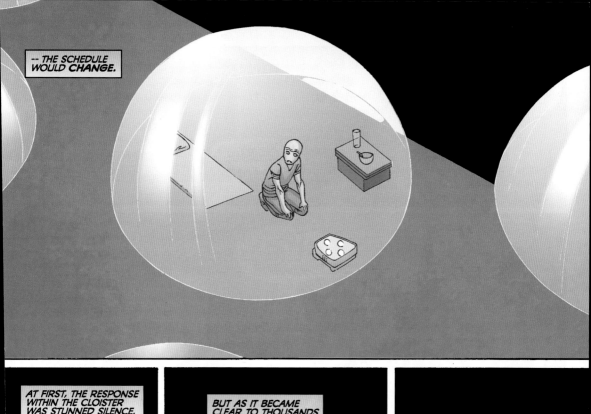

-- THE SCHEDULE WOULD *CHANGE.*

AT FIRST, THE RESPONSE WITHIN THE CLOISTER WAS STUNNED SILENCE.

BUT AS IT BECAME CLEAR TO THOUSANDS THAT SOMETHING HAD CHANGED --

-- THE RESPONSE CHANGED, TOO.

MMMWWWAAAAHH!

MMFF. MMFF.

WAAAAAAAAAAAAHHHH!

DIDJA EVER HEAR SUCH HOWLIN'? YOU'D THINK TH' BRATS HAD NEVER SEEN THE DARK BEFORE!

NOT IN THIS PLACE, THEY HAVEN'T. TELL THE FOLKS UPSTAIRS IT'S DONE, *MURL.* THAT IS -- IF THEY CAN'T HEAR THEM ALREADY!

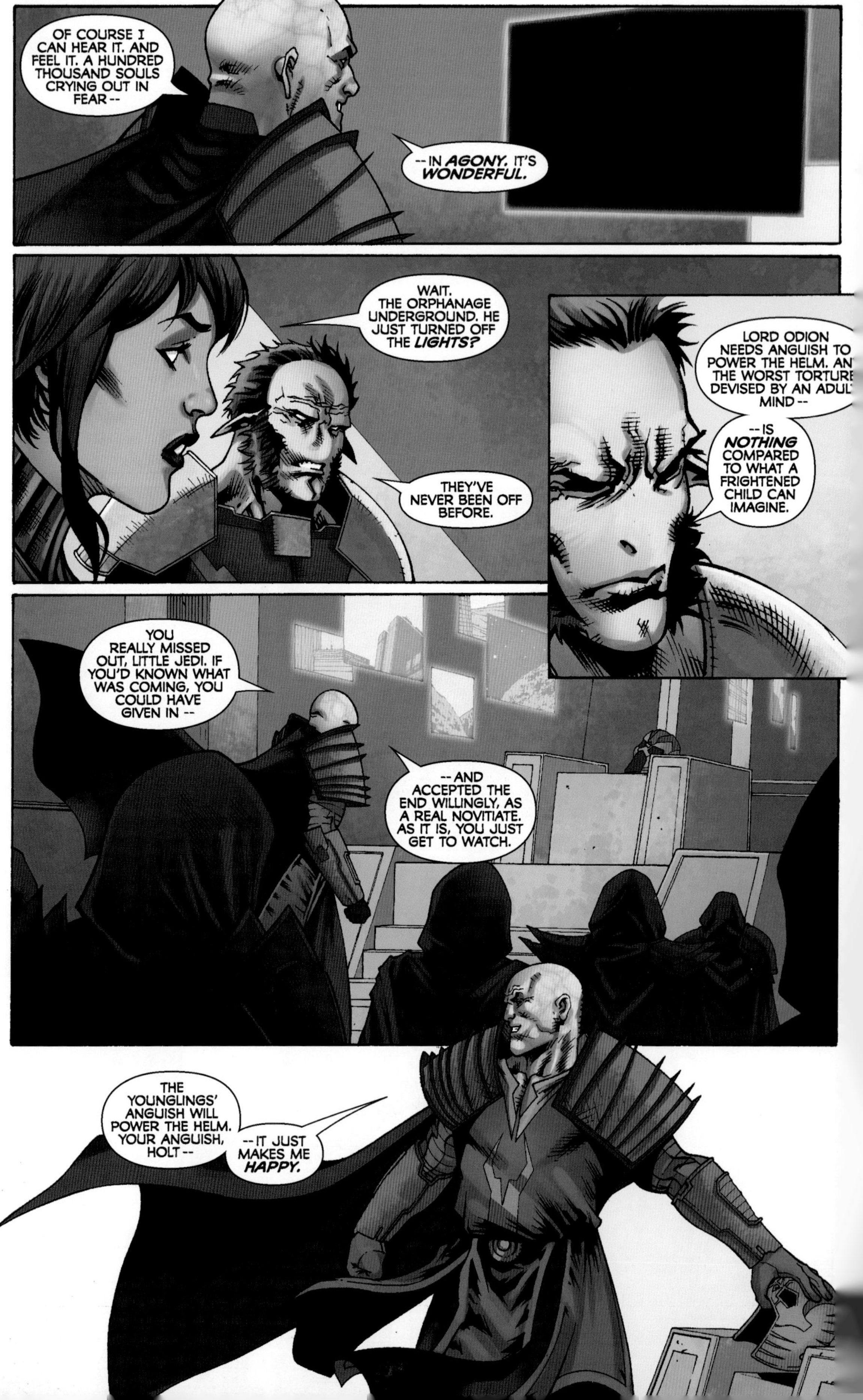
OF COURSE I CAN HEAR IT. AND FEEL IT. A HUNDRED THOUSAND SOULS CRYING OUT IN FEAR --
--IN AGONY. IT'S WONDERFUL.
WAIT. THE ORPHANAGE UNDERGROUND. HE JUST TURNED OFF THE LIGHTS?
THEY'VE NEVER BEEN OFF BEFORE.
LORD ODION NEEDS ANGUISH TO POWER THE HELM. AN THE WORST TORTURE DEVISED BY AN ADUL MIND --
--IS NOTHING COMPARED TO WHAT A FRIGHTENED CHILD CAN IMAGINE.
YOU REALLY MISSED OUT, LITTLE JEDI. IF YOU'D KNOWN WHAT WAS COMING, YOU COULD HAVE GIVEN IN --
--AND ACCEPTED THE END WILLINGLY, AS A REAL NOVITIATE. AS IT IS, YOU JUST GET TO WATCH.
THE YOUNGLINGS' ANGUISH WILL POWER THE HELM. YOUR ANGUISH, HOLT --
--IT JUST MAKES ME HAPPY.

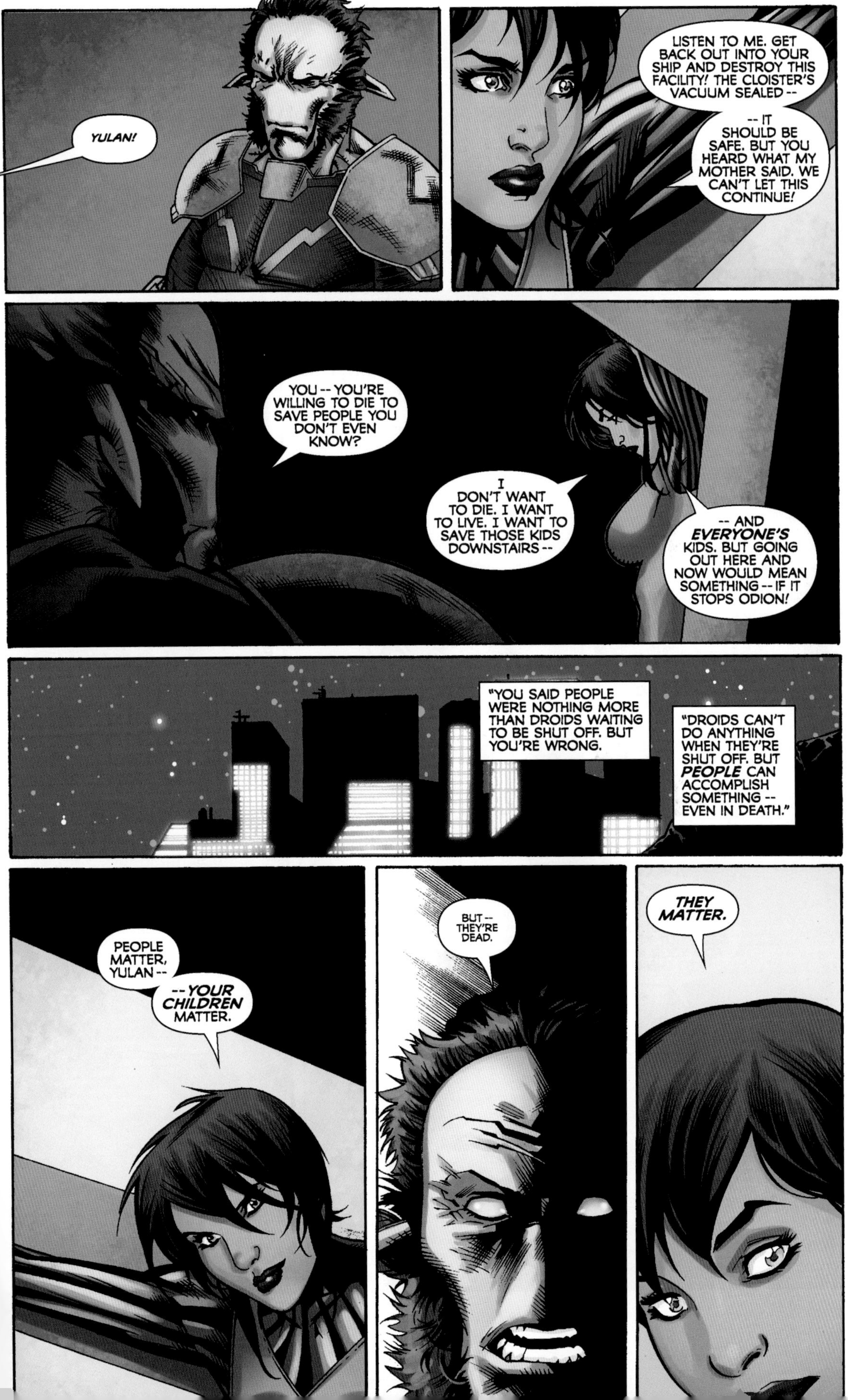
YULAN!
LISTEN TO ME. GET BACK OUT INTO YOUR SHIP AND DESTROY THIS FACILITY! THE CLOISTER'S VACUUM SEALED --
-- IT SHOULD BE SAFE. BUT YOU HEARD WHAT MY MOTHER SAID. WE CAN'T LET THIS CONTINUE!
YOU -- YOU'RE WILLING TO DIE TO SAVE PEOPLE YOU DON'T EVEN KNOW?
I DON'T WANT TO DIE. I WANT TO LIVE. I WANT TO SAVE THOSE KIDS DOWNSTAIRS --
-- AND EVERYONE'S KIDS. BUT GOING OUT HERE AND NOW WOULD MEAN SOMETHING -- IF IT STOPS ODION!
"YOU SAID PEOPLE WERE NOTHING MORE THAN DROIDS WAITING TO BE SHUT OFF. BUT YOU'RE WRONG.
"DROIDS CAN'T DO ANYTHING WHEN THEY'RE SHUT OFF. BUT PEOPLE CAN ACCOMPLISH SOMETHING -- EVEN IN DEATH."
PEOPLE MATTER, YULAN --
-- YOUR CHILDREN MATTER.
BUT -- THEY'RE DEAD.
THEY MATTER.

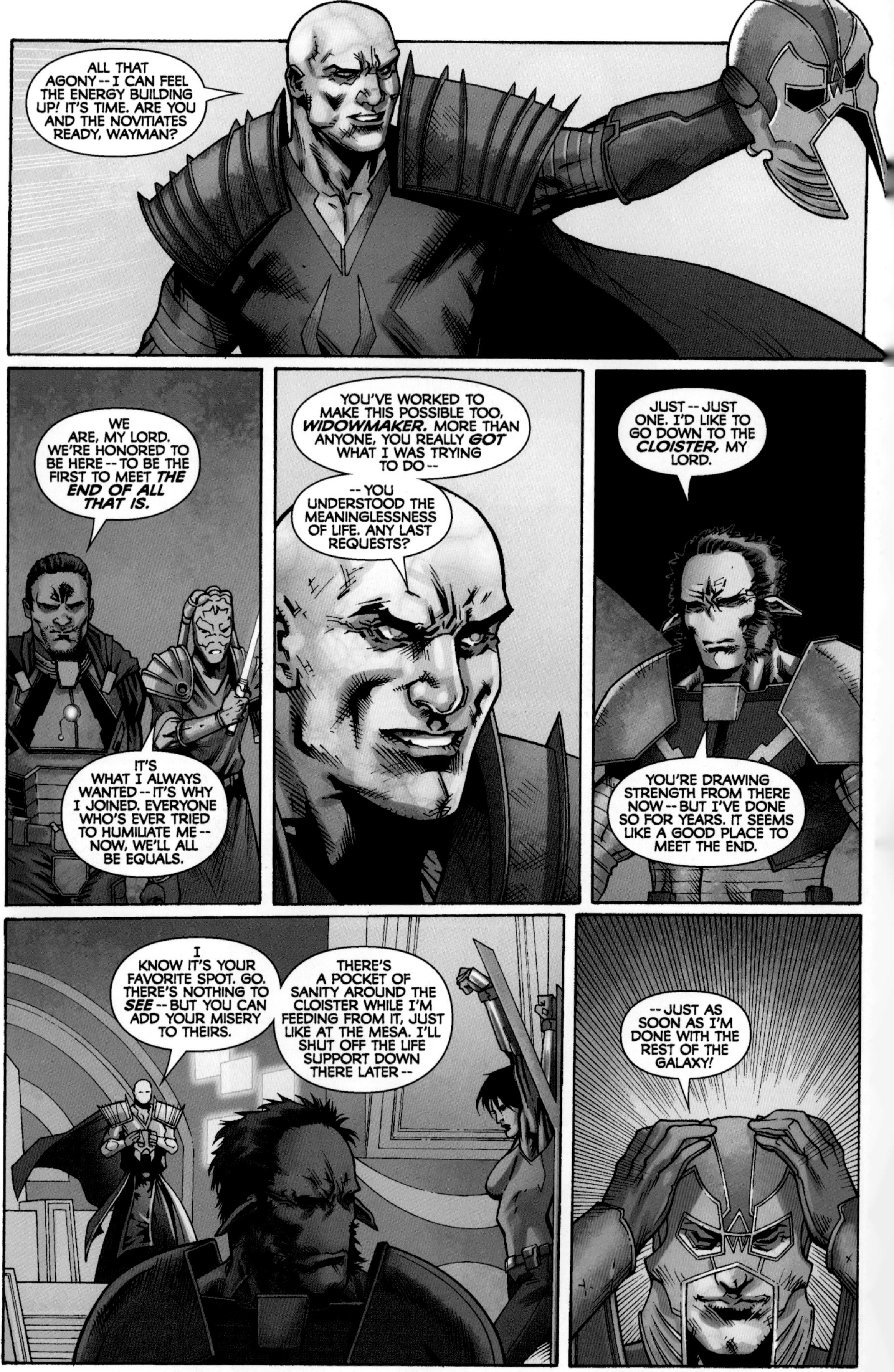
ALL THAT AGONY -- I CAN FEEL THE ENERGY BUILDING UP! IT'S TIME. ARE YOU AND THE NOVITIATES READY, WAYMAN?
WE ARE, MY LORD. WE'RE HONORED TO BE HERE -- TO BE THE FIRST TO MEET ***THE END OF ALL THAT IS.***
IT'S WHAT I ALWAYS WANTED -- IT'S WHY I JOINED. EVERYONE WHO'S EVER TRIED TO HUMILIATE ME -- NOW, WE'LL ALL BE EQUALS.
YOU'VE WORKED TO MAKE THIS POSSIBLE TOO, ***WIDOWMAKER.*** MORE THAN ANYONE, YOU REALLY ***GOT*** WHAT I WAS TRYING TO DO --
-- YOU UNDERSTOOD THE MEANINGLESSNESS OF LIFE. ANY LAST REQUESTS?
JUST -- JUST ONE. I'D LIKE TO GO DOWN TO THE ***CLOISTER,*** MY LORD.
YOU'RE DRAWING STRENGTH FROM THERE NOW -- BUT I'VE DONE SO FOR YEARS. IT SEEMS LIKE A GOOD PLACE TO MEET THE END.
I KNOW IT'S YOUR FAVORITE SPOT. GO. THERE'S NOTHING TO ***SEE*** -- BUT YOU CAN ADD YOUR MISERY TO THEIRS.
THERE'S A POCKET OF SANITY AROUND THE CLOISTER WHILE I'M FEEDING FROM IT, JUST LIKE AT THE MESA. I'LL SHUT OFF THE LIFE SUPPORT DOWN THERE LATER --
-- JUST AS SOON AS I'M DONE WITH THE REST OF THE GALAXY!

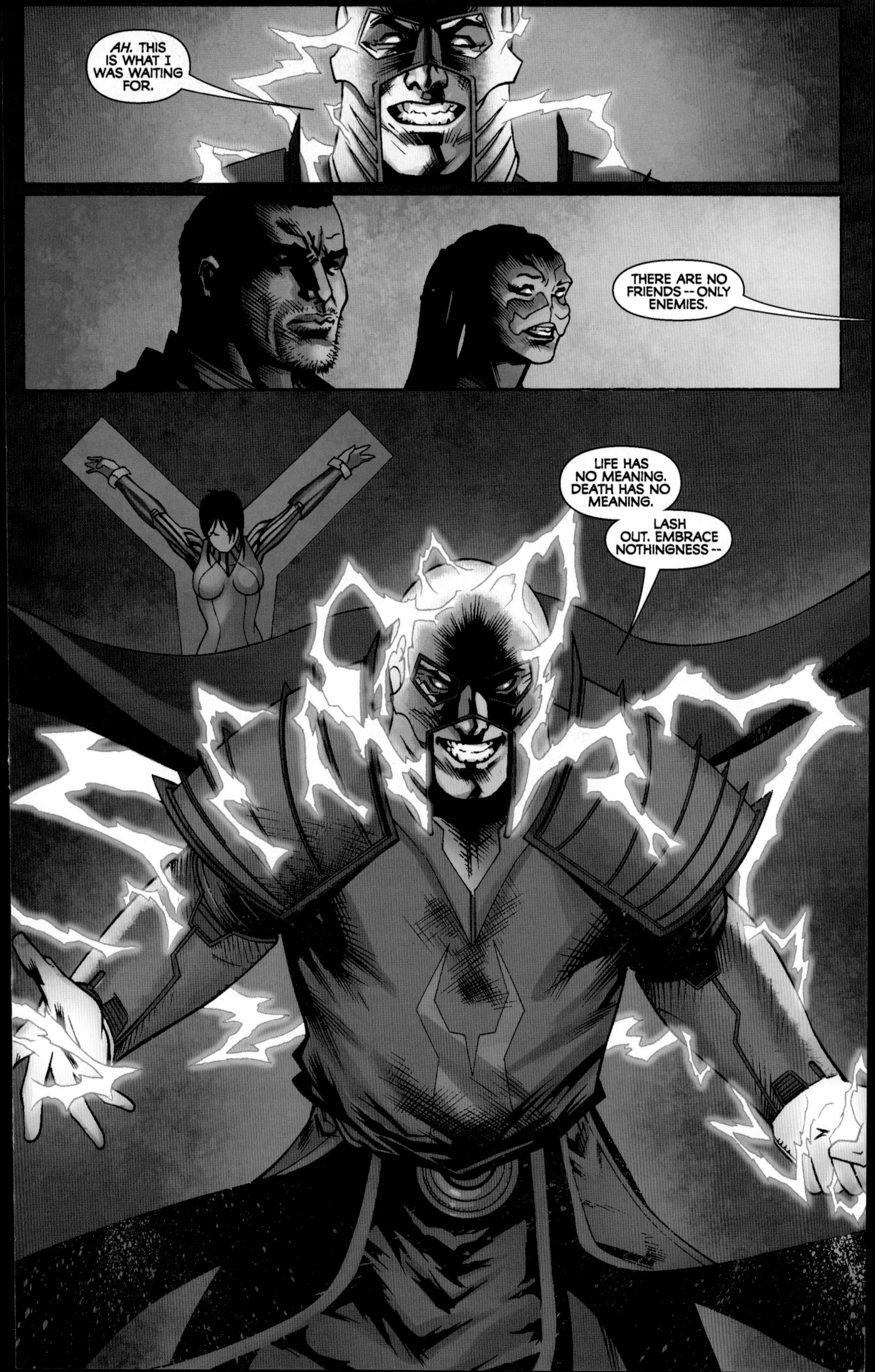
AH. THIS IS WHAT I WAS WAITING FOR.
THERE ARE NO FRIENDS -- ONLY ENEMIES.
LIFE HAS NO MEANING. DEATH HAS NO MEANING.
LASH OUT. EMBRACE NOTHINGNESS --

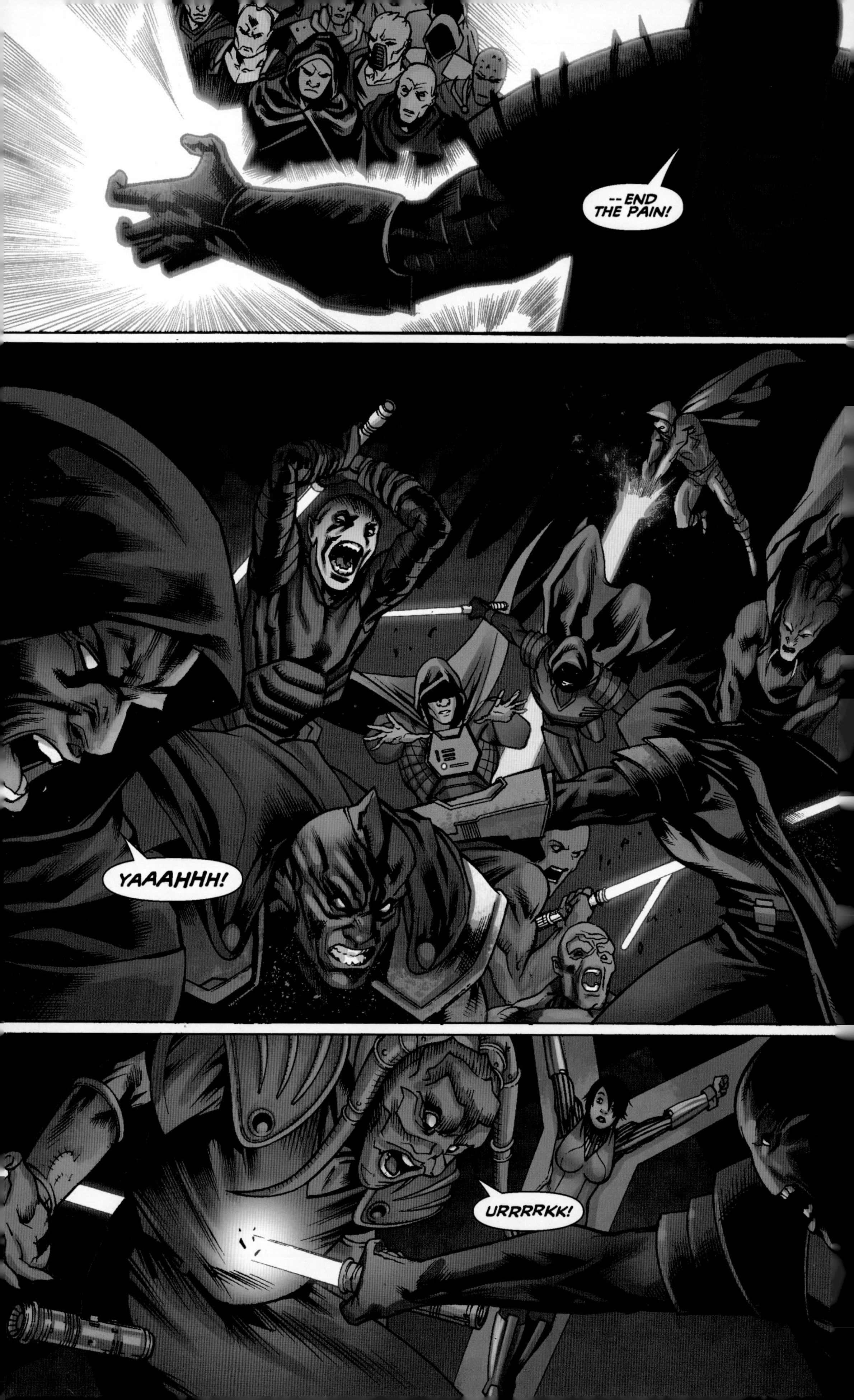
-- END THE PAIN!
YAAAHHH!
URRRRKK!

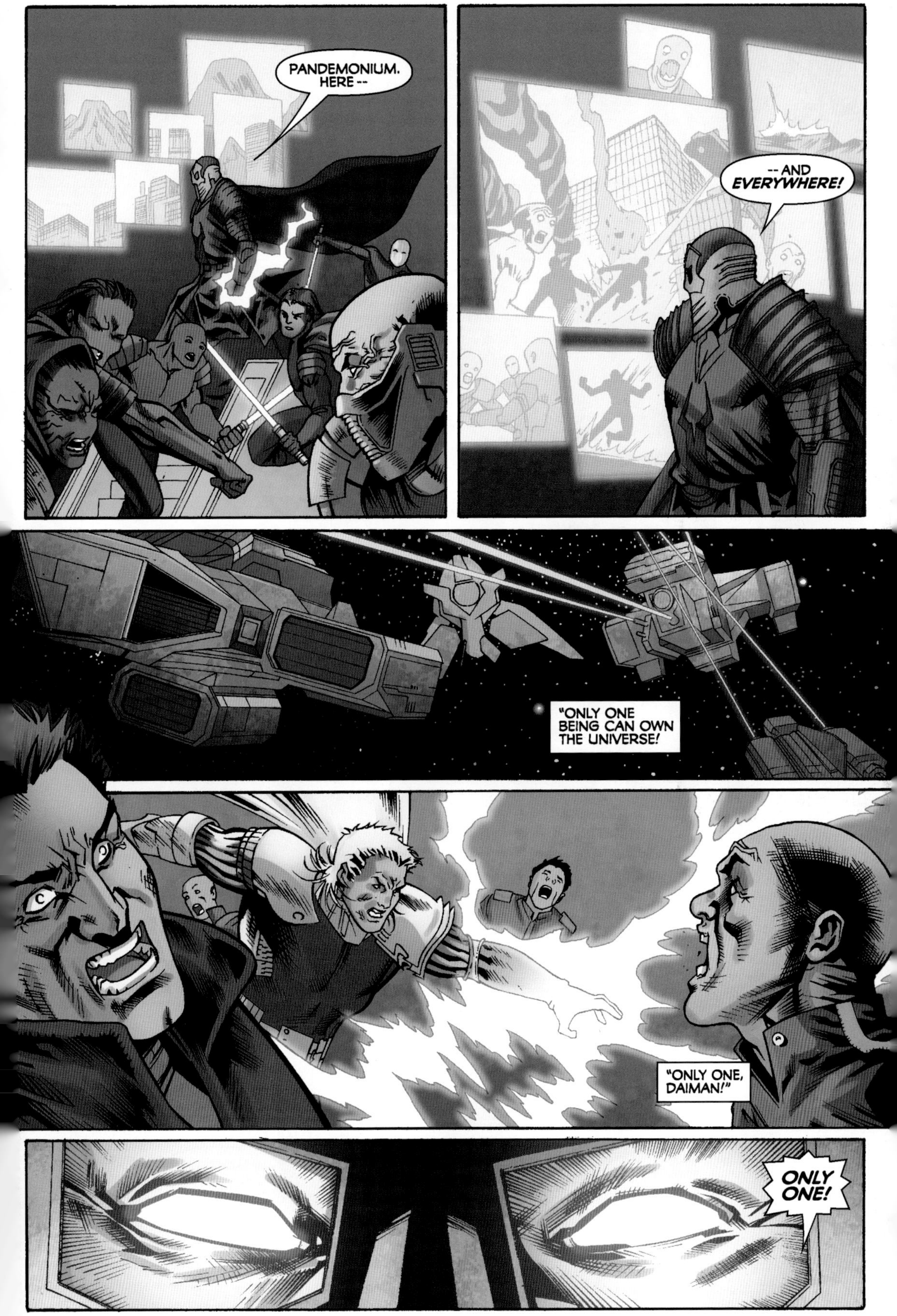
PANDEMONIUM. HERE --
-- AND EVERYWHERE!
"ONLY ONE BEING CAN OWN THE UNIVERSE!
"ONLY ONE, DAIMAN!"
ONLY ONE!

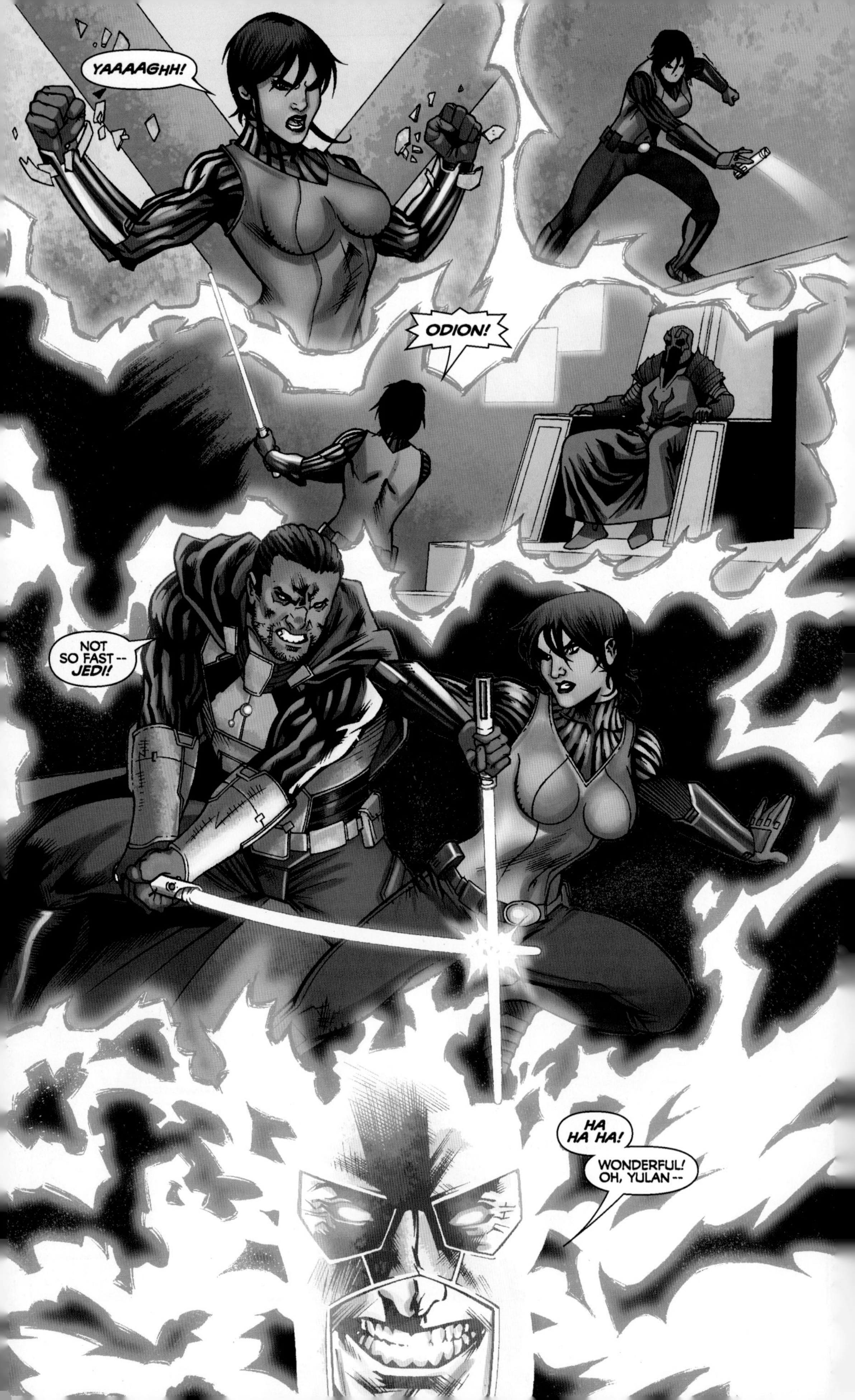
YAAAAGHH!
ODION!
NOT SO FAST -- JEDI!
HA HA HA!
WONDERFUL! OH, YULAN --

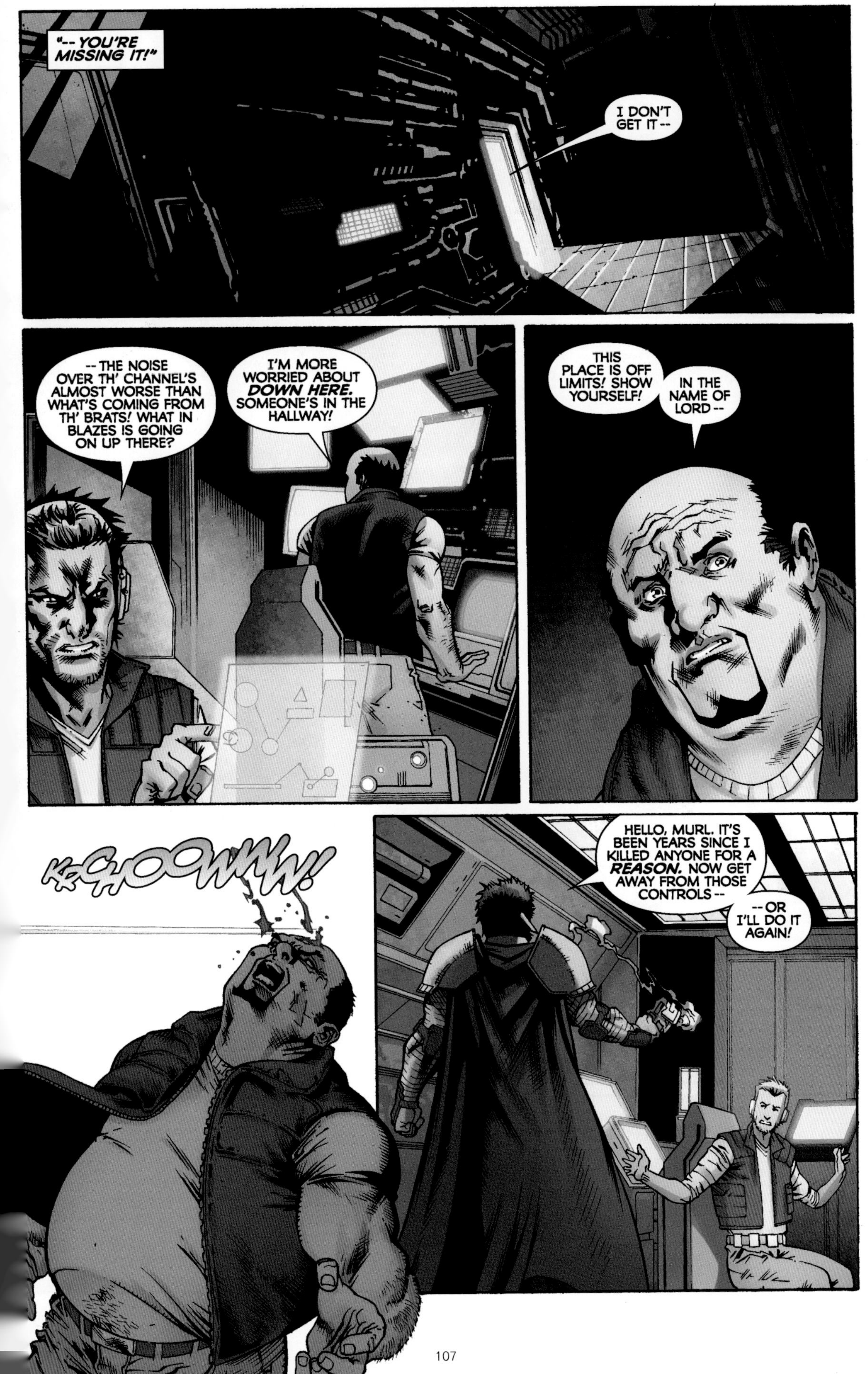
"-- YOU'RE MISSING IT!"
I DON'T GET IT --
-- THE NOISE OVER TH' CHANNEL'S ALMOST WORSE THAN WHAT'S COMING FROM TH' BRATS! WHAT IN BLAZES IS GOING ON UP THERE?
I'M MORE WORRIED ABOUT DOWN HERE. SOMEONE'S IN THE HALLWAY!
THIS PLACE IS OFF LIMITS! SHOW YOURSELF!
IN THE NAME OF LORD --
KRCHOOWWW!
HELLO, MURL. IT'S BEEN YEARS SINCE I KILLED ANYONE FOR A REASON. NOW GET AWAY FROM THOSE CONTROLS --
-- OR I'LL DO IT AGAIN!

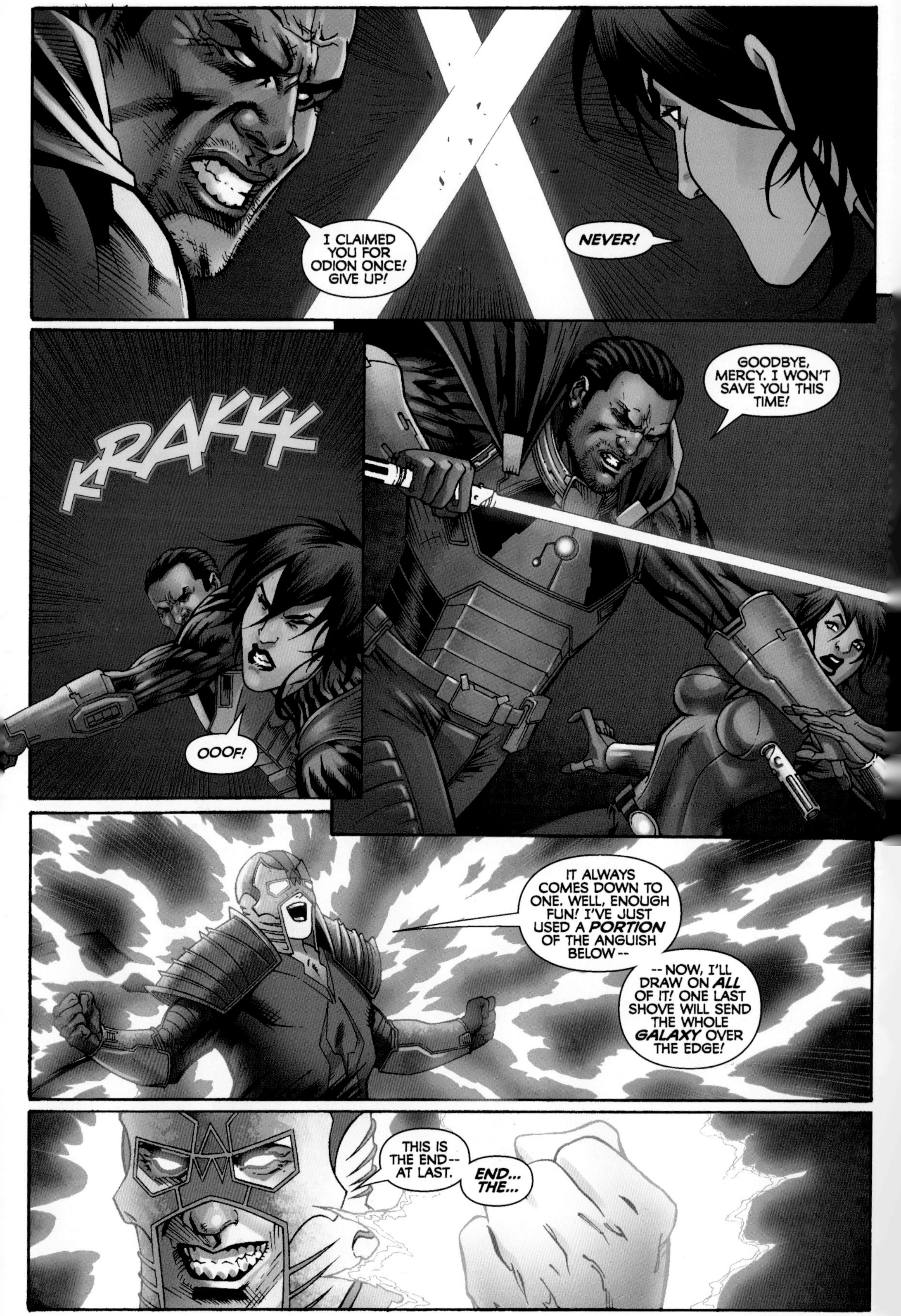
I CLAIMED YOU FOR ODION ONCE! GIVE UP!
NEVER!
KRAKKK
OOOF!
GOODBYE, MERCY. I WON'T SAVE YOU THIS TIME!
IT ALWAYS COMES DOWN TO ONE. WELL, ENOUGH FUN! I'VE JUST USED A PORTION OF THE ANGUISH BELOW--
--NOW, I'LL DRAW ON ALL OF IT! ONE LAST SHOVE WILL SEND THE WHOLE GALAXY OVER THE EDGE!
THIS IS THE END-- AT LAST.
END... THE...

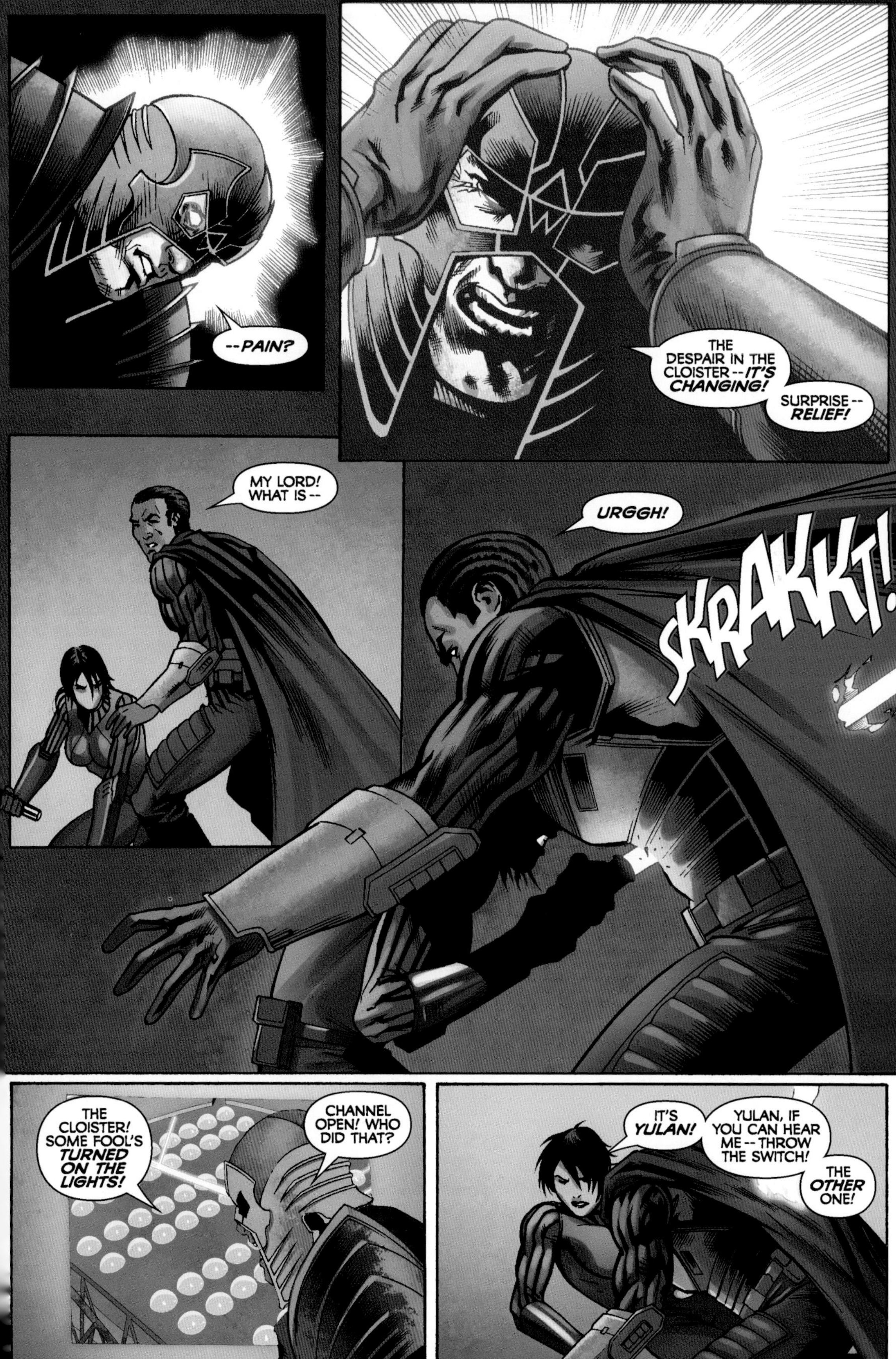
--PAIN?
THE DESPAIR IN THE CLOISTER--IT'S CHANGING!
SURPRISE--RELIEF!
MY LORD! WHAT IS--
URGGH!
SKRAKKT!
THE CLOISTER! SOME FOOL'S TURNED ON THE LIGHTS!
CHANNEL OPEN! WHO DID THAT?
IT'S YULAN!
YULAN, IF YOU CAN HEAR ME--THROW THE SWITCH!
THE OTHER ONE!

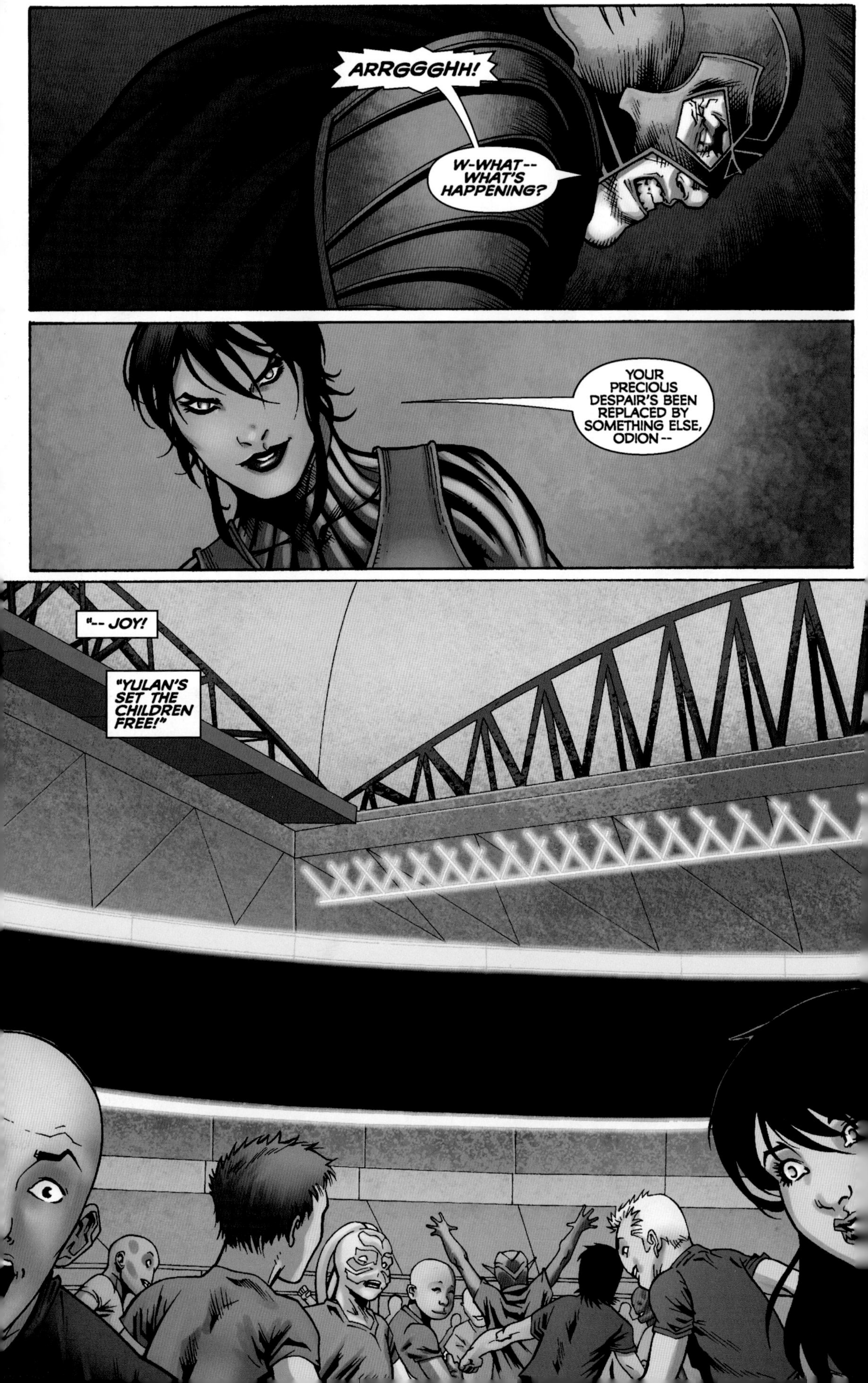
ARRGGGHH!
W-WHAT-- WHAT'S HAPPENING?
YOUR PRECIOUS DESPAIR'S BEEN REPLACED BY SOMETHING ELSE, ODION --
"-- JOY!
"YULAN'S SET THE CHILDREN FREE!"

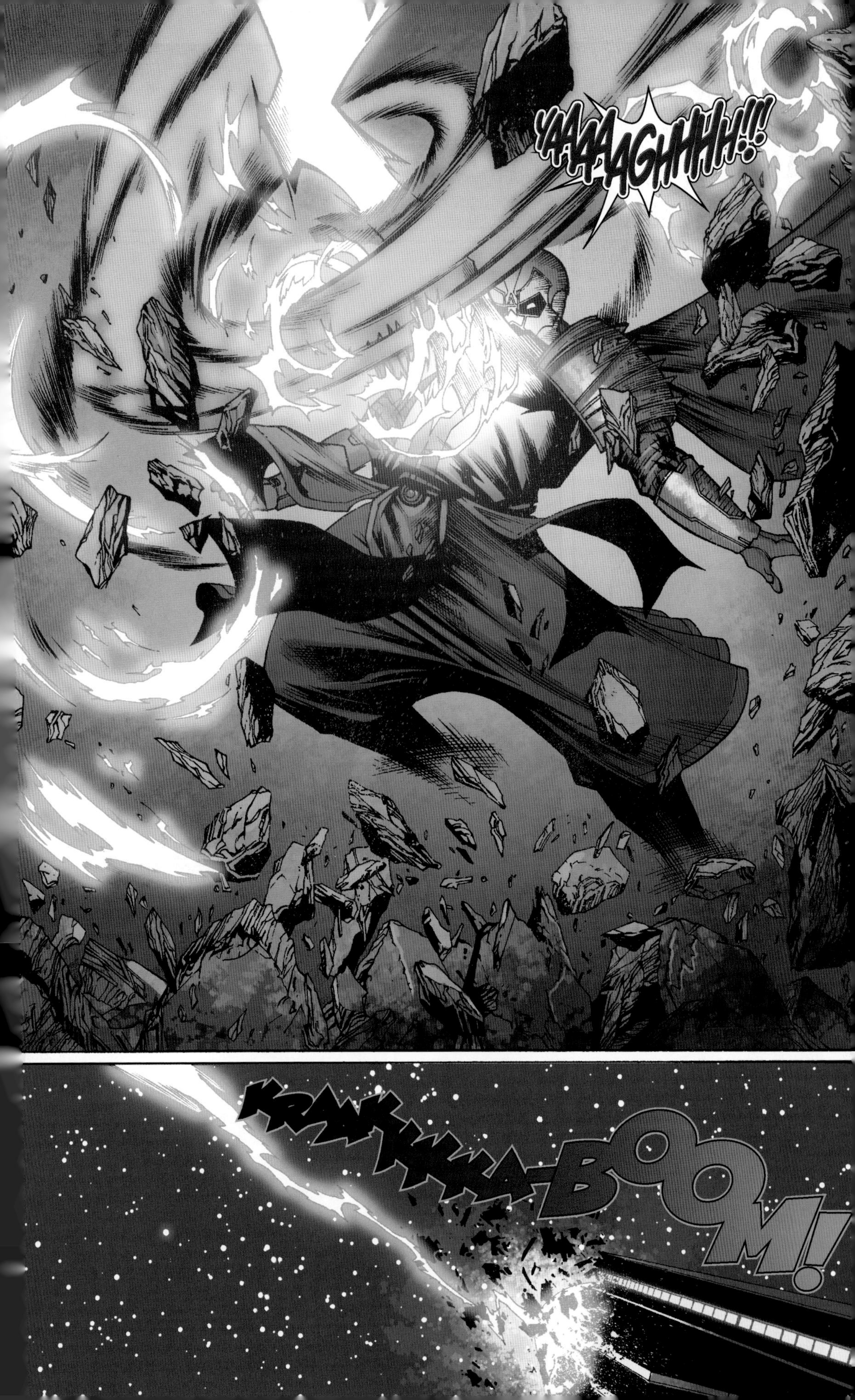
YAAAAAGHHHH!!!
KRAKKKKA-BOOM!

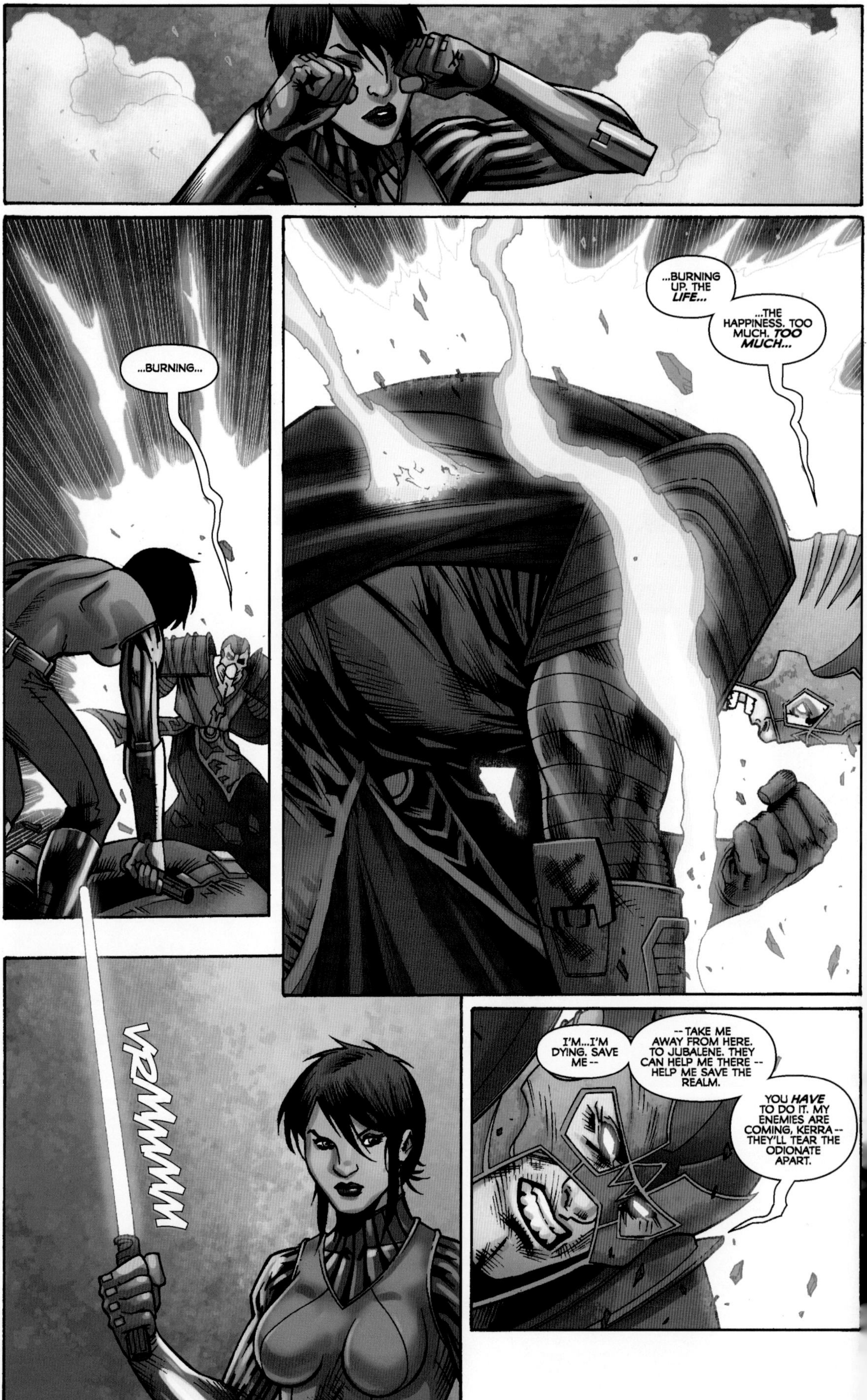
...BURNING...
...BURNING UP. THE LIFE...
...THE HAPPINESS. TOO MUCH. TOO MUCH...
VRMMMM
I'M...I'M DYING. SAVE ME --
-- TAKE ME AWAY FROM HERE. TO JUBALENE. THEY CAN HELP ME THERE -- HELP ME SAVE THE REALM.
YOU HAVE TO DO IT. MY ENEMIES ARE COMING, KERRA -- THEY'LL TEAR THE ODIONATE APART.

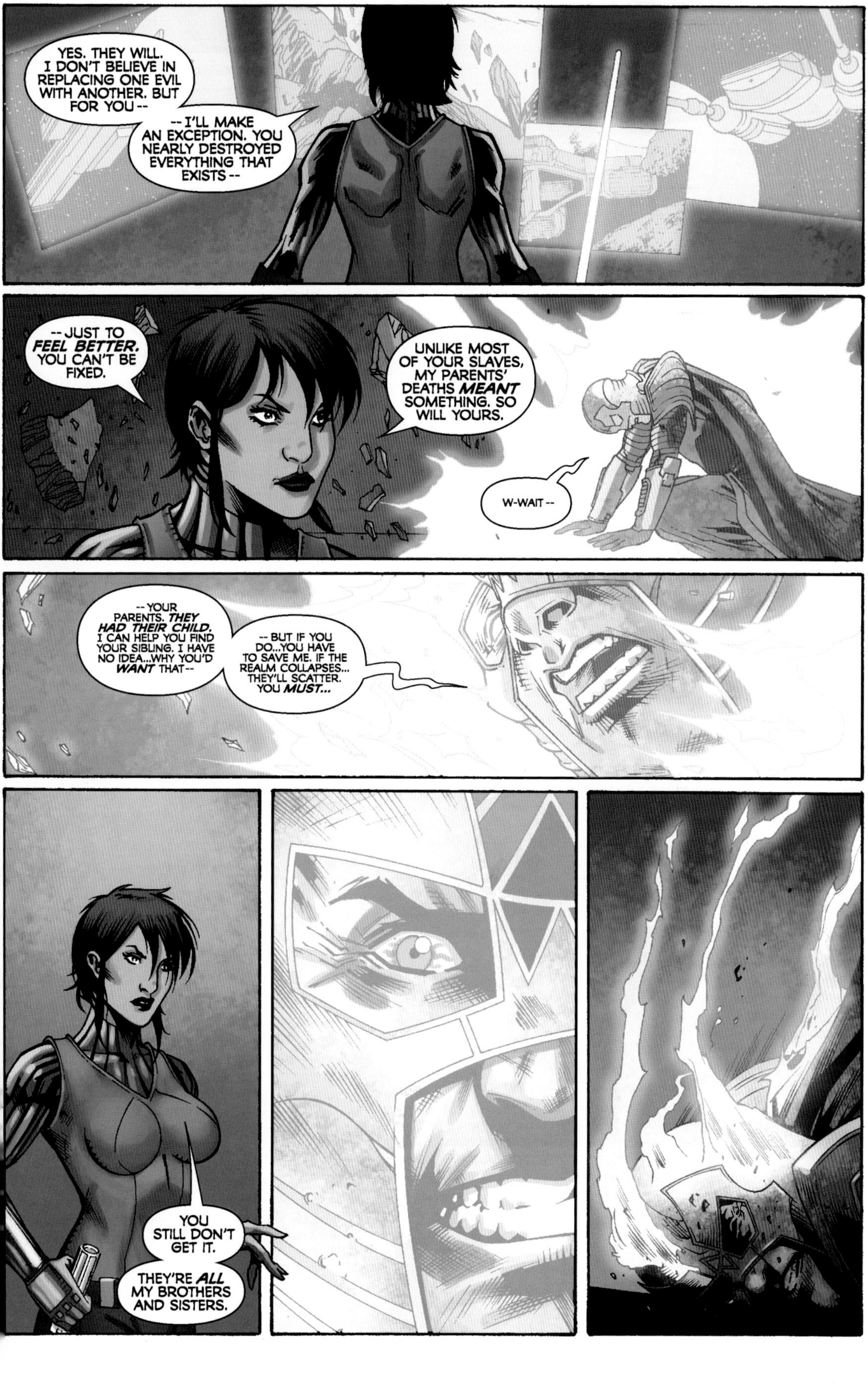
YES. THEY WILL. I DON'T BELIEVE IN REPLACING ONE EVIL WITH ANOTHER. BUT FOR YOU --
-- I'LL MAKE AN EXCEPTION. YOU NEARLY DESTROYED EVERYTHING THAT EXISTS --
-- JUST TO FEEL BETTER. YOU CAN'T BE FIXED.
UNLIKE MOST OF YOUR SLAVES, MY PARENTS' DEATHS MEANT SOMETHING. SO WILL YOURS.
W-WAIT --
-- YOUR PARENTS. THEY HAD THEIR CHILD. I CAN HELP YOU FIND YOUR SIBLING. I HAVE NO IDEA...WHY YOU'D WANT THAT--
-- BUT IF YOU DO...YOU HAVE TO SAVE ME. IF THE REALM COLLAPSES... THEY'LL SCATTER. YOU MUST...
YOU STILL DON'T GET IT.
THEY'RE ALL MY BROTHERS AND SISTERS.

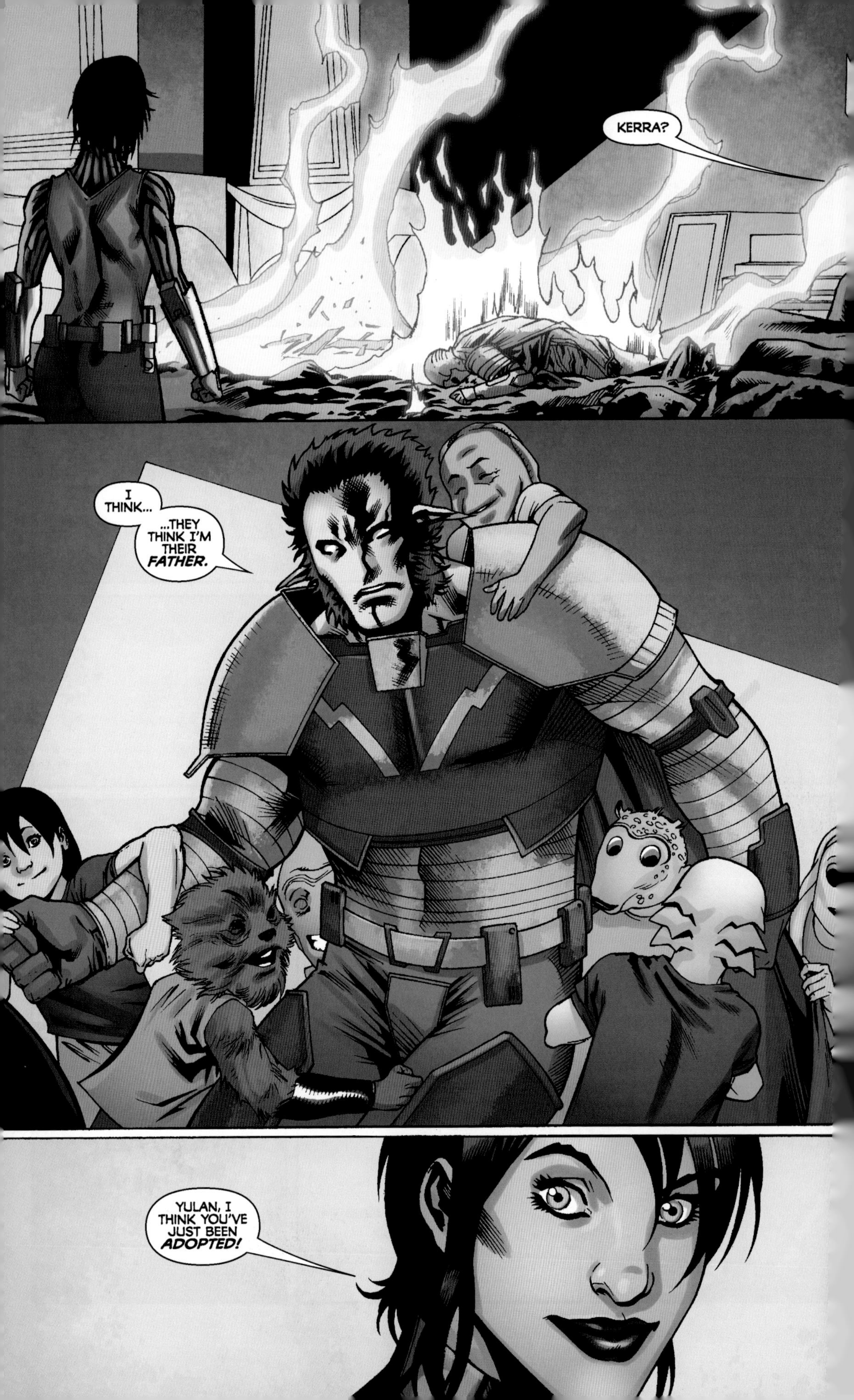
KERRA?
I THINK...
...THEY THINK I'M THEIR *FATHER.*
YULAN, I THINK YOU'VE JUST BEEN *ADOPTED!*

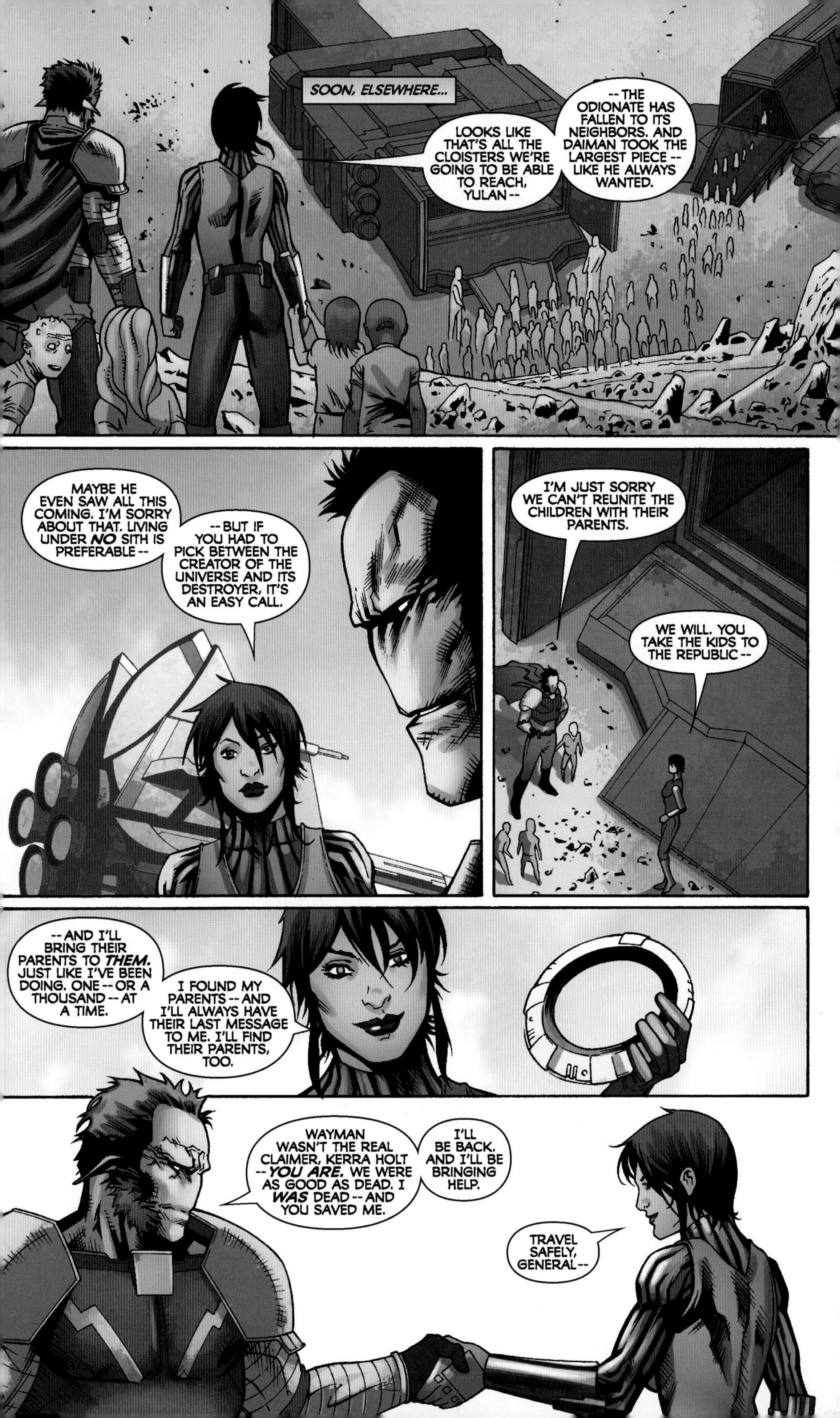
SOON, ELSEWHERE...
LOOKS LIKE THAT'S ALL THE CLOISTERS WE'RE GOING TO BE ABLE TO REACH, YULAN --
-- THE ODIONATE HAS FALLEN TO ITS NEIGHBORS. AND DAIMAN TOOK THE LARGEST PIECE -- LIKE HE ALWAYS WANTED.
MAYBE HE EVEN SAW ALL THIS COMING. I'M SORRY ABOUT THAT. LIVING UNDER NO SITH IS PREFERABLE --
-- BUT IF YOU HAD TO PICK BETWEEN THE CREATOR OF THE UNIVERSE AND ITS DESTROYER, IT'S AN EASY CALL.
I'M JUST SORRY WE CAN'T REUNITE THE CHILDREN WITH THEIR PARENTS.
WE WILL. YOU TAKE THE KIDS TO THE REPUBLIC --
-- AND I'LL BRING THEIR PARENTS TO THEM. JUST LIKE I'VE BEEN DOING. ONE -- OR A THOUSAND -- AT A TIME.
I FOUND MY PARENTS -- AND I'LL ALWAYS HAVE THEIR LAST MESSAGE TO ME. I'LL FIND THEIR PARENTS, TOO.
WAYMAN WASN'T THE REAL CLAIMER, KERRA HOLT -- YOU ARE. WE WERE AS GOOD AS DEAD. I WAS DEAD -- AND YOU SAVED ME.
I'LL BE BACK. AND I'LL BE BRINGING HELP.
TRAVEL SAFELY, GENERAL --

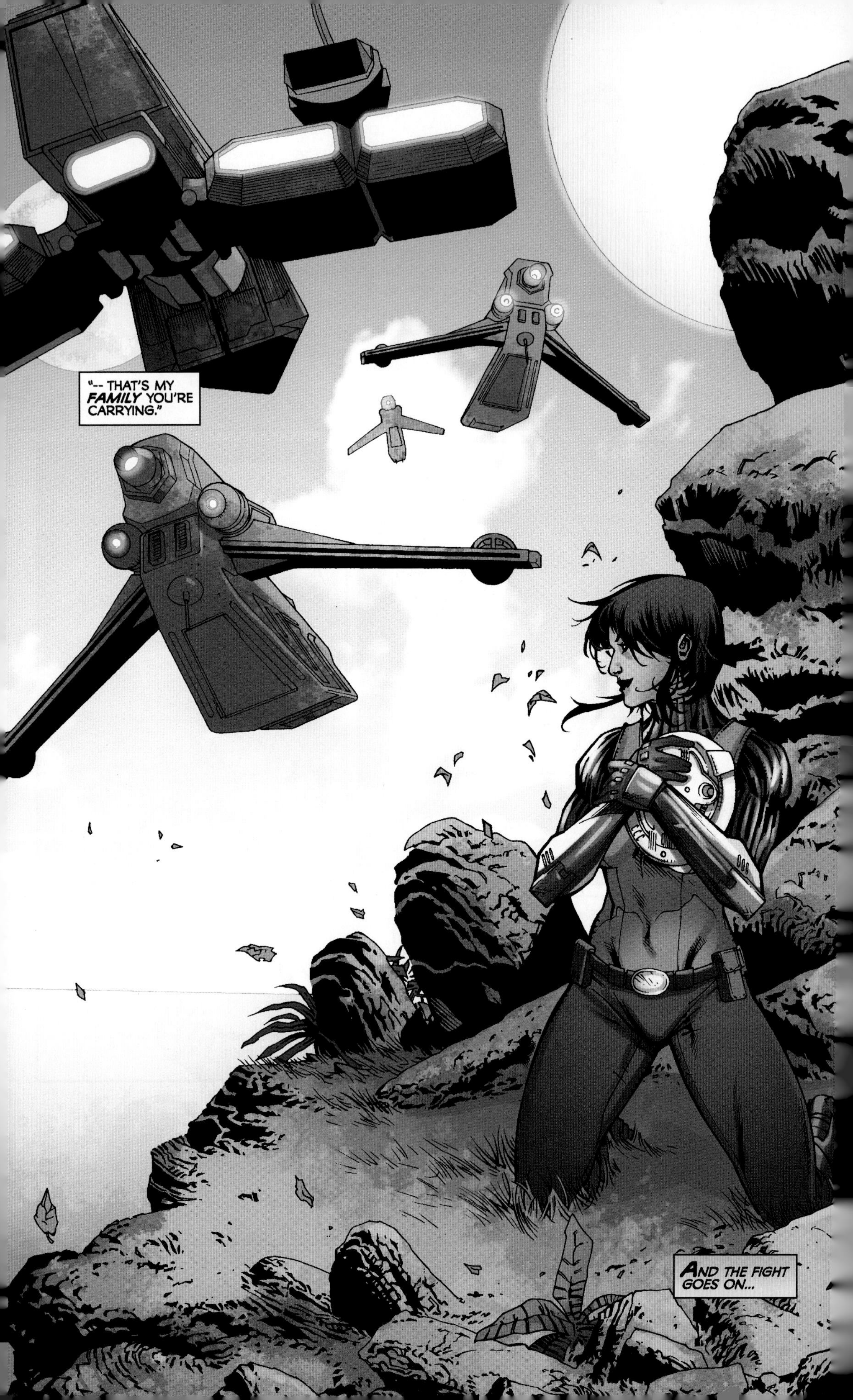
"-- THAT'S MY FAMILY YOU'RE CARRYING."
AND THE FIGHT GOES ON...

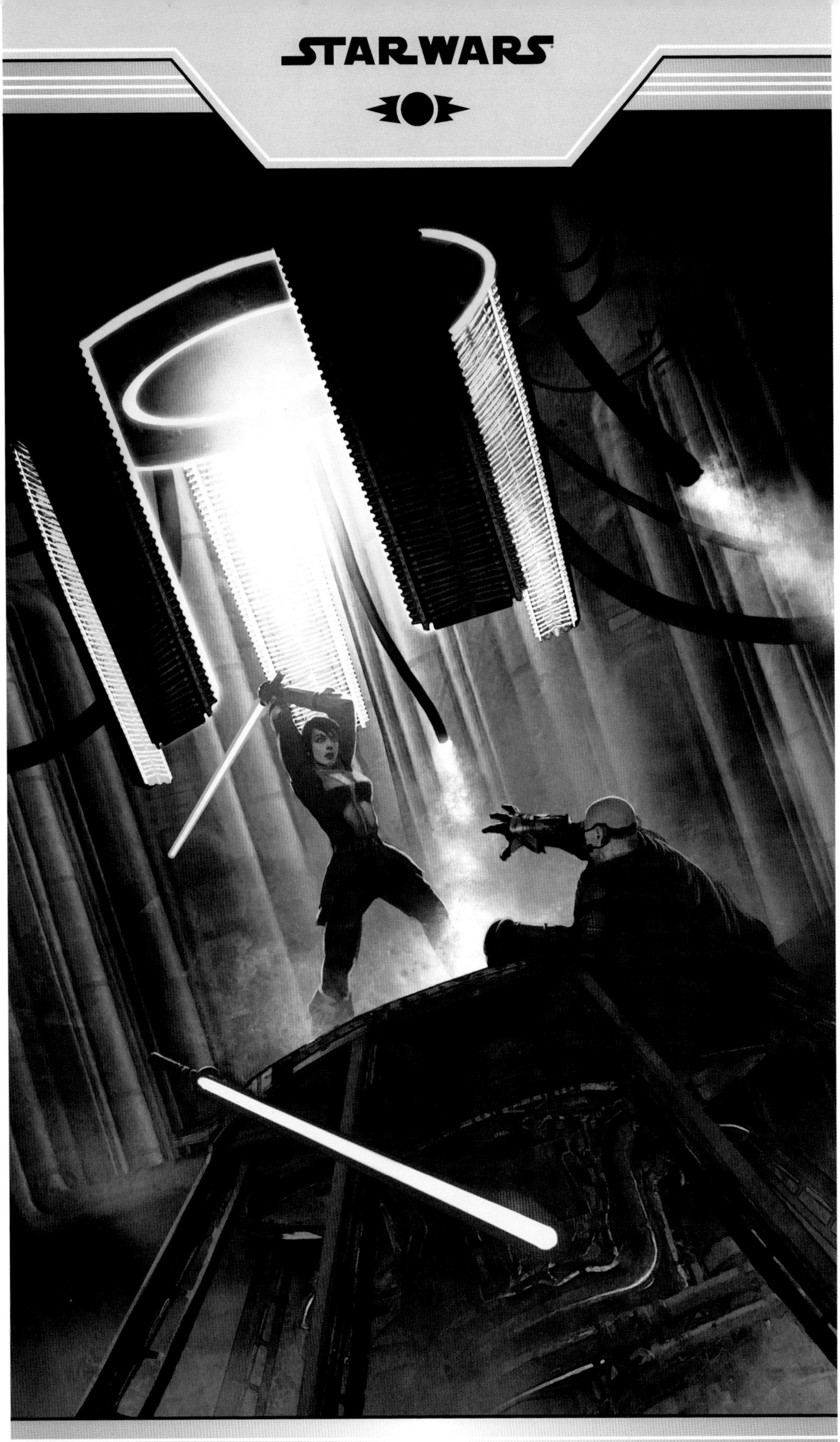
STAR WARS

ILLUSTRATION BY BENJAMIN CARRÉ

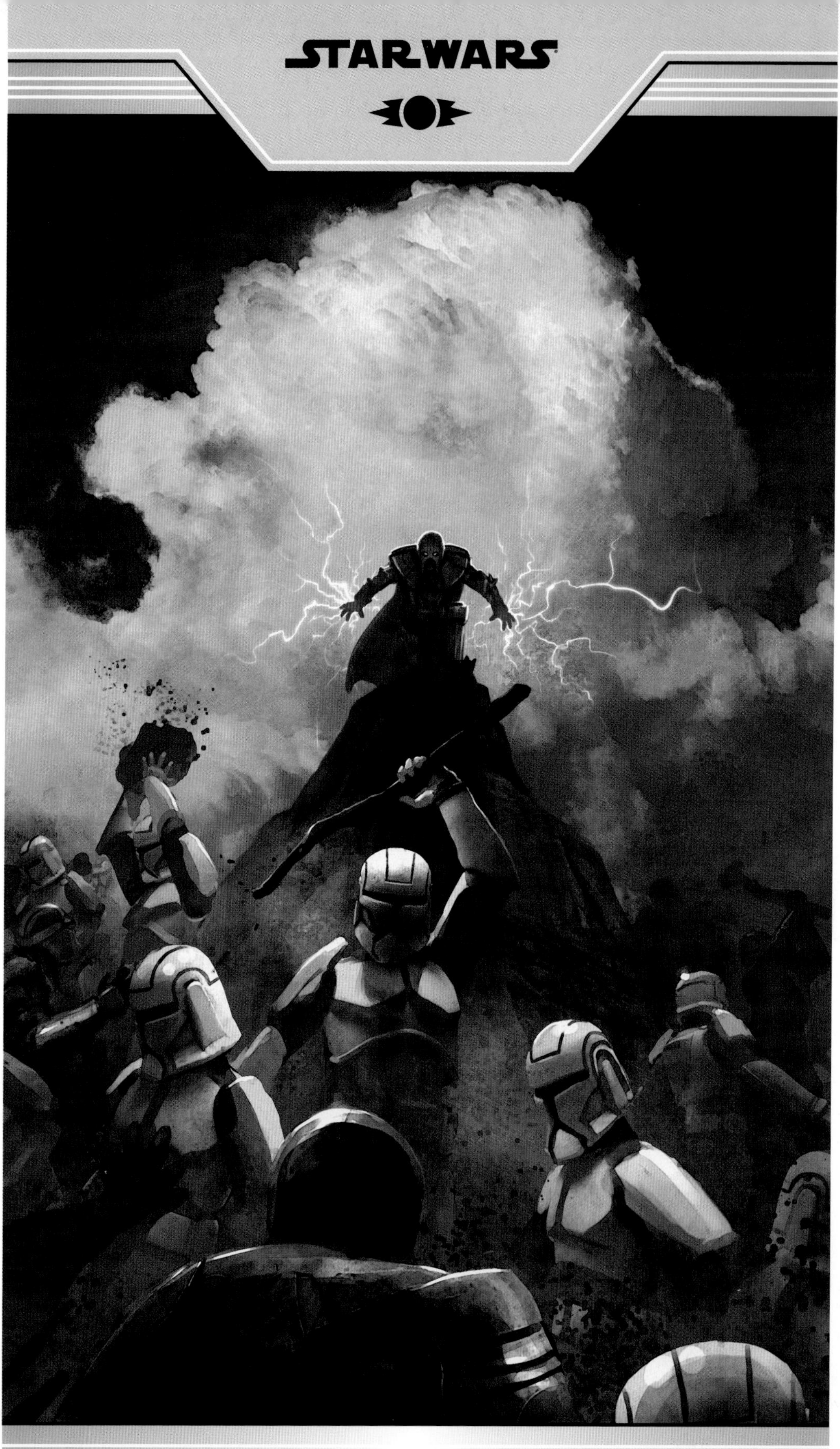
STAR WARS

ILLUSTRATION BY BENJAMIN CARRÉ

STAR WARS GRAPHIC NOVEL TIMELINE (IN YEARS)

Omnibus: Tales of the Jedi—5,000–3,986 BSW4

Knights of the Old Republic—3,964–3,963 BSW4

The Old Republic—3653, 3678 BSW4

Knight Errant—1,032 BSW4

Jedi vs. Sith—1,000 BSW4

Omnibus: Rise of the Sith—33 BSW4

Episode I: The Phantom Menace—32 BSW4

Omnibus: Emissaries and Assassins—32 BSW4

Omnibus: Quinlan Vos—Jedi in Darkness—31–30 BSW4

Omnibus: Menace Revealed—31–22 BSW4

Honor and Duty—22 BSW4

Blood Ties—22 BSW4

Episode II: Attack of the Clones—22 BSW4

Clone Wars—22–19 BSW4

Clone Wars Adventures—22–19 BSW4

General Grievous—22–19 BSW4

Episode III: Revenge of the Sith—19 BSW4

Dark Times—19 BSW4

Omnibus: Droids—5.5 BSW4

Omnibus: Boba Fett—3 BSW4–10 ASW4

Omnibus: At War with the Empire—1 BSW4

Episode IV: A New Hope—SW4

Classic Star Wars—0–3 ASW4

Omnibus: A Long Time Ago . . .—0–4 ASW4

Empire—0 ASW4

Omnibus: The Other Sons of Tatooine—0 ASW4

Omnibus: Early Victories—0–3 ASW4

Jabba the Hutt: The Art of the Deal—1 ASW4

Episode V: The Empire Strikes Back—3 ASW4

Omnibus: Shadows of the Empire—3.5–4.5 ASW4

Episode VI: Return of the Jedi—4 ASW4

Omnibus: X-Wing Rogue Squadron—4–5 ASW4

Heir to the Empire—9 ASW4

Dark Force Rising—9 ASW4

The Last Command—9 ASW4

Dark Empire—10 ASW4

Crimson Empire—11 ASW4

Jedi Academy: Leviathan—12 ASW4

Union—19 ASW4

Chewbacca—25 ASW4

Invasion—25 ASW4

Legacy—130–137 ASW4

Old Republic Era
25,000 – 1000 years before
Star Wars: A New Hope

Rise of the Empire Era
1000 – 0 years before
Star Wars: A New Hope

Rebellion Era
0 – 5 years after
Star Wars: A New Hope

New Republic Era
5 – 25 years after
Star Wars: A New Hope

New Jedi Order Era
25+ years after
Star Wars: A New Hope

Legacy Era
130+ years after
Star Wars: A New Hope

Vector
Crosses four eras in the timeline

Volume 1 contains:
Knights of the Old Republic Volume 5
Dark Times Volume 3
Volume 2 contains:
Rebellion Volume 4
Legacy Volume 6

BSW4 = before *Episode IV: A New Hope*. ASW4 = after *Episode IV: A New Hope*.

STAR WARS OMNIBUS COLLECTIONS

STAR WARS
OMNIBUS
BOBA FETT

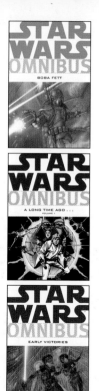

STAR WARS: BOBA FETT

Boba Fett, the most feared, most respected, and most loved bounty hunter in the galaxy, now has all of his comics stories collected into one massive volume!

ISBN 978-1-59582-418-9 | $24.99

STAR WARS
OMNIBUS
A LONG TIME AGO . . .

STAR WARS: A LONG TIME AGO. . . .

Star Wars: A Long Time Ago. . . . omnibus volumes feature classic *Star Wars* stories not seen in over twenty years! Originally printed by Marvel Comics, these recolored stories are sure to please *Star Wars* fans both new and old.

Volume 1: ISBN 978-1-59582-486-8 | $24.99
Volume 2: ISBN 978-1-59582-554-4 | $24.99
Volume 3: ISBN 978-1-59582-639-8 | $24.99
Volume 4: ISBN 978-1-59582-640-4 | $24.99
Volume 5: ISBN 978-1-59582-801-9 | $24.99

STAR WARS
OMNIBUS
EARLY VICTORIES

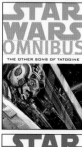

STAR WARS: EARLY VICTORIES

Following the destruction of the first Death Star, Luke Skywalker and Princess Leia find there are many more battles to be fought against the Empire and Darth Vader!

ISBN 978-1-59582-172-0 | $24.99

STAR WARS
OMNIBUS
AT WAR WITH THE EMPIRE

STAR WARS: AT WAR WITH THE EMPIRE

Stories of the early days of the Rebel Alliance and the beginnings of its war with the Empire—tales of the *Star Wars* galaxy set before, during, and after the events in *Star Wars: A New Hope*!

Volume 1: ISBN 978-1-59582-699-2 | $24.99
Volume 2: ISBN 978-1-59582-777-7 | $24.99

STAR WARS
OMNIBUS
THE OTHER SONS OF TATOOINE

STAR WARS: THE OTHER SONS OF TATOOINE

Luke's story has been told time and again, but what about the journeys of his boyhood friends, Biggs Darklighter and Janek "Tank" Sunber? Both are led to be heroes in their own right: one of the Rebellion, the other of the Empire . . .

ISBN 978-1-59582-866-8 | $24.99

STAR WARS
OMNIBUS
SHADOWS OF THE EMPIRE

STAR WARS: SHADOWS OF THE EMPIRE

Featuring all your favorite characters from the *Star Wars* trilogy—Luke Skywalker, Princess Leia, and Han Solo—this volume includes stories written by acclaimed novelists Timothy Zahn and Steve Perry!

ISBN 978-1-59582-434-9 | $24.99

STAR WARS
OMNIBUS
X-WING ROGUE SQUADRON

STAR WARS: X-WING ROGUE SQUADRON

The greatest starfighters of the Rebel Alliance become the defenders of a new Republic in this massive collection of stories featuring Wedge Antilles, hero of the Battle of Endor, and his team of ace pilots known throughout the galaxy as Rogue Squadron.

Volume 1: ISBN 978-1-59307-572-9 | $24.99
Volume 2: ISBN 978-1-59307-619-1 | $24.99
Volume 3: ISBN 978-1-59307-776-1 | $24.99

AVAILABLE AT YOUR LOCAL COMICS SHOP OR BOOKSTORE!

To find a comics shop in your area, call 1-888-266-4226

For more information or to order direct: • On the web: DarkHorse.com • E-mail: mailorder@darkhorse.com • Phone: 1-800-862-0052 Mon.–Fri. 9 AM to 5 PM Pacific Time